AF522359

Indian Education and Humanity

Indian Education and Humanity

Edited by
Dr. G. VISVANATHAN
Professor, Department of Education,
Annamalai University, Tamil Nadu
and
Dr.S.K.PANNEER SELVAM
Assistant Professor, Department of Education
Bharathidasan University, Tamil Nadu

RANDOM PUBLICATIONS
NEW DELHI (INDIA)

Indian Education and Humanity

ISBN 978-93-5111-315-7

Published in 2014 in India by

RANDOM PUBLICATIONS

4376-A/4B, Gali Murari Lal, Ansari Road
NewDelhi-110 002
Phone : +9111-43580356, 011-23289044
E-mail: randomexports@gmail.com; sales@randompublications.com; info@randompublications.com

Type Setting by : Shah Computer Graphics, Delhi-110094
Digitally Printed at: Replika Press Pvt. Ltd.

Contents

1

Role of NCTE, NCERT, CIET and SCERT for the Cause of Teacher Education

Teacher is a national builder. Education is a powerful instrument of national development

—***Sri Sarvepalli Radha Krishnan.***

Introduction

Education is a solution of all types of problems in the society. Through education we get knowledge, good habits, character, morals and values. We have thousands of years of tradition and culture. In Vedas the teacher was called 'Guru'. According to Indians teacher is third god. We give more respect to teacher after mother and father in the society. Teacher is a national builder. It is necessary to give importance to teacher education. Today's children are tomorrow's citizens. By taking good steps in the framing of teacher education curriculum, we can give good quality and value based education to the teachers.

National Council for Teacher Education, National Council of Educational Research and Training, Central Institute of Educational Technology, State Council of Educational Research and Training etc. are the institutions for the strengthening the teacher education in India.

National Council for Teacher Education (NCTE)

The National Council for Teacher Education, in its previous status since 1973, was an advisory body for the Central and State Governments on all matters pertaining to teacher education, with its Secretariat in the Department of Teacher Education of the National Council of Educational Research and Training (NCERT). Despite its commendable work in the academic fields, it could not perform essential regulatory functions, to ensure maintenance of standards in teacher education and preventing proliferation of substandard teacher education institutions. The National Policy on Education (NPE), 1986 and the Programme of Action there under, envisaged a National Council for Teacher Education with statutory status and necessary resources as a first step for overhauling the system of teacher education. The National Council for Teacher Education as a statutory body came into existence in pursuance of the National Council for Teacher Education Act, 1993 (No. 73 of 1993) on the 17th August,1995.

Objective of NCTE

The main objective of the NCTE is to achieve planned and coordinated development of the teacher education system throughout the country, the regulation and proper maintenance of Norms and Standards in the teacher education system and for matters connected therewith. The mandate given to the NCTE is very broad and covers the whole gamut of teacher education programmes including research and training of persons for equipping them to teach at pre-primary, primary, secondary and senior secondary stages in schools, and non-formal education, part-time education, adult education and distance (correspondence) education courses.

Organizational Structure of NCTE

NCTE has its head quarter at New Delhi and four Regional Committees at Banglore, Bhopal, Bhubaneshwar and Jaipur to look after its statutory responsibilities. In order to enable the NCTE to perform the assigned functions including planned and co-ordinated development and initiating innovations in teacher education, the NCTE in Delhi as well as its four Reginal Committees have administrative and academic wings to deal respectively with finance, establishment and legal matters and with research, policy planning, monitoring, curriculum, innovations, co-ordination, library and documentation, in-service programmes. The NCTE Headquarters is headed by the Chairperson, while each Regional Committee is headed by a Regional Director.

All teacher education colleges are under the control of NCTE. There are 24 Government D.Ed. colleges, 324 B.Ed., Government, aided and un-aided colleges, 17 Telugu pandit training colleges, 5 UGDPEd colleges, 7 B.P.Ed. Colleges, 5 Urdu pandit training colleges and 20 M.Ed., colleges under the control of NCTE in Andhra Pradesh. Nearly 50 thousands of trainee teachers are studying in all the above colleges. It is the duty of NCTE to provide quality education in all the above colleges. It is the duty of NCTE to frame curriculum for teacher education.

The Parliament appreciated the role of quality teacher education in providing quality teachers for quality school education and passed an Act in 1993 for setting up of the National Council for Teacher Education (NCTE) as a statutory body. The broad mandate given to the NCTE is to achieve planned and co-ordinated development of the teacher education system throughout the country, the regulation and proper maintenance of norms and standards in the teacher education system and for matters connected therewith.

The NCTE has been conducting orientation programmes on education in human values for teacher educators and repackaging electronically the contributions of the experts and those of the participants. The outcomes of its programmes are distributed to each of its recognized institutions on multimedia CD-ROMs and through the World Wide Web of the Internet. Full texts of publications on value education in easily downloadable form have been made available on the NCTE web site (http://www.ncte-in.org). Titles related to value education available from the NCTE web site are: Education for Character Development; Education for Tomorrow; Report of the Working Group to Review Teachers' Training Programme; Role and Responsibility of Teachers in Building up Modern India; Gandhi on Education; Sri Aurobindo on Education; and Tilak on Education. The titles of the NCTE CD-ROMs on value education are New Education for New India - Integral Education of Sri Aurobindo, Jeevan Vigyan and Teachers as Transformers. A CD-ROM based on the workshop that was organised by the NCTE jointly with the Chinmaya World Centre will be released shortly. Recently, in December 2001 two workshops on value orientation in teacher education for teacher educators of the Southern States were organised by the RIMSE (Ramakrishna Institute for Moral and Spiritual Education).

It may be appreciated that the role of the NCTE in bringing any curricular change in teacher education programme, even providing facilitation in integration of education in human values in it, at best, is that of a catalytic agent. What NCTE is trying is to make available a basketful of resource materials on education in human values to teacher education institutions.

National Counsel of Educational Research and Training (NCERT)

The National Council of Educational Research and Training (NCERT) is an apex resource organisation set up by the Government of India, with headquarters at New Delhi, to assist and advise the Central and State Governments on academic matters related to school education. NCERT doing so many researches to improve the quality of teacher education. The objective of NCERT is to assist and advise the Ministry of Education and Social Welfare in the implementation of its policies and major programmes in the field of education, particularly school education. The NCERT provides academic and technical support for improvement of school education through its various constituents, which are:

- National Institute of Education, New Delhi
- Central Institute of Education Technology, New Delhi
- Pandit Sunderlal Sharma Central Institute of Vocational Education, Bhopal
- Regional Institute of Education, Ajmer
- Regional Institute of Education, Bhopal
- Regional Institute of Education, Bhubaneswar
- Regional Institute of Education, Mysore.
- North Eastern-Regional Institute of Education, Shillong

Priorities

- Among the top priorities of NCERT are:
- Implementation of National Curriculum framework
- Universalization of Elementary Education (UEE)
- Vocational education
- Education of groups with special needs
- Early childhood education
- Evaluation and examination reform information technology (IT) education
- Value Education
- Educational Technology
- Development of exemplary textbooks/workbooks/teacher's guide/ supplementary reading materials
- Production of the girl child
- Identification and nurturing of talent
- Guidance and counselling
- Improvement in teacher education
- International relations

By conducting national seminars, workshops and conferences NCERT gives valuable recommendations to teacher education. Now we are living in the technological world.

Programmes and Activities

The NCERT undertakes the following programmes and activities.

Research

Being an apex national body for research in school education, the NCERT performs the important functions of conducting and supporting research and offering training in educational research methodology. The different Departments of the National Institute of Education (NIE), Regional Institutes of Education (RIEs), Central Institute of Educational Technology (CIET) and Pandit Sunderlal Sharma Central Institute of Vocational Education (PSSCIVE) undertake programmes of research related to different aspects of school education, including teacher education.

Besides conducting in-house research, the NCERT supports research programmes of other institutions/organizations by providing financial assistance and academic guidance. Assistance is given to scholars for publication of their Ph.D. theses. Research fellowships are offered to encourage studies in school education to create a research base for developmental, training and extension programmes and to create a pool of competent research workers. It also organizes courses for educational research workers. The NCERT also organizes educational research in the country. It has computer facilities for storing, processing and retrieval of data. It collaborates with international agencies in inter-country research projects.

Development

Developmental activities in school education constitute an important function of the NCERT. The major developmental activities include development and renewal of curricula and instructional materials for various levels of school education and making them relevant to changing needs of children and society. The innovative developmental activities include development of curricula and instructional materials in school education in the area of pre-school education, formal and non-formal education, vocationalisation of education and teacher education. Developmental activities are also undertaken in the domains of educational technology, population education, and education of the disabled and other special groups.

Training

Another important dimension of NCERT's activities is the pre-service and in-service training of teachers at various levels; pre-primary, elementary, secondary and higher secondary, and also in such areas as vocational education, educational technology, guidance and counseling, and special education. The pre-service teacher education programmes at the Regional Institutes of Education (RIEs) incorporate innovative features such as integration of content and methodology of teaching, long-term internship of teacher trainees in the actual classroom setting, and participation of students in community work. The RIEs also undertake the training of key personnel of the states and of state level institutions and training of teacher educators and in-service teachers.

Extension

The NCERT has comprehensive extension programmes in which various Departments of the NIE, RIEs, CIET, PSSCIVE and the offices of the Field Advisers in the states are engaged in various ways. It works in close collaboration with various agencies and institutions in the states and also works extensively with Extension Service Departments and Centres in teacher training colleges and schools with the purpose of providing assistance to various categories of personnel, including teachers, teacher educators, educational administrators, question-paper setters, textbook writers, etc. Conferences, seminars, workshops and competitions are organized *as* regular on-going programmes as a part of the extension activities. Several programmes are organized in rural and backward areas in order to reach out to the functionaries in these areas where special problems exist and where special efforts are needed. Special programmes are organized for the education of the disadvantaged sections of the society. The extension programmes cover all States and Union Territories of the country.

Publication and Dissemination

The NCERT publishes textbooks for different school subjects for Classes I to XII. It also brings out workbooks, teachers guides, supplementary readers, research reports, etc. In addition, it publishes instructional materials for the use of teacher educators, teacher trainees and in-service teachers. These instructional materials, produced through research and developmental work, serve as models to various agencies in States and Union Territories. These are made available to state level agencies for adoption and/or adaptation. The textbooks are published in English, Hindi and Urdu.

For dissemination of educational information, or the NCERT publishes six journals: *The Primary Teacher* is published both in English and Hindi and aims at giving meaningful and relevant educational inputs to primary school teachers for direct use in the classroom; *School Science* serves as an open forum for discussion on various aspects of science education; *Journal of Indian Education* provides a forum for encouraging original and critical thinking in education through discussion on current educational issues;

Indian Educational Review contains research articles and provides a forum for researchers in education; and *Bharatiya Adhunik Shiksha,* published in Hindi, provides a forum for encouraging critical thinking in education on contemporary issues and for dissemination of educational problems and practices. Besides these, a house journal called *NCERT Newsletter* is also published in English and Hindi. The title of the Hindi version of the newsletter is *Shaikshik Darpan.*

Exchange Programmes

The NCERT interacts with international organisations such as UNESCO, UNICEF, UNDP (United Nations Development Progammes), NFPA (National Federation of Paralegal Associations) and the World Bank to study specific educational problems and to arrange training programmes for personnel from developing countries. It is one of the Associated Centres of APEID (Asia-Pacific Programme of Educational Innovation for Development). It also acts as the Secretariat of the National Development Group (NDG) for Educational Innovations. The NCERT has been offering training facilities, usually through attachment programmes and participation in workshops, to educational workers of other countries. The NCERT also acts as a major agency for implementing the Bilateral Cultural Exchange Programmes entered into by the Government of India with the governments of other countries in the fields of school education and teacher education by sending delegations to study specific educational problems relevant to Indian requirements and by arranging training and study visits for scholars from other countries. Educational materials are exchanged with other countries. On request, the faculty members are deputed to participate in international conferences, seminars, workshops, symposia, etc.

Central Institute of Educational Technology (CIET) – India

Central Institute of Educational Technology (CIET) is a constituent unit of the National Council of Educational Research and Training (NCERT), an autonomous organisation under the Ministry of Human Resources Development, Government of India. Established in 1984 with the merger of the Centre of Educational Technology and Department of Teaching Aids. Its chief aim is to promote Educational Technology especially mass media singly or in combinations (multimedia packages) to extend educational opportunities and improve quality of educational processes at the school level.

As a premier institute of Educational Technology at the apex level, major functions of the CIET are:

To design, develop, try out and disseminate alternative learning systems to achieve the national goal of universalisation of primary education and

- To address various educational problems at micro and macro levels. The broad areas of activities of the CIET are as given below:
- To design and produce media software materials viz., television/ radio (for both broadcast as well as non-broadcast use) film, graphics and other programmes for strengthening the transaction of curricular and co-curricular activities at the school level.
- To create competencies in development and use of educational software materials mentioned above through training in areas such as script development, media production, media communication, media research, technical operations, setting up studios, repair and maintenance of equipment.
- To train the faculty of Institutes of Advanced Study in Education/ Colleges of Teacher Education and District Institutes of Education and Training in the use of Educational Technology in their teacher education programmes.
- To undertake research evaluation and monitoring of the systems, programmes and materials with a view to improving the materials and increasing their effectiveness.
- To document and disseminate information, materials and media programmes for better utilization and to function as a clearing house / agency in the field of Educational Technology.
- To advise and coordinate the academic and technical programmes and activities of the SIET set up by the MHRD in six states of India.
- To ensure a continuous progress in the quality of production, various evaluation studies are carried out on a regular basis. Some of the important research programmes undertaken during the year 1997-98 are:
    - Monitoring and evaluation of Training
    - Analysis of viewer's mail
    - Field-testing of media programmes
    - Review of research with implications for media production
    - A need assessment for media programmes for the middle schools.

Sate Counsel of Educational Research and Training

The State Council of Educational Research and Training (SCERT) Andhra Pradesh was established on 27-07-1967, amalgamating the following institutions:

- The State Institute of Education.

- The State Bureau of Education and Vocational Guidance.
- The State Science Education Unit and
- The State Evaluation Unit

Objectives

- To organize in – service training for teacher educators and to teachers of Primary, Upper Primary and Secondary Schools.
- To Act as a clearing house for ideas and information to keep the teacher educators and teachers abreast of the latest developments in the field of Education
- To provide academic guidance to the schools through extension services.
- To undertake studies, investigations and surveys relating to educational matters on the appraisal of educational programmes.
- To Undertake and co – ordinate action research projects on instructional practices, Educational problems etc.
- To undertake publication of books, periodicals and other literature necessary for furtherance of knowledge for teachers.
- To undertake evaluation and research studies to find out the impact of educational programmes in the state.

Functions

Based on its objectives as the academic wing of the Department of School Education. The following are the functions of SCERT.

- Preparation of curricula, syllabi, instructional material for Primary, Upper Primary, Secondary and alternative systems of education.
- Department of evaluation procedures and material which are helpful to the practicing teachers.
- Bridging gaps between the methods and techniques advocated in training and the actual classroom practices.
- Dissemination of knowledge to improved methods and techniques to be followed by educational institutions.
- Co-ordination with national and international organizations in academic programmes.
- Organization of orientation programmes for the professional growth of teachers, teacher – education, supervisor's etc.
- Publication of journals, periodicals, books etc. ,
- Resource support to implement the academic policies lay down by the Government.

Services

Constituent Units

SCERT has some constituent units spread over the entire state. They are:-

- Institutes or Advances Study in Education (IASEs) Colleges of Teacher Education. (CTEs)
- District institutes of Education and Training (DIETs) / Teacher Training institutes (T. T. I. s)
- Extension Service Departments.
- Science Teacher's Centres.

Professional Growth

For the professional growth of teachers, SCERT takes up in-service training courses for Primary, Upper – Primary, Secondary teachers and teacher–educators, besides providing sources material like hand books, manuals and other publications.

SCERT also organizes seminars. Workshops, conferences involving teachers, teacher - educators, supervisors and administrators.

Research and Evaluation

SCERT undertakes action research, studies, experimental research and evaluation of the programmes implemented by it. It also promotes research and evaluation studies by teacher educators and action research by the practicing teachers.

Co–ordinate Efforts

SCERT co-ordinates various academic programmes of IASE's CTE's. DIETs. TTIs and the Extention Services Departments functioning in IASE, CTEs and DIETs.

Future Vision of the Department

National Policy of Education 1986 and Programme of action lay a lot of stress on the qualitative improvement of education. The Govt. of India has made the State Councils of Education Research and Training as nodal agencies to look into the task of qualitative improvement of Elementary Education at Elementary and Secondary Education levels. Teacher Education Institution like DIETs, IASEs, CTEs etc., co-ordinate and implement UNICEF projects like UGC, EFA (Education For All) and other projects like MLL (Minimum Level of Learning), Distance Education. The institution's major responsibility is to ensure quality in teacher education.

SCERT organizes seminars, workshops, conferences with the help of NCERT, NCTE AND NIEPA to give quality education for teachers.

Conclusion

We know teacher is a national builder. He has a power to change the world. It is necessary to take care about teacher education. NCTE, NCERT, CIET and SCERT have to play prominent role in the development of quality in teacher education. NCTE has major role in framing of teacher education curriculum and establishment of teacher education institutions. We are living in the modern world. It is necessary to use technology. It is necessary to provide computer and technology labs and other type of labs.

2

Role of Information Technology in Teacher Education

*Education is the learning of human souls to what is best, and making what is best out of them?–**John Ruskin***

Now we are living in the modern world. A lot of change is occurring in every day. With the help of science and technology we have developed in all the fields. With the help of technology now it is easy to know any type of information within seconds throughout the world.

Radio, Television, Phone, Mobile, Computer and Internet have changed the human life. Through education we can learn anything easily with the help of these instruments. According to Mahatma Gandhi, the father of Indian Nation, by giving good education to each and every one we can remove poverty and develop good character.

India is a developing country. Now we have very much demand in the IT filed. The development of IT is a wonder. Now lacks of student are entering in to the IT filed. Our central and state governments are also giving more importance for Information Technology.

There is a separate department for Information Technology under the Ministry of Communication and Information Technology.

Definition of Information Technology

Information technology (IT): The science and activity of using computers and other electronic equipment to store and send information.

Information Technology is also defined as, "The technology involved with the transmission and storage of information, especially the development, installation, implementation, and management of computer systems within companies, universities" and other organizations".

Goals and Objectives

1. To provide in-service training to teachers and teacher educators on computers and IT.
2. To incorporate all the IT facilities into teacher education model.
3. To extend internet, e-mail facilities to all teachers and students in teacher education.
4. To provide network how to operate computers and internet to all the student teachers.
5. To provide network to teacher education centres all over India.
6. To extend distance mode of teacher education online and also include a live interactive practical teaching.
7. To restructure teacher education curriculum.
8. To incorporate use of IT in special education.
9. To use IT in teacher education research.
10. To create a virtual teacher education centre.
11. To incorporate good hidden curriculum strategies to restore the humanistic tendencies required for a teacher.
12. Ensure the protection and security of data.
13. Minimize duplication of effort, services and resources.
14. Eliminate inefficient and costly redundancies.
15. Define what services, if any, should be restructured or eliminated.
16. Eliminate non-compatible standards and architectures.
17. Identify obstacles for departments wanting to move computing operations to the Division of Information Technology.
18. Recommend a strategy for evaluating the university-wide impacts of major information technology purchases including analysis of total cost of ownership.
19. Evaluate the complexity and risks of managing a complex distributed computing environment, including system security, exposure to data loss and virus protection.
20. Identify issues and trends in technology that may affect the university's technology infrastructure and long-term architecture.
21. Recommend the most effective balance of central and distributed technology services, staffing and resources. Detail any logical alternatives. Recommendations will include background, advice and alternatives that address the following:

- Create a cost efficient blend of centralization and decentralization of information technology resources - properly aligning the university's information technology infrastructure to best meet the needs of its teaching, research and outreach missions.
- Create a coherent campus-wide information technology computing architecture and a solid foundation for the university's information technology infrastructure.
- Develop a long-term organizational process and structure to ensure the best utilization of the university's information technology resources for the future.
- Estimate the costs of infrastructure and support, including personnel and training, in the current distributed environment and to estimate the same costs for the alternatives proposed.

Need of Information Technology in Teacher Education

It is well known fact that IT and Cyber age have brought a revolutionary transformation and drifted the whole life style of people. No area left untouched with it. We have arrived at global village concept with all virtual realities on our desktops. But is it the teacher education, which has remained untouched in this direction.

We have a lot of educational institutions in the filed of Information Technology like 'Indian Institute of Information Technology (IIIT), 'International Institute of Information Technology, 'Tata Institute of Information Technolgoy' and 'Deerubai Ambani Institute of Information Technology'. There are so many Information Technology departments in the universities at both state and central level. The effect of Information Technology in our daily life is very much. It is very necessary to take Information Technology help for teacher education. There is a separate subject for trainee teacher 'Educational Technology'. With the help of Information Technology it is possible to give quality and effective education for trainee teachers.

A nation's development potential depends upon its ability to continuously educate its population and its ability to create armies of skilled manpower. In particular, use of Information Technology (IT) in acquiring knowledge and skill has become an essential element in education and training. These IT elements in the educational process have magical effects.

Higher education without the support of IT makes the lives of learner and teachers equally difficult. A nation's intellectual strength depends on IT support. The use of computing and communication technology to enhance the efficacy of transaction and productivity is the driving force in this new era of social and economic transformation in the new society called Information Society.

A strong IT infrastructure can give an institution a competitive advantage for the best students and faculty and an advantage in competition for absorbing external research grants to execute studies, research etc. in a short time and with great resolution. The quality of an institution's environment for digital information storage and retrieval has, for any disciplines, become more important than the institution's conventional, library resources in print media.

Virtually every economic sector that is labour intensive has managed to improve productivity through the use of technology except education. Faculty/student ratios in higher education have changed significantly in more than 50 years. The most advanced technology in common use in the classroom today in our country is the overhead projector, and it took nearly three decades to migrate from the national level training institute to the classroom. Institutions like UGC, IGNOU, and CIET have begun to transact curriculum on DD 1 but the ETV programmes are mostly of enrichment type and not as per the demand of the students. It is unlikely that IT will have a major impact on teaching and learning if the current paradigm for instruction changes.

Generally majority trainee teachers have no knowledge about usage of technology. Because their lower classes curriculum is separate. It is necessary to change curriculum at school level and implement Information Technology at school level also. 'Today's children are tomorrow's citizens', so it is necessary to take care about school curriculum. It is government duty to provide Information Technology labs for all type of Educational Institutions in the country.

Uses of Information Technology

Now we are using Information Technology in all the fields like education agriculture, banking, transport, medicine, research and manufacturing and in social service mode.

Specific Uses of Information Technology

- Animation for simulation of urban environments and video for assembling and disseminating results of the analysis and design work.
- Graphic Information System (GIS) for the study of housing and development patterns.
- Computer Aided Design (CAD) for geometric modeling: Digital image archival systems for compiling data about the built environment.

Role of Information Technology in Teacher Education

In-service Training

There is a need to provide in-service training to all the teachers and teacher educators with updated computer operation skills and provide with IT know how. To utilize the facilities to access updated information and solutions to their problems in their areas of specialization, it can be provide on-line.

Teacher Education Training Programmes through IT facilities

A virtual teacher education centre can be created. All the necessary skills and training can be provided in different modes on the network. It should incorporate all the available facilities like, tele-education, teleconferencing, floppy diskettes and CD-ROMs in teacher education. Networks like ERNET, INTERNET and futuristic concept of bringing satellite channels directly to homes by DTS (Direct to Home) service and expert talks through virtual classrooms can also be made available.

Distance Mode of Education

The present practice of TV and other media in distance mode of education can be substituted by multimedia systems which have an extra advantage of intractability through GUI (Graphics User Interface) which controls the response of information transfer process according to the learners pace. It helps in using screen as an instructor for self-learning.

IT in special Education

IT is providing solutions for the education of physically challenged people as well. As reported by BBC web-site (web-site at BBC news, science), the Germans have developed a technology and associated software for which people, where computer will sense the signals from the head of a paralyzed person through two attached electrodes, and thereby, allow him to surf the net like a normal person. These facilities will transform the lives of the physically challenged and IT can be used even for diagnosing.

Research and INTERNET

Internet facilities should be made available to research students, teacher educators. All the departments should have internet connectivity. It helps in accessing information about the ongoing research in their respective fields and it also avoids overlapping.

Restructuring Curricula of Teacher Education

1. Teacher education curriculum needs drastic changes by incorporating all facilities available through IT. Primarily IT can be

used to keep on par with the existing knowledge structure. It can be thoroughly incorporated into methodologies of teacher education.

2. There should not be exclusive theoretical orientation in curriculum. It shall have more practically demonstrable skill and strategies in the curriculum.
3. All possible attempts should be made to train teachers apart from virtual classrooms, to incorporate the necessary live interactive experiences to understand the significance of physical interaction with the child in the classroom.
4. Humanistic and affective hidden curriculum and an effective training to acquire all traits and qualities required in teacher to handle human society should also be included in the curriculum.

Conclusion

Information Technology has a prominent role in the filed of teacher education. With the help of information technology it is easy to know any type of information with in seconds through out the world. The advanced knowledge of information technology is much helpful for research in all the fields of education. With the help of Information Technology it is easy to educate trainee teachers. By knowing the usage of technology they have a change to share their opinions with other teacher through out the world. Information Technology motivates the teacher to learn lot of things in their subject area.

Now we are happy that our State and Central Governments have taking good steps to introduce online education in the educational institutions. There are separate subjects in D.Ed., and B.Ed., like Computer Education and Educational Technology. Now teachers are using computers and internet in the educational institutions. But the percentage is very less. It is more important to give equal importance to theory and practical in the computer education and educational technology subjects. It is the duty of the Government to provide Computer and Educational technology labs for each and every teacher education institution in the country.

Now NCTE, CIET, NIEPA, NCERT, SCERT and other educational departments have recognized the advantages of Information Technology in the field of education. They motivate the students to use IT. They are conducting national seminars, workshops, and conferences about Information Technology. Teachers must be given excellent training in setting, grading papers and preparing assignment, etc. These can be used in teacher training network. Excellent stimulated models can be made available to access on network.

3

Impact of Globalization on Teacher Education

A teacher who establishes rapport with the taught, becomes one with them, learns more from them than he teaches them. He who learns nothing from his disciples is, in my opinion, worthless. Whenever I talk with someone I learn from him. I take from him more than I give him. In this way, a true teacher regards himself as a student of his students. If you will teach your pupils with this attitude, you will benefit much from them

—***Gandhi.***

Introduction

Education has been around for as long as man has been, though its structure and perception has varied over centuries and civilizations. Now we are living in the highly scientific and technological world. Enormous changes are occurring in the day to day life of human beings because of globalization, privatization and liberalization. Education is seen as central to economic competitiveness, the reduction of poverty and inequality, and environmental sustainability. So, it is necessary to provide education for all; then only India will become developed country by 2020.

Globalization

Globalization is a term describing the increasing interdependence, integration and interaction among people, companies and corporations in disparate locations around theworld. This umbrella term refers to a complex medley of economic, trade, social, technological, cultural and political relationships. The term has been used as early as 1944; however Theodore Levitt is usually credited with its first use in an economic context.

In defining and explaining globalization, Nsibambi (2001), incorporated five concepts. He defined globalization as "a process of advancement and increase in interaction among the worlds, countries and peoples facilitated by progressive technological changes in locomotion, communication, political and military power, knowledge and skills, as well as interfacing of cultural values, systems and practices". He noted that globalization is not a value-free, innocent, self-determining process. It is an international socio-politico-economic and cultural permeation process facilitated by policies of governments, private corporations, international agencies and civil society organizations. It essentially seeks to enhance and deploy economic, political, technological, ideological and military power and influence for competitive domination in the world.

Globalization is the worldwide process of homogenizing prices, products, wages, rates of interest and profits. Globalization relies on three forces for development: the role of human migration, international trade, and rapid movements of capital and integration of financial markets.

From the culture point of view, David (2002), states that globalization is the process of harmonizing different cultures and beliefs. Globalization is the process that eroding differences in culture and producing a seamless global system of culture and economic values (Castells, 1997). The harmonization, according to Awake (2002), is achieved due to advancement in communication and countries are increasingly being forced to participate. Therefore, globalization can be viewed as a process of shifting autonomous economies into a global market. In other words, it is the systematic integration of autonomous economies into a global system of production and distribution.

The world of separate nation-states is said to be ending enabling the process of globalization to run its logical course. The new technology, based on the computer and satellite communication have indeed revolutionized our traditional conception of the media, both print and electronic. Books, newspapers, radio, television and video programme are now being transposed into the multimedia world of the cyber space and available to all people of the world wherever they may live. Ajayi (2001) remarks that globalization is about competition and struggle for dominance which encourages more than anything else, the continuation and expansion of western imperialism in the new millennium.

Importance of Education

During the Vedic and Upanishadic period, India had some of the prominent institutions of higher education, which attracted scholars from distant places located in different parts of the world to come to India in pursuit of knowledge. The ancient universities of Takshashila and Nalanda, which survived till the end of the fifth and twelfth Century AD respectively, imparted knowledge in different areas according to the requirements of the contemporary society.

The importance of education is quite clear. Education is the knowledge of putting one's potentials to maximum use. One can safely say that a human being is not in the proper sense till he is educated.

This importance of education is basically for two reasons. The first is that the training of a human mind is not complete without education. Education makes man a right thinker. It tells man how to think and how to make decision.

The second reason for the importance of education is that only through the attainment of education, man is enabled to receive information from the external world; to acquaint him-self with past history and receive all necessary information regarding the present. Without education, man is as though in a closed room and with education he finds himself in a room with all its windows open towards outside world.

Education means the gradual process of acquiring knowledge. Education is a preparation for life. Swami Vivekananda, the great thinker and reformer of India had remarked: "We want that education by which character is formed, strength of mind is increased, intellect is expanded and by which one can stand on one's own feet. Education is the manifestation of the perfection already in man." The great Nobel Laureate and writer Rabindra Nath Tagore was one of the earliest educators to think in terms of the global education village, and his educational model has a unique sensitivity and aptness for education within multi-racial, multi-lingual and multi-cultural situations.

Development through Educational Institutions

Independent India has witnessed an upsurge in the growth of higher education. Yet from an international perspective, we are relatively slow, despite being steady in registering advancements in learning. Today India has the second largest education system in the world, next only to the USA. Yet, the total number of students represents hardly six percent of the relevant age group, i.e. 18-23 years, which is much below the average of developed countries which is about 47 percent. The gap is glaring. Hence the phenomenal challenge. The journey from being 'Good' to being 'Great' appears to be long and arduous.

India is a developing country. 70% of people are living in the villages. The rural area literacy percentage is very low when compared to urban area literacy rate. The main occupation of Indians is cultivation. The duty of higher educational institutions is to introduce courses which help to improve the rural people socio-economic status in the society. Through education it is possible to change the world. Because of globalization now world become a village. We get any type of information with in the seconds. Educational institutions have prominent role in the development of rural people in the society.

The first citizen of India today, Dr.A P J Abdul Kalam, while envisioning India of 2020, recently observed - "Spirit of Inquiry, creativity, entrepreneurial and moral leadership are the capabilities central to nation building in a democracy. Educators should develop in our children these capacities and make them autonomous learners who are self-directed and self-controlled."

Earlier all over the world, education, especially higher education, was available only to a privileged few. In the context of a knowledge society and the goals of sustainable development, higher education/teacher education needs to percolate to the masses, not only just in terms of quantity, but also quality. In the last few years, this shift has been slowly taking place. Still, glaring deficiencies remain in the access to higher education, overall development of the student, sensitivity to human needs and equality in our society.

Also come into play, concerns in teacher education that come with globalization and rapidity of change like fast rate of obsolescence of knowledge, quality, competitiveness of education services, networking of institutions and innovations and new practices in delivery, combined with this are the concerns for sustainable development of the world.

Role of Teacher in Building Modern India

The role of the modern teacher is not confined to teaching alone. He/she is expected to participate in the development programmes of the community life. The question arises as to how this could be integrated with the teacher education programmes. Mudaliar Commission (1952-53) Report stated rightly, "we are convinced that the most important factor in the contemplated education reconstruction is the teacher-his personal qualities, his educational qualifications, his professional training and the place that he occupies in the school as well as in the community". On similar lines

Kothari Commission (1964-66) stated that, "Nothing is more important than securing a sufficient supply of high quality recruits to the teaching profession, providing them with the best possible professional preparation and creating satisfactory conditions of work in which they can be fully effective".

The importance of the teachers in the Educational Programme of a country is too great. The greatness of a country does not depend on lofty buildings, gigantic projects and large armies, but on the quality of its citizens. If a nation has young men of sterling character and unimpeachable patriotism, she is found to make rapid progress in all fields. Young men are entrusted to the care of the teacher and it is therefore the sacred duty of the teacher to impart the right type of knowledge and make them good citizens. It is the teacher who impresses his children with his personality.

The teacher, a national integrator as he is, is the backbone of society, particularly so in the remote villages. He stands as an outstanding figure among the illiterate and semi-literate families. He is their friend, Philosopher and guide. The teacher actively shares the responsibility of reconstructing a social order, with all the cherished values and traditional beliefs, which are being eroded by the surge of new ideals and practices. He acts as a social reformer and counsellor to the community.

Impact of Globalization on Teacher Education

In the knowledge economy, the objectives of a society changes from fulfilling the basic needs of all round development to empowerment. The education system instead of going by text-book teaching will be promoted by reactive, interactive self learning, both formal and informal, with focus on values, merit and quality. The workers instead of being skilled or semi-skilled will be knowledgeable, self-empowered and flexibly skilled. Finally, the economy will be knowledge driven and not industry driven.

All fields of human activity, including education, have been influenced by the process of globalization clubbed with unexpected advancements in information and communication technology. Within the various sectors of education, teacher education has been affected the most. It is now increasingly realized that knowledge is universal and its creation and dissemination cannot be confined within national boundaries. The world is now like a global village, and continuous international interaction has become an essential component of human survival. The globalization of economy has led to internationalization of higher education including teacher education, not merely for economic benefits, but also for increased social interaction and promotion of international understanding.

Positive impact of Globalization on Teacher Education

1. A number of teacher educational institutions were increased.
2. Usage of technology increased in the educational institutions.
3. Information and communication technology were increased.
4. Teacher educational institutions were established in rural areas.
5. Government and private partnership in the field of teacher education.
6. Extension of internet facilities even to rural areas educational institutions.
7. Teachers are less worried for government jobs as MNC's and private or public sector are offering more lucrative jobs.
8. Free education for bright students.

Negative impact of Globalization on Teacher Education

1. Indian youths leaving education in mid-way and joining MNC's.
2. There has been an increase in the violence, particularly against women in the educational institutions.
3. Quality in education is decreasing (liberalization).
4. Degradation of values.
5. More availability of cheap and filthy material (CD's or DVD's of Hollywood movies, porn movies, sex toys, foreign channels like MTV) in the name of liberalization. It affects the psychology of teachers. Some teachers are miss-behaving with students.
6. Values of teacher are decreasing.

Conclusion

It is left to one's discretion to use a knife either to cut a fruit or to kill a person/animal. In the modernized and globalized world, it is necessary to be very cautious. Every single step should be taken with utmost care. It is the first duty of policy makers, politicians, officials and leaders to give priority for mother society and well being of their people. Globalization undoubtedly offers great opportunities for growth and development. However, no one can deny that its benefits are unevenly shared and its costs are unevenly spread among, across and within countries. This is particularly true with respect to developing and underdeveloped countries. Inspite of economic reforms the rates of unemployment and poverty in India are still high. Both in concept and practice, while globalization has positive, innovative, dynamic aspects, it also has negative, disruptive and marginalizing aspects (UNDP HDR 1999). Nsibambi (2001) suggested that globalization must be seen as a change process full of opportunities and challenges that must be carefully and skilfully harnessed and managed to ensure human development.

Teacher is a national builder. According to Indian philosophy teacher is a third god. It is very important to take care about teacher education. Through education only it is possible to preserve values and culture. Through education it is possible to solve any types of problems in the society.

It is apt to quote Mahatma Gandhi "I do not want my house to be walled in on all sides and my windows to be stuffed. I want the cultures of all the lands to be blown about my house as freely as possible. But, I refuse to be blown off my feet by any".

4

Role of Universities

(Calestouos Juma, Professor, practice of international development, Harvard University)

African universities need to make sweeping changes if they are to benefit from aid offered by the G8. The week, have agreed to help develop professional skills through networks between higher education institutions and centres of excellence in science and technology. This is a high shift in aid policy from the current focus on primary education.

But funding for such activities will have little impact unless African countries reform their universities and research institutions to focus on solving local problems. Many African universities were created to train civil servants, but times have changed. Today Africa needs to stimulate economic growth so it can work its way out of poverty. Universities must contribute to this task.

The good news is Africa can learn from successful efforts to bring technical knowledge to development. In 1948, Costa Rica abolished the army and used part of the saved revenue for higher education. This helped the country prosper and become an economic force in Central America. Costa Rica's Earth University pioneered a new teaching mode that focuses on training young people to create enterprises.

A large part of the reconstruction of Rwanda after the genocide was done through the Kigali Institute of science, Technology and Management. The institute is at the forefront of providing alternative energy sources such as biogas. Its students at Ghana's University could use radio and other tools such as pod casting to extend its mission to the wider community.

African countries will need to take steps to benefit from a new focus on support for higher education. They must align their policies and Government structures with the need to put science and technology at the centre of development of science and innovation advisers to help leaders focus on the role of innovation in development.

Governments will need to rehabilitate university infrastructure, especially their communications and information facilities, to become part of the global knowledge community. Such links will also help them to tap into their experts in Diasporas. Outmoded curricula that focus on training students to become paper shufflers and pen pushers must be replaced by new approaches that encourage creativity, enquiry and entrepreneurship.

It is also crucial that emphasis sis placed on bringing research, teaching and community outreach together. Medical schools should be more directly integrated into hospitals, just as agricultural research stations should have a strong teaching role. Finally, universities should enjoy greater autonomy from state control so that they can adapt in a timely manner to changing world.

In African universities do not make these changes, they will become increasingly marginal and their status will decline. Governments will do no better if they fail to make knowledge the driving force for improvement. These reforms need to be made even if financial aid is not available because the times have changed. As philosopher Eric From once observed in times of change only learners inherit the earth.

EDUCATIONAL RESPONSE TO COMPETITIVENESS

In the past decades, academic institutions depended upon a packaged set of knowledge and information organized around syllabi, textbooks and handbooks. Since private sector jobs were far fewer than the Government jobs, the education and training were directed towards the responsibilities of public sector. It was a period of slow growth in scientific and technological disciplines, and hence the pace of acquisition of new knowledge was also slow.

Emerging trends

The graduates of tomorrow are expected to be far more creative and innovative, with greater need for self-learning than relying on syllabi and handbook. With explosive growth rate in sciences and technologies, some of the acquired knowledge will become obsolete. Migration from one discipline to another will be seamless.

The career opportunity in private sector will be much larger than in Government with much less job security and greater mobility than the past. Many would be better off by self employment or by starting their own enterprises. The professional opportunities will be global and so will be the competition requiring competencies that are internationally recognized. Career growth rate will be faster, reaching peak level at a much younger age than in the past. Higher Education system is beginning to respond to the demands of Global demands for new kinds of programmes providing multidimensional, multidisciplinary educational experiences. An increasing number of programmes are offering degrees, diplomas and certificates in several cross - disciplinary fields.

New Directions

The rapidly changing professional scenario requires the young learners to be aware of their own talents, aptitudes and preferences so that they are not carried away by popular clichés and end up drifting in the winds of changes.

Intelligent career guidance, group discussions and professional monitoring by mature knowledge able persons should be available while pursuing university education, to avoid disappointments and frustrations in later life. All need not look outside the national borders nor should they all flock towards a single professional market. Some may even opt for lower initial emolument but can overtake others in due course.

During the last decade, urged by compulsions of competitiveness - national and international educators and researchers have been working to wards the development of principles and ideas for multidisciplinary modes of research and education. It is generally accepted that the knowledge of intricacies of design and the skill for the development of products and processes are fundamental to sustainable economic growth.

India is full of opportunities for anyone who could design and develop products, system and applications that can improve an existing one or replace it. The effort should be launched during the first year of the student in small groups encouraging them to brainstorm the potential opportunities and identify a few that are worth pursuing with the help of the faculty, laboratory facility and with some level of mentoring from a competent guide from the industry of service.

FOR CHILD INSPIRED EDUCATION SYSTEM

Children's questions do not respect the insularity of disciplines normally taught in our schools and colleges. Creativity often resides at the boundaries of disciplines. Besides several other points of difference, I would like to give some examples of the wonder and curiosity children and bring to the attention of teachers and schools in general that is not covered by our courses. Giving respect to children's questions does not mean blindly accepting what they say. They do bring some knowledge that after critical examination can enrich the curriculum. But more often they bring questions. The mere existence of questions among the young is a precious thing. They often reflect independent perception and exploration. Many a time children discover these questions themselves. The occurrence of these questions is more important than a densely packed slate full of answers given by grownups and scholars. At least for the children they represent important footsteps towards a creative life. And if such questions are often discussed in class they would benefit all the children and, I dare to say also their teachers.

Children's questions serve another important function. They do not respect the insularity of disciplines normally taught in our schools and colleges. That might be the reason for many discipline-imprisoned scholars feeling uncomfortable with them. Life is seldom, if ever, contained within any one discipline, surely we cannot stay within a culture where life as it is lived is considered to lie completely outside the hallowed grounds of schools and universities. This is not to imply that we do not get into the depts. of various disciplines. But it has been found that creativity often resides at the boundaries of disciplines. You do end up worrying about geology, archaeology, sociology, biology, chemistry, physics and cosmology, but such connections are seldom made in organized disciplinary courses. Children's questions keep reminding us that interconnections are necessary for the human mind. To the extent we deal with these questions we end up enriching the ecology of knowledge in our brains. That is often the real source of creativity. I take it for granted that one of the major objectives of education should be to encourage the emergence of creative individuals.

When our talks of individual creativity, one might be accused of "neo-liberal" tendencies. I do not know what sort of abuse that implies, but I cannot accept that any society should feel threatened by the encouragement of individual passion to understand in preference to voluminous short-term memorization. Long sermons to avoid communalism do not go very far; a deep understanding of the inevitability and value of cultural diversity is far more effective. It is no one's case that there should be complete absence of information. But information and misinformation without understanding is best used for advertising or brainwashing or for filling up the limited storage space of the brain with junk in which every new idea gets stuck. I fail to understand why I should be deprived of marks if I do not remember the name of Mussolini's mother.

One is thrilled by several examples of engagement of students with the land and cultural life around them. An effort to understand local history should not be ridiculed. Scientific exploration of flora and fauna around otherwise familiar environs surely cannot work against a similar understanding at the state and national level. A National Framework should not try to erase your knowing relationship with the sands of Rajasthan, or the vibrant beaches of Kerala, or the snowy hills of the North, or the majestic fury of the Brahmaputra. Everyone has a right to feel that they live on top of the globe; what we need to foster is the understanding that you that right only if you grant it to every one else. This is a requirement for us and for the world as a whole. This is global consciousness and not globalization.

A comment has been made questioning that knowledge can be provided by children because we do not have it encapsulated in our genes! Yes, our genes have no knowledge of our culture. Our religion or caste, no subjects such as physics or algebra, no history or geography. But there is immense capacity to experiment, to learn skills – sitting down. Crawling, standing, walking and talking. We learn more during the years before we enter school than through the rest of our lives. Such capabilities of observation, perception and urge to experiment dim with age. Some of this dimming is the result of how we try to educate our young!

I have received thousands of questions from the children of this country. While answering them I have made it clear that I am not a data bank, that I would entertain only those questions they have themselves discovered. Furthermore I also state that I would like to share my way of addressing their queries but there might be other ways of doing the same. I have not been overwhelmed by bigotry, though there are questions about astrology, *Vastushastra, and* modes of worship, but they are all questions and none of them is useless or insulting. Quite often they come because they are not captured in any single discipline. These questions come to me because they are usually not entertained in school. I wish they were and I wish we would learn not to avoid them. We should not only learn from children what to teach them but out education should also become child-inspired.

DOWN THE INFINITE CORRIDOR OF LEARNING

MIT's Open Course Ware, which provides those with internet connectivity free access to some 1600 courses taught at one of the world's top entries of learning, is an exciting initiative. To the intellectually curious, OCW offers the possibility of lifelong learning in a wired world- Vijaysree Venkatraman

Professor R.S. Kumarn, the unassuming head of the computer science department of an engineering college founded by a South Indian Industrial conglomerate, still remembers the fateful Google search from five years ago. Sitting at his desk in the Bannari Amman College of Technology in Tamil Nadu, he keyed in the search strings "Computer science" and "course material". Within minutes, he stumbled on a semester's worth of first-rate course material on several subjects of interest from software engineering to artificial intelligence – meticulously laid out on a Massachusetts Institute of Technology website.

The chance discovery gave him insight into a teaching model that places value on application not just on theory. You can say that I am an addict of ocw.mit.edu," says Prof.Kumar, who uses some of the content to teach his graduate and post-graduate classes.

The MIT open course ware site (OCW) provides those with internet connectivity free access to some 1600 courses taught at the 142 year old campus in Cambridge, Massachusetts. On this website formalities like registration necessary even for reading most American newspapers online are dispensed with. There is no tuition fee. Un like traditional distance learning successfully working through the OCW course material the lecture notes, reading assignments, the problem sets, and the final exams – will not earn the user any academic credits. Yet if site traffic and user testimonials are anything to go by, this portal launched in thing to go by, this portal launched in September 2002 serves self-learners, students, and educators, across the globe well.

Many find the 'intellectual philanthropy" baffling – why would one of the world's top universities give its teaching model and course material away free of cost? "The OCW philosophy stems from the institute faculty's belief that knowledge should be free and open to all – not just to those can afford it," says Anne Margulies, the Director of MIT OCW. "Innovations and discovery are possible only if resources are shared".

The internet serves as an effective medium for knowledge dissemination. The MIT OCW site receives approximately 1.4 million visits each month from several countries, including those in sub Saharan Africa, and the Middle East, With India ranking consistently among the top five users, says Steve Carson, Director of External Relations and OCW. Non profit organization has translated the content into many languages, increasing the impact and reach of this initiative.

MIT's example has inspired other universities, including Johns Hopkins Bloomberg School of Public Health, the Berkman Center for Internet and society at the Harvard. Law School, and the Tokyo Institute of Technology to initiate similar efforts, Some 150 like minded universities, including those in China, Japan and Spain, has formed an international consortium to publish their educational material online. Consortium members bring in valuable content that lies outside MIT's traditional area of expertise. Even with universal subjects like basic sciences, there are different approaches to teaching the same material. Users can pick what works best for them.

Many courses are text only, but the physics videos lectures by Prof. Walter H.G. Lewin – with classroom demonstration bring in feedback that can best be described as fan mail. A high school student from India writes: "The day I become a big man I will give MIT a million dollars for this".

Kandasamy Sivasakthival, a mainframe professional with TATA consultancy services, uses the sit to brush up on his engineering fundamentals, as he will be pursuing an advanced degree this fall. Good textbooks are available everywhere, but the assignment on OCW make students think rather than mug up formulae mindlessly, he says. At work, he has started initiatives on the strength of knowledge gained from the site. Particularly in Artificial Intelligence, Shaik Ibrahim, a 35 year old Chennai, businessman, has been using OCW from the pilot phase. "Some of the first courses I looked up were from the Sloan's School of Management because I was an MBA student at Madras University back then," he recalls. Now he visits the site to learn about relativity, robotics, or any topic that catches his fancy.

However, the academic riches on offer can sometimes seem overwhelming. "One of the future goals is to make the site easier to use and facilitate reuse of the vast material,' says Ms.Margulies whose team works to ensure that there is no copyright violation. The consortium portal could become an academic resource of first choice as it grows organically with contributions from institutes across the globe, she adds.

Even supporters of Open Course Ware belief there can be no substitute for interaction with professors and fellow students. "Good education is a contact sport", says M.S. Vijay Kumar, director of the office of Educational Innovation and Technology, MIT, But the creditors of the consortium foresee the formation of global learning communities centered on the site's contents.

Examinations will always be a reality for students – "an ordeal they have to get through", as Professor Kumar points out. But thanks to MIT's initiative, life long learning minus the exams falls within the realm of possibility for the intellectually curious in a wired world.

IMPORTANCE OF PROBLEM BASED LEARNING

It takes more time and energy to deliver the content this way, but is very gratifying as it is interesting, *Sudha Vidyasagar*

Priya Narayanana's Suggestions regarding open book exams (Open page, January 13) is very relevant in the context of evaluation. The aim of any open book exam is to stimulate thinking in a student and test his ability to seek and retrieve information. This is what we all do, later on in real life, in every field. To achieve this aim, not only should evaluation change, but the methods of learning also have to change.

At present right from school to even professional colleges, the teacher has to "finish the portions" before the exam. Little thought is given to whether this system makes the student a self learner. Since the examination papers contain predominantly questions which demand only recall, the whole system is in perfect equilibrium expected that the student who passes out in the end is a memory machine.

In contrast, problem based learning, which was started by MC Master University, uses the model of giving problems in the syllabus and encouraging activate learning by the student. This model is closest to real life situations and has been adapted by prestigious colleges all over the world.

Let us take the example of the medical field which is what I am familiar with. Every patient comes to a doctor with a complaint. The doctor with listens to what the patient has to say, examines him and orders tests, all with a single goal in mind: to find out what he is suffering from. In effect he is solving a problem applying his medical knowledge.

Of course experience fine tunes all these processes, but solving problems in something doctors do all their lives. The emotional aspect of healing is yet another dimension. Which demands empathy and understanding which are not easy to teach?

Application of knowledge

To make professionals good problem solvers, the curriculum too has to be delivered differently; emphasizing application of knowledge, the teacher can construct problems in the subject which can be solved using principles which govern the subject matter. Learning points can be pointed out and reinforced.

This takes imagination and effort on the part of the teacher and clarity regarding what should be highlighted. It takes more time and energy to deliver the content this way, but is very gratifying as it is interesting and students cannot sleep off while discussing a problem! It is also better remembered as all of us recollect examples and use them as memory hooks to latch on our knowledge to.

The end product of this kind of learning will be an individual who can think things out in any situation. With the vas expansion of knowledge in every field, it is humanly impossible to remember every fact in one's head

Further with the internet revolutionizing the availability of information, it is no longer necessary to strain one's memory thus. It becomes more important to know what information is needed in a particular situation, and where to look for it. Learning should be tuned to this aim, and teachers and students have to align themselves to this goal.

Of course the examination system too has to change simultaneously. With the continuous emphasis on marks right from childhood, most students will not learn anything that does not fetch marks, which are considered the surrogate for one's intelligence!

The evaluation thus drives the learning process, which is where the suggestions regarding open book exams are particularly relevant.

Further students must be encouraged, right from the school level, to question, discuss and apply facts and understand rather than mug up. The exams here too must be designed to test these abilities.

The resistance change methods of teaching are more often with us teachers who are set in our old comfortable ways. We find it easy to teach in the lecture format, and set papers which demand mugged up answers (which we too know by heart), as any other system shakes us out of our comfort zones).

But in the interests of future professionals, it is time we tried to implement these to make the next generation of graduates and post graduates better than us.

5

Children Must Be Warmly Hopped

(Professor Krishna Kumar, Director, National Council of Education Research and Training, New Delhi)

There is no alternative to evolving a child - centered system of governance. Kusum Nair's classic, Blossoms in the Dust, which was first published in 1961, provides a benchmark for judging India's progress. The book describes her travels and conversations with villagers across many regions of India. Her conclusion about the prospects of development in rural India was that modern means of production alone will not succeed unless there is a change in values and attitudes. Her major advice to planners was that they must recognize the sharp diversity of values and perceptions that prevails between and within different regions. Apparently, she hoped that education would play a big role in bringing about social change. This expectation was share by several social scientists and commentators of the 1960s.

Perceived as a panacea for many familiar ills, education was itself in dire need of reform. It is colonial character had exacerbated the very malaise that it was supposed to cure. For instance the stigma attached to manual work was at the heart of caste and gender based hierarchies. The spread of education has undoubtedly helped to develop fissures in these hierarchies. But the outcomes of this significant change are unevenly distributed. Between caste and gender, the latter provides far more visible and pervasive evidence of change than does the former. Educational and employment opportunities have changed the lives of millions of women along lines that had already surfaced in the late colonial period. Women's autonomy and lack of fear have become increasingly more manifest in our public life, but there is an irony in this. From the early decades of the 20th century onwards, educated women started to face a rough time in seeking social acceptance. Their personal and emotional experiences got tougher as their levels of educational attainment increased. The reason was that while education opened up a new world to women, it failed to socialize men into a new, corresponding mould, Men's expectations from women remained unchanged, and hence women's emancipation evoked conflict, aggression, even violence. Looking around, we can witness this state of affairs daily. Searching for causes responsible for this lopsided impact of education, we would soon realize that what education teaches. Its curriculum, has failed to keep pace with the requirements of sensitizing society to new realities. An assumption prevailed that the bonds of caste would on their own; somewhat magically loosen up as a result of literacy and success in examination.

Neglecting teacher training has further compounded the losses incurred on account of indifferently induced, or entirely absent, curricular changes. Teachers constitute the most important factor in determining the quality of children's experience at school. Today millions of children born to illiterate parents are expected to attend school, yielding the exciting potential to nurture a thoughtful and tolerant society of the kind the constitution envisions. Yet hardly any State is in a position to realize this potential because the welfare and training of teachers have been ignored everywhere. Instead of moving forward, in this sector we have actually regressed. Schools teachers had played an important role in the national movement, both as individuals and as a professional group. Far from treating them as national resources for deeper social churning, independent India treated them as a faceless mass of literate workers. The Chattopad hyaya commission appointed by Indira Gandhi in 1983 noted that "today the average teacher's perception of his role and responsibility is far too limited and is concerned with his own immediate tasks" The commission felt that the teacher must "actively and feeling associate himself, as an essential and responsible partner, in the great tasks which face the nation". This recommendation filed to save the school teacher's status as it declined rapidly over the decade of the 1990s and continues to do so today. The profession has lost all attraction for the young, due to which only those who fail to materialize all other aspiration accept teaching as a last resort.

A great opportunity was lost when the constituent Assembly failed to mobilize consensus on making elementary education a fundamental right of every child. That mistake was corrected a few years ago when the constitution was amended. However, necessary follow up steps to make the amendment meaningful have not been taken. Given the sad condition of the infrastructure of education in most states (most accurately reflected in the sad physical and academic condition of most state councils of educational research and training and District Institutes of Education and Trainings), there seems little alternative to Centre led reforms and a bill passed by Parliament. Those who oppose this assert that the responsibility to pass the necessary legislation and to provide resources lies with the States.

Historically, the vague division of education at responsibilities between the centre and the states has harmed India's children since colonial days. The lone instrument of Centre State dialogue on education, namely the Central Advisory Board or Education (CABE), has no executive authority or powers. As far as our elementary school children are concerned, India continues to be reluctant to own them. The case of pre-school children is worse, for they are not even nominally covered in the constitutional amendment. Even as our rural masses now face the worst ever crisis of survival, which the Magsaysay award winner P.Sainath has amply described in his regular writings in *The Hindu* the wrangling over the bill on right to elementary education and the hesitation to allocate adequate resources for it casts a tragic shadow over the remarkable economic growth rate we have achieved six decades after independence.

Any agenda for educational reform must start by recognizing that children belong to a special category of citizens because they cannot protect their own rights. Children must be warmly hugged by the State in respect of all their needs, namely health and nutrition, safety security and education. Significant reforms in governance are required to ensure that the efforts to be made by different departments come together. This is not easy, but there is no alternative to evolving a child –centered system of governance so that India stops wasting its huge human resources potential on account of malnutrition, illiteracy and child abuse. With widespread low hemoglobin levels and frequent illness, especially among girls India cannot compete with its neighbors like China and Japan, let alone the Europeans and the Americans. For greater focus and efficiency in the delivery of child related services, the entrenched Centre – State impasse must be overcome. While no one can deny the Center's role in setting policy goals and providing funds for systemic reform, we can hardly overlook the lack of rig our and accountability in the States response to policy directions. One glaring evidence is that 40 years after the Kothari commission wrote its laudable report, even the pattern of stages it recommended has not been implemented in all the States. Adoption of the National Curriculum Frame work 2005, though it has the approval of CABE and has been implemented by CBSE, presents similarly story.

State level issues of education governance are ignored by the national media as well as by civil society groups. A vast number of systemic problems simply never get resolved. Territorial disburse between SCERTs and Boards the isolation of SCERTs and DIETs from universities and the multiplicity of structures (eg. the existence of more than one Board in Tamil Nadu) are illustrative instances of the kind of long standing problems that keep the system stymied. Even small decisions require a mountain of pressure. Consider for instance the eligibility of Delhi University's B.El.Ed (Bachelor of Elementary Education) Degree holders for the salary scale of a Trained Graduate Teacher (TGT). This is the least than Delhi Government could do for a world class programme of teacher education. Almost a decade has passed since the first batch of remarkable teacher's cam out of this programme, but the modest honour of a TGT grade still eludes them why? Because, the world 'elementary' has no operative value in the lexicon of scales. If you teach up to Class V, you get a TGT scale if you are qualified to teach up to class X not if you stop at Class VIII where the constitution defines the end of elementary education, apparently the Constitution can guide the nation but have little value for those who decide salary scale.

6

For Pleasing Personality Skills

(Dr. R.V. Baskar, Professor of English, University of Aden Republic, Yemen)

Personality refers to certain qualities in a person's character which distinguish him from other people. Personality is defined as the organization of the Psycho physical systems in an individual that moulds his thoughts and actions.

The person's family, education, environment, social values, philosophy of life, religion, culture and civilization influence his personality. Active participation in sports and games and considering victory and defeat as two facets of life, practice of yoga and mediation endow a person with pleasing personality traits.

There are different types of personality, like aggressive, sensitive, jovial, pleasing and dynamic. Assertive behaviour starts in the adolescent age, because the abundant energy available in youth is not properly channelized. Certain activities like watching adult stuff of television and computer, pornography, use of tobacco and intoxicants, make them physically and mentally weak. Parents, teachers and elders must guide them in a friendly way and channelize their youthful potential in constructive activities.

Self-esteem means respecting and thinking positively of one's own self and his capabilities. It should be cultivated from childhood. It helps to avoid inferiority complex, leads to emotional and integral growth and facilitates a human and balance personality

The right altitude and approach to issues and events pave the way for success. Attitude and aptitude alter the altitude of live. Punctuality and skilful management of time are the essential features of a successful personality. Planning leads to perfection. Plan your work and work your plan. Schedule the work and mcticulously execute it.

Plan the day's work, prioritize it, write it on a piece of paper, and refer to it often and do the work methodically. In the evening, verify your checklist and feel satisfied that you have successfully carried out the day's assignment. Spend the rest of the evening with the family, friends and relatives.

Apparel always proclaims the personality. Distinguish yourself by smart dressing and appearance. Emotional intelligence refers to administering emotions like determination, desire, joy, sorrow, gluttony, love, lust, envy, jealousy, hatred and anger. Do not fall a prey to emotions; remain cool, calm and well collected at critical hours.

Every organization needs potential leaders. Physical fitness mental alertness and moral correctness are the hallmarks of leadership.

A leader should possess a sound knowledge, good experience and rapport with his people. He leads others by his personal example and inspires them. Ability to converse and convince; address and attract the audience is essential qualities of leadership. Commanding voice and good command over language add value to a leader.

Educational institutions, social, cultural and religious organizations must play the lead role in shaping the personality of the younger generation. Sound personalities make a sound nation. Positive and pleasing personalities permanently live in the memory of the people and inspire them.

7

Human Rights, National Security, and Terrorism

(Ramesh Thakur, Distinguished Fellow at the centre for international Governance Innovation and Professor of Political science at the University of Waterloo in Canada)

Who would have thought that India would need to tutor Australia on protecting individual human rights? Yet here we have the case of the Government of India summoning the Ambassador of Australia to remind his Government of the need for due process in the treatment of an Indian doctor detained in Brisbane.

The case highlights the importance of proper balance between civil liberties, individual human rights, and the responsibility of the state to protect inhabitants from terrorists. Before 9/11, western governments and human rights champions were prone to moral ambivalence between perpetrators of terrorism and efforts of legitimate governments to maintain national security and assure public safety. After 9/11 western governments began to view other countries parallel wars against terrorism through the prism of a fellow government facing agonizing policy choices in the real world, rather than single-issue groups whose vision is not anchored in any responsibility for policy decisions. Many governments used to be at the receiving end of moral and political judgment about robust responses to violent threats posed to their authority and order from armed dissidents. They now get a more sympathetic hearing and mature understanding forged in the crucible of shared suffering.

This does not give any government a license to trample rights won at great cost over many centuries: rights of people against government. A human right, owed to every person simply as a human being, is inherently universal. Held only by human beings, but equally by all, it does not flow from any office, rank or relationship. The language of human rights embodies the intuition that the human species is one and every individual is entitled to equal more consideration. It is vividly captured in the Second World War joke that they came after the workers; I was not a worker, so I did not object. They cam after the homosexuals: I wasn't one, so I did not object, they came after the Jews; I wasn't one, so I did not object, Then they came after me: There was no one left to object.

Success in defeating terrorism can come only if we remain true to values that terrorists reject. It is possible to resort to the lesser evil of curtailing liberties and using violence in order to defeat the grater evil of terrorism, but only if we do not succumb to the greater evil of destroying the very values for which democracies stand.

They way to this is to require of Governments that they justify all restrictive measures publicly, submit them to judicial review, and circumstances them with sunset clauses to guard against the temporary becoming permanent. The safeguards are especially important because the history of the great democracies themselves suggests that most people privilege the security of the majority over the harm done to minorities deprived of their rights in the name of national security.

After 9/11, some western democracies recalibrated the existing balance between national security and civil liberties in their laws and practices. American priorities shifted to subordinate human rights to victory in the 'war' against terrorism, A counter terrorism expect testified that "After 9/11 the gloves came off" while another official remarked that "if you don't violate someone's human rights, you aren't doing your job". There developed also the distasteful practiced of "rendition to torture". Sending prisoners to their home countries precisely because the later were known to practice torture as a routine part of their interrogation.

Many other democracies jointed the United States in shifting the balance of laws and administrative practices towards state security. In Australia, the post 9/11 hysteria was harvested by the Government to introduce tough detention laws against illegal immigrants in defense of a policy of Fortress Australia that led to the detention of dozens of Australian citizens, one whom was deported to her country of birth and another, a mentally ill woman, spent ten months in detention.

Thus terrorism has an impact on human rights in three ways. First, it is itself an extreme denial of the most basic human right, namely to life, and it creates an environment in which people cannot live in freedom from fear and enjoy their other rights. Secondly, the threat of terrorism can be used by governments to enact laws that strip away many civil liberties and political freedoms. One simple yet popular technique is to reverse the burden of proof; those accused of terrorist activities sympathies or even guilt by association on the basis of accusations by anonymous people are to be presumed to be guilty until they can prove their innocence of unspecified charges. Thirdly, without necessarily amending laws or enacting new ones, governments, can use the need to fight terrorism as an alibi to stifle dissent and criticism and imprison or threaten domestic opponents.

This is where the case of Dr. Mohamed Haneef is so very disturbing. On the evidence presented to the Brisbane court, he made the mistake of giving his prepaid SIM card to a second cousin in the United Kingdom because the card would not be of any use to him in Australia for whose sunny shores he was departing. The card was found in a car used by a terrorist a year later.

Hardly surprising that the magistrate granted bail. This is where the case gets cursor and curioser as Alice remarked in her wonderland. Having spent 12 days in custody before being questioned, then grated bail pending trail, Dr. Haneef had his multi year work visa canceled on 'Character' grounds.

No country will strip its immigration Minister of the power to cancel a visitor's visa. But the purpose is to prevent someone from entering or, if he is already in the country, to terminate his presence and deport him. In Dr.Haneefs case the primary motivation would appear to be to keep him in Australia under detention – and require him to pay for the privilege at the end of it all, even if he should be acquired.

To top it all, the government has made it clear that Dr.Haneef will be deported even if he is ultimately found innocent. A case perhaps of guilty even if proven innocent? It is hard not to infer that this is a case of serious misuses of power and political interference in the process of criminal justice.

The dream of a world ruled by law is a shared vision. We must not privilege security and order to such an extent as to destroy our most cherished values of liberty and justice in the search for an unattainable absolute security. As Benjamin Franklin, One of the fathers of American independence, said, those who would sacrifice essential liberty to temporary safety deserve neither liberty nor safety.

The robustness and resilience of the civilest world's commitment to human rights norms and values will be judged in the final analysis not be the breaches in the aftermath of 9/11, but by the reversal and attenuation of the breaches through judicial and political processes as well as the pressure of domestic and international civil society. This is where the response of the Australian community to the prima facie abuse of executive power of the Australian Government is so reassuring the legal fraternity, civil liberties groups, other sectors of society, an even the state premier have either roundly condemned the extra judicial detention of detention of Dr. Haneef or demanded a public explanation from the government. The one disappointment has been the federal opposition labor party, which frightened of being wedged on an issue of national security, has once again resorted to "metabolism".

If and when Dr.Haneef is tried in a court of law, the trail will be about him: his beliefs, actions, and links to terrorism. The manner, forum, and rules of procedure of the trial are not about him, but about the quality and credibility of the Australian justice system, specifically, do the Australian Government belief in, respect and abide by the rule of law or disregard it as a mere inconvenience when judicially tested? The question of indifference or active concern about Dr.Haneef's fate in a foreign land is about Indian values and beliefs. A failure by the Government to demand justice for him would be an abdication of its responsibility to protect citizens.

Tough on terrorists, Tougher on the causes of terrorism. But toughest of all on safeguarding the virtues of tolerance, human rights, civil liberties, and due process.

THE NOBLEST CALLING

The best teacher furthers the life chances of his students without necessarily doing anything beneficial to his own. Income from a family of teachers. My mother taught in a school through much of her adult life. My sister, a highly qualified doctor, choose to teach in a medical college rather than go into private practice. My father was a research scientist through whose hands passed numerous doctoral candidates. And the tradition goes back further. Three of my granduncles were teachers, as were two of my great grandfathers.

In this respect I am black sheep of the family. Although I had the necessary qualifications, and opportunities, I chose a career that is in many respects diametrically opposed to that of teaching. To be a writer is to privilege your individual self, and (Especially) signature. Your name is carried alongside all you say; the credit (and, it must e added, discredit) that the work brings is yours alone. Writing is a profoundly egoistical enterprise; and writers are in deed the most self – centered and self – absorbed of men (and, of course, women). On the other hand, to be a teacher is to subordinate you're self and your ego, your needs and your ambitions, to the self and ego of others. The best teacher furthers the life chances of his students without necessarily doing anything beneficial to his own.

Vial difference

Writing is all about, "me mine, myself"; teaching about, "his, hers, theirs". It may be because of this conceptual (and moral) distance between my profession and theirs that I have always had a profound respect for caring and conscientious teachers. The teacher I most admired died in the last weeks of the year that has just ended. His name was sub has Chandra Bhargava, and for more than three decades he taught physics and integrity at St.Stephen's college, Delhi.

I first got to know Bhargava Saab in the mid 1970s, while I was a student at Delhi University. I was registered for a degree in economics, so I was never in fact formally taught by him. But we had a common interest in the game of bridge (Which he played brilliantly, and I no more than adequately); and a common physical affliction, bronchial asthma. Through exchanging bidding conventions and bronchodilators we forged a friendship that endured for 30 years.

Bhargava Saab was a tall, thin man with a shock of thick, dark hair, He was upright in his bearing and even more so in his character. The physics students, naturally, adored him because, unlike most other teachers, he did serious scientific research himself. But beyond his discipline and his college, he was known throughout Delhi University for his generosity and his integrity. Student who could not find a hostel room stayed with him for months on end; students in trouble with the (instinctively authoritarian) authorities found him an able interlocutor on their behalf. Ex-Students visiting Delhi could always count on free board and lodging. I was one of those who extravagantly abused this privilege; over the years, I must have spent at least 300 days at his home, working in the achieves in the day and discussing bridge and other matters with him at night. (His democratic instincts extended to his politics; he was an early critic of the Emergency and also active in the civil liberties movement.

I have spoken of the veneration we students had for Bhargava Saab; if anything, his fellow teachers admired him even more. As the physicist lay dying one old colleague wrote to me of how "For 30 years he has been a kind of fixture in my moral universe. On all the 'small' things which constitute personal integrity and friendship, he was always a guide and at important moments it has often been “What would Bhargava Sahib say?”

Just another Rahul

One day in the mid 1980s Bhargava Saab received a call from a high school student named Rahul, who wished to consult him as to which subject to study in college. An appointment was fixed for 9.30 a.m. the next day. At 8.30 Bhargava Saab went to the lab to set up some experiments. When he next looked at his watch it was 9.20. He put down his instruments and rushed back to his apartment. The route from lab to home was normally leafy and quiet. But on this day it was swarming with policemen. About 50 yards from his house he was stopped and not allowed to proceed further. “*Mujhe Jaane do, ghar mein ekladka mera intezar kar raha hai*”, pleaded Bhargava Saab (“Let me go, there is a student waiting to meet me at home”). The cops would not relent; policemen and professors argued, back and forth, until it finally dawned on the former that this was the man their boss’s son had come to meet.

Some credit in this story accrues to Rahu Gandhi’s advisers. They had done their homework, thus to find that the Delhi University teacher most likely to give the best, or most fair-minded, career advice was a man who did not carry an elevated title such as Dean or vice Chancellor. But most of the credit must remain with Bhargava Saab. All Rahuls were akin to him, be one the son of the college Chaprasi or another the son of the serving Prime Minister of India. (It is characteristic that he did not bother to ask the caller his surname). We can be sure that for any other Rahul he would still have arrived on the dot.

FRUITFUL COLLABORATION FOR FUTURE

Recent years have seen universities actively pursuing a different role – signing memorandum of understanding (MoU) with foreign universities, industrial establishments and multinational companies. Madras and Anna Universities are among those universities. Which have been in the MoU mode?

They received impetus when the University Grants Commission, during the X Plan period (2002-2007), took the initiative, promotion of Higher Education Abroad (PI HEAD). As part of the initiative, the UGC embarked upon a focused nationally – coordinated programme to attract international students and promote Indian institutions to offer programmes abroad.

“As of now, the university of Madras has a very extensive network of about 71 international institutions/universities for academic collaboration and joint research", says S.Ramachandran, Vice Chancellor. As for Anna University, it is having collaborative projects with 50 foreign universities, 25 leading industrial houses of India and 10 multinational corporations, according to D.Viswanthan, Vice chancellor.

Exchange programmes of the faculty and students are one of the prominent characteristics of the experiment, the two universities have entered into partnership with many pending institutions from countries including United States, United Kingdom, South Korea, New Zealand and Canada. Under the project, crossing the boundaries, the Wageningen University of Netherlands is supporting a five year programme of providing scholarship to women scholars of the Anna University for higher studies in integrated water resources management. Efforts are on to introduce disaster management in the Madras University curriculum utilizing the expertise of Kyoto University, Japan. Sharing his experience, S.P. Thyagarajan former Madras University vice-chancellor, says that as a follow up to his participation in an international conference of universities in the US five years ago, he set up the International Centre of Madras University (ICOM) with a director and coordinators drawn form broad areas of teaching and research to initiate MoUs with the foreign institutions.

Prof. Thyagarajan, who conducted a study of the status of MoU projects two years ago, says that about 50 percent of the Mous got translated into significant activity in terms of student exchanges and faculty visits. Talking of the difficulties encountered in implementation of the MoUs, he points to the absence of a world class hostel for foreign students and financial limitation in extending the require level of local hospitality to the faculty who visited the Madras University and in supporting the visits of Madras University students and faculty to the respective foreign universities [even though local hospitality is extended by the host university]. However, Prof. Viswanathan is emphatic that the MoU mode has become essential when not many people are coming forward for teaching. This will primarily help strengthen the faculty. In future, the focus should be on twinning programems whereby students of Anna University will spend a portion of their study period in a foreign university and vice-versa.

For such projects to be successful, Prof. Thyagarajan says each university should establish en exclusive body to facilitate all activities connected with the projects. It will have to structure study India programmes, summer research programmes and on demand curricula as per foreign students' requirements. It will have to make them known through their websites.

SERENE BRILLIANCE

A year ago Faber and Faber reissued Wallace Stevens' Collected Poems in a handsome new volume. Its distinctive dark blue cover will serve any new reader well as a clue to one of Steven's most cherished natural features; the sea which he used resonantly throughout many of his best poems. For a fan rediscovering this poet she loves, it is just a surface to the immense intellect, insight and emotional power flowing through Steven's work.

Stevens is unique in the rich and diverse mechanics of 20th century English poetry. He is enigmatic as a poet in that he published his first groundbreaking collection, Harmonium, only when he was 45 in 1923. Many other great poets have published at a much earlier age. Prodigies W.H. Auden and Paul Muldoon effectively published as undergraduates while Ted Hughes and Seamus Heaney made their debut an age of 27.

Intensely Philosophical

Furthermore, although Stevens is categorized as a modernist, his work never had the gloom that gripped T.S. Eliot's "Wasteland", W.B. Yeat's Second coming or Auden's "Spain 1937". This was despite the fact that he lived in the same compelling times. Contrarily, he was intensely and deeply philosophical but never politically engaged the way Auden or Vladimir Mayakovsky were. His poetic voice retained the same thematic direction throughout his career and was principally concerned with the problematic relationship between the 'outside world' and the 'inside world' or 'reality' and 'imagination'.

In other poets, their themes have changed. Hughes was initially inspired by nature and then went to myth and finally confessional with "Birthday Letters". Stevens follows a very flat trajectory by comparison.

However, this does not detract from the seriousness of the task Stevens was immersed in. He thought that the separation between what humans call "reality" and 'imagination' was not as firm as we would like to believe. Reality and imagination as concepts are like porous rocks; they look waterproof but let the water drip in. Even worse is the idea that they are interchangeable.

This possibility provides the basis for Steven's oeuvre and he approaches it with profound sophistication. Often, he writes in a grand manner where many of the poems speak to the reader as long philosophical mediations. Steven's style and subject matter make him a difficult, but rewarding, poet to read with the reader having to engage deeply with his intellect.

What makes Stevens tough to interpret is his unique diction, which is a mixture of the hymn, the ornate and the bizarre. The bizarre is definitely worth exploring as it is more prevalent in his early work but is gradually weeded out as his voice matures and becomes more solemn.

Numerous examples of eccentricity can be located in Harmonium but a favorite is from “Bantams in Pine-Woods” Where “Chieftain Iffucan of Azcan in catf tan / of tan with henna hackles, halt!” Some of these short lyrics can be looked on with humour but others such as “Life is Motion” just baffle. In its entirety it reads: “In Oklahoma / Bonnie and Josie / Dressed in Calico / Danced around a stump. / they cried / ‘Ohoyaho / Ohoo’.../ Celebrating the marriage / of flesh and air”.

Remarkable beauty

On the other hand, Stevens wrote some of the most emotionally stunning lyrics of the 20th century. His famous “The Snowman” takes one’s breath away literally. The reader feels the ‘misery in the sound of the wind” and the “Nothing that is not there and the nothing that is”

In longer lyrics, Stevens could be very musical and unbelievably plain Speaking. In ‘Academic Discourse at Havana” the first pat of the poem says, “Canaries in the morning, orchestras / in the afternoon. That is / A difference, at least, from nightingales / Jehovah and the great sea worm. The air / is not so elemental nor the earth / so near. But the sustenance of the wilderness / Does not sustain us in the metropoles”.

These lines and images say nothing of solid philosophical substance, especially for Stevens, but here he demonstrates a different quality as a poet: an ability to say something with remarkable beauty.

Conceptually, “Thirteen ways of looking at a blackbird” is one of Steven’s most crucial poems as it examines the topography of the world in the metaphor of a blackbird through imagination. In this poem, perspectives change and Stevens Point to reality shifting as imagination accompanies it in tandem. In part VIII, Stevens reflects, “I know noble accents / and lucid, inescapable rhythms; / But I know too the blackbird is involved / in what I know”.

Stevens established a specific terminology to talk about his theme and this in turn allowed him to create a special grid where he was able to discuss ‘reality’ and imagination’. Poet Jay Parini writes that ‘reality’ was summed up in the words of “Sky, day north, rock, sun and blue” while “mind, night, south, wind, moon and green” was imagination.

Stevens saw a lot of what he was articulating as “things dark on the horizons of perception”. He says this in one of his last great poems. “To an old Philosopher in Rome”. What is critical though is realizing these, “things” are “Two alike in the make of the mind”. Stevens thinks our world is a human construct and that 'imagination' and 'reality' in this poem are two sides of the same coin.

Philosophical detachment

Originally Stevens was more of an idealist regarding the powers of the poet and poetry. In "Another Weeping women" Stevens wrote, "The magnificent cause of being / the imagination, the one reality / in this imagined world," The poet is here to locate and express this magnificence.

A primary concern for Stevens with modern human society was that since religion had lost much of its power, something had filled the void artistically, emotionally, spiritually and so forth. This was of course to be poetry but like any great poet, Stevens never let go of his skeptical side. There remained a philosophical detachment in all his work. In "Man Carrying Thing", he declared "the poem must resist the intelligence / Almost successfully". Perhaps Stevens by this statement meant that poetry is a tight rope; it must be an incentive which gives a participant something she wants but simultaneously allows room for intelligent criticism.

Stevens was like Yeats in that, as his career moved towards its end, he formulated the conclusion that his poetry and vision was less world making in reality then in imagination. Wallace Stevens as an artist is up there with William Shakespeare, Leo Tolstoy and Yeats. These people were not only thought provoking but transformed the way we perceive ourselves.

Reading Stevens gives us as he says in his final poem, "Not Ideas about the Thing but the Thing Itself; A new knowledge of reality".

DOES REAL LEARNING TAKE PLACE IN SCHOOLS?

The all too familiar Indian School classroom - Students chorusing a mathematical formula or an important scientific principle at the top of their voices over and over, with most of them totally oblivious to what they are 'learning'.

What is more, they are made to sit through arduous sessions dedicated to such pointless yelling. This is just one instance that reflects the functioning of the countries fault-plagued school education system.

Having spread my schooling across four Indian States (I am now an engineering student in Chennai), I found the sorry state continuing in every school I attended, Primary Schools are increasingly becoming places where students manifest a sharp predilection for rote behaviour and insatiable appetites for grades and percentages.

Thanks to this method of running schools in the country, and innate thinking or creativity on the part of students is nipped in the bud.

Raise intelligent or thought based questions in class and you get public remonstrations and a one-way ticket into the teacher's bad books. Such proclivities are largely responsible for lackadaisical outlook among students, who finally become devoid of independent thought. The grim situation extends across all levels of schooling.

How did such a system, imparting superficial education, come into existence in the first place? I am sure it was not a well chalked out plan for things to pan out the way they have. Rather, it became a situation no one could really help.

A school handling 5,000 students with vast syllabi waiting to be taught will undoubtedly fall prey to such pressure. Teachers and students succumb to this pressure alike.

With burgeoning peer pressure, all eyes (and minds) are on the high percentage that would set the scorecards ringing and not on the subjects parse.

Teachers have their own time constraints and this translates into their teaching becoming all the more examination centric. Students find their way around exams very easily, without having to acquire the necessary lore.

Implications

The situations are all hunky-dory so long as you are schooling and the transition from school to college academics is not always flowery. Students are suddenly brought out their reclusive and narrow intellectual shells and they start flunking even the simplest of tests in colleges.

Another disturbing consequence is their inability to relate what they "Study"? Vis-à-vis real world situations, on that count, the very principle of education seems to have been refuted. I agree that Indian scooters and engineers are among the best in the business but the fact is that we will be able to churn out better professionals in the future should things fall into place quickly.

I think it is never too late to pull back things a bit. The emphasis should be on instigating qualitative education methods and on making it more holistic in approach. We can very well afford to cut down on the quantum of curricula laid out each year. I would rather students spend an hour on calisthenics than having to memorize a few of Tennyson's poems or two-line long algebraic formulate.

Examinations, usually cursory and awash with frenzy, could use a through reformulation possibly the only measure of academic excellence, examinations need to be contrived in way that puts students' true learning and though to test. We need, not put up with the system fate de mieux, let us do what we do best – think across all dimensions without bounds and expend the full potential of the human mind. Let us also help posterity do it. The onus is on us.

The Problem of Non employability

Our Engineering graduates are brilliant and acquire the necessary technical skills during their studies. Some of them are successful at campus recruitments. Of these a good number are shown the door during training.

In real case situations, a batch of graduates from a well known engineering college was recruited by a prestigious IT company. The individuals of this batch were consistently scoring above 85 percent from class X onwards and alter graduated without arrears in any semester. Two weeks into training, they were rejected.

Why were they rejected? The basic reason was they were not adequately groomed to move from campus to corporate life. The skill sets required from students include an attitude to learn ability to work in teams, ability to work around obstacles and analytical skills.

Employers demand employable professionals who could start bringing in the dollars as early as possible In short, they want "industry ready candidates".

A teacher teaches and a trainer trains. This is the most basic concept. Unfortunately this is not understood by many, at the adult level, a teacher can only impart knowledge that is technical or otherwise but it requires something more to bring about the right mind set and synergies for corporate life.

People who have not been through corporate life or large government run organizations cannot deliver the goods when it comes to higher level preparation and grooming. To draw an analogy, a doctor with an MBBS degree is both a physician and a surgeon. He is empowered and licensed to perform surgeries. Will any patient in his senses approach such a doctor for an open heart surgery?

The lesson drawn form the above is that, if you want goods and services of a high quality, you have to pay for them. Colleges should produce engineers who would be successful in corporate life. This has become an absolute necessity in today's employment scenario. Today leading IT companies are finding that B.A., B.Com., B.Sc and BCA graduates are more suitable for employment in the IT sector than engineering graduates.

Commerce, Arts, Science and Computer application graduates are emerging as qualitative employee who can handle clients' requirements better. Their process of education is more wholesome and they are taught to interact with people and develop what are called "People skills".

Engineers are taught to interact with machinery and electronic gadgets without emphasis on people. This affects them later in their life and career. Corrective action is the need or the hour and it is incumbent on the engineering colleges to produce employable engineers. The statistics will prove that there is an increase in demand for IT and communication related engineering seats. The fast buck syndrome is the only driving force.

The irony, however is that low cost education (B.A., B.Com., B.Sc., and BCA etc) is generating better employability.

8

Globalization and Legal Education

(C. Rajkumar, Associate professor of Law at City University of Hong Kong and Chief Executive Officer of Legal Education and Research Society)

Globalization has been a subject of debates and discussions from numerous perspectives. There is no doubt that globalization has profound implications for the future of higher education worldwide. While the debate relating to foreign universities coming into India or private investment in higher education is very important, it is critical to examine how India as a country will face up to the competition posed by institutions world wide in attracting Indian students for pursuing educational opportunities abroad. Inevitably, the need for raising academic standards, creating a better research environment, developing sound infrastructure formulating good governance, models, creating better career opportunities, and promoting professional advancement of academics are all central issues for formulating the necessary policies for higher education.

Within this larger debate relating to reform of the higher education sector in India, there is an urgent need to examine, the situation with regard to legal education and how globalization is going to impact the agenda for it. There are four important consequences for legal education. Global curriculum, global faculty, global degrees, and global interaction. These deserve public attention.

A few decades back, law schools in India could do well as long as their curriculum was focused on Indian law and issues relating to the country's legal system. While there was some limited impetus to the study of international and comparative law, the larger focus was primarily on issues relating to the Indian Legal system. This was of course, necessary and ought to have been the approach. There is indeed greater scope for improvement in promoting excellence in teaching and research relating to Indian Law and to addressing the challenges facing the legal system, including the need for establishing a society that respects the rule of law and meets the challenges of globalization.

However, new and emerging law schools cannot afford to limit their focus to teaching and research on issues relating to Indian Law. In fact, the appetite of Indian law students for understanding international and comparative law has significantly increased over the years, given their participation in international moot competitions that range from issues such as maritime law to humanitarian law to dispute resolution. The most challenging task is to strike proper balance to ensure that students are taught a fair mix of course that give them knowledge and training in Indian law. But at the same time prepare them for facing the challenges of globalization, whereby domestic legal mechanisms interact with both international and foreign legal systems. This interaction is going to deepen in the years to come and our law schools must prepare themselves to face this challenge posed by globalization.

Hiring of good faculty has been a challenge in law schools in India and abroad. Generally the financial incentives offered by the private sector both in India abroad are far more attractive than those available in the public sector, including law schools, for good lawyers to make commitment to academia. But it is possible to attract good lawyers to academia by promoting a range of educational reforms and institutions initiatives, including better financial incentives. Globalization has in deed provided new opportunities to address some of the challenges in this regard. Issues relating to the Indian legal system are not only taught and researched in India but also in many other parts of the world. Growing numbers of Indian lawyers and scholars are involved in this effort. There is need for having a global focus in hiring faculty for Indian law schools. Of, course, success will depend on the schools, ability to provide the right kind of intellectual environment and finical and other incentives for Indian or foreign scholars to teach and pursue research in India and to contribute to its growth story.

Indian law schools need to consider innovation when it comes to the degree programmes offered by them. At present, there are two models: the three year bachelor of Law (LLB) programme offered by many universities in India; and the five year integrated B.A (Hons) cum LLB programmes offered by the National law Schools in Indian starting with the one in

Bangalore. It will be useful to look at the experience of the United States and others in examining whether Indian law schools should consider offering the Juris Doctor (JD) Programme. The starting the JD programme in the U.S. is largely credited to Christopher Columbus Lang dell when he was Dean of Harvard Law School during 1870 – 95, although the University of Chicago was the first law schools to offer a JD degree. Increasing many parts of the common law would are beginning to offer JD programems; law schools in Australia, Canada and Hong Kong are in the forefront. Obviously, there is an emerging trend infavour of JD programme.

There could be many sound justifications for offering a JD Programme in Indian. One of the important reasons for starting an integrated B.A., LLB programme was to attract some of the brightest schools leavers to the legal profession and to raise the standards of the Bar by providing sound legal education. This objective was indeed achieved to some extent, but the context and circumstances have changed. Law is increasingly becoming a preferred career not only among school leavers, but also among students holding other professional degrees. For example, there is a growing interest among students who have pursued a liberal arts undergraduate education in history, sociology, economics, political science, and other disciplines in pursuing legal studies. Under the existing five-year integrated law programme in the National Law schools, it will be a long term commitment (3+5 years) on the part of other degree holders to study law, unless they decide to enter one of the three year. LLB programmes offered by many universities. In this context, it will be useful to examine whether a graduate entry JD programme can be established in India. It is relevant to note that starting 2008, Melbourne Law School, one of Australia's oldest and most reputed law schools will offer only a graduate entry JD programme because it scrapped its LLB programmes last years. The rationale for this has been articulated thus: "The school firmly believes that the Melbourne JD, as designed and taught by the school, represents the right response to the challenge of providing the highest quality legal education in the demanding and competitive international environment of the 21st century".

The law schools of the future ought to provide academic space for engaging in teaching and cutting edge research on issues of global significance. The institutions ought to constantly reinvent themselves for facing the challenges of globalization through exchange and collaboration programmes. This has different implications for faculty. Students and for the development of teaching and research programmes. In this regard, it is important to note that token arrangements of collaboration may not be helpful to the institutions involved. There is a need to develop a shared understanding of the nature of exchange and collaborative programmes being established for them to be effective and beneficial for all the parties concerned. Globalization has posed multiple challenges to the future of legal education in India but it has provided an opportunity to challenge the status quo, which is an essential condition for seeking any reform.

SIXTY YEARS OF HIGHER SCIENCE EDUCATION

The constitution of India (Seventh Schedule) together with the amendment of 1976 places the responsibility for coordination and determination of standards in the institutions of higher learning and research with the centre and the state governments. These institutions include universities (both Central and State), the Indian Institute of Sciences (IISc) the Indian Institute of Technology (IITS), and institutes of national importance declared by Parliament.

At the time of Independence, there were only 25 universities in the country, most of them imparting science education through affiliated colleges. In the last six decades, the number of institutions for higher science education has grown enormously. Today there are 20 Central universities, 215 state universities, 100 deemed universities, 13 institutions of national importance, and more than 17,000 colleges. Under the Ministry of Human Resources Development (MHRD), the government evolved a machinery to discharge these responsibilities, it established the University Grants Commission (UGC) in 1956 and the All Indian Counsel for Technical Education (AICTE) in 1987 through ACts of Parliament to administer, regulate and supervise and functioning of higher science and technology (S &T) education in the country. However, the discharge of this constitutional responsibility by the Government over the years has left a great deal to be desired.

The proportion of India's population that enters higher education is around seven percent, which is half the average for Asia. There is about one university for nearly four million people. This figure is too small for any significant impact of higher education, science education in particular, on the country. The number of universities has not grown in relation to the population, thus greatly restricting the opportunities for higher education. The system needs a massive expansion to establish about 1500 universities countrywide so that the country can achieve a gross enrolment ratio of about 15 percent by 2015. China for example, has authorized the certain of 1250 new universities in the last three years. Unfortunately, the expansion that is evident in India is only in the form of dubious deemed universities and unregulated private engineering colleges that have mushroomed mainly as commercial ventures.

Compared to an enrolment of 5.7 million (1995 data) at the tertiary level in India, it is 14.20 million in the Unites States, which works out respectively to 613 and 5399 tertiary students per 100,000 populations. Even though enrolment at the tertiary level has been low, the absolute numbers have been increasing. In particular, enrolment in the science stream has increased from 127,200 in 1950-51 to about 1.5 million at the turn of the millennium. However, there are disquieting features in these numbers.

The number of students opting for science after the secondary school stage has dropped from 32 percent in the early 1950s to 19.7 percent in recent years. More significantly, in the 1950s the brightest entered science but today's 19.7 percent is from the lower middle level. This shows that young students, particularly the brighter ones, are drifting away from science. The choice of the national Talent search awardees also reflects this trend in recent years. Of the 750 awardees, hardly 100 opt for science and only 15-20 percent pursues science to the post-graduation level. Peer pressure, the changing socio-economic situation, and market mechanisms have further added to the process of the drift away from basic sciences to professional courses with the lure of high salaries as you step out, like information commerce, management, information technology and biotechnology.

A study by K.C. Garg and B.M. Gupta of the National Institute of Science, Technology and Development studies (NISTADS) in 2003 based on 10 year enrolment data (1992-2002) both at Plus – Two and college levels in Delhi, showed that priority for science disciplines as a whole is o the decline even at the Plus-Two level. Data of college enrolment in the sciences between 1990-91 and 1997-98 revealed that, on an average, about 48 percent of the students drifted out of B.Sc courses to join professional courses. These students are those who got admission after securing 80-90 percent marks at the Plus-Two level. Data from a few colleges outside Delhi too showed a similar trend, which indicates that this disturbing phenomenon in countrywide.

The above also indicates that students who remain in science do so as a last resort thus leading to a situation where most students in higher science education are unmotivated and uninterested. To compound matters is the fact that 88 percent of the students who opt for science after school are taught in affiliated colleges, which are ill-equipped have woefully inadequate library and laboratory facilities are overcrowded and poorly staffed.

Even those highly motivated few who choose to remain in science and move into universities for post graduation and research are only confronted with outdated curricula, uninspiring teaching and disinterested teachers, entrenched bureaucracy and improper administration, poor infrastructure obsolete laboratory equipment, lack of an academic environment, and to top it all, lack of opportunities for the youngsters to do even reasonable research, let alone be creative and engage in front – end work. Data since the 1980s bear this out this as well. While the absolute numbers of student enrolment and universities have increased, the number of research degrees awarded in natural science has almost stagnated, whereas in engineering sciences the numbers have actually declined.

"There is in fact, a quite, crisis in higher education in India that runs deep". Observed the recently released National Knowledge Commission's Report to the nation" "It is not yet discernible simply because there are pockets of excellence, an enormous reservoir of talented young people.... And in some important spheres, we continue to reap the benefits of what was sown in higher science education 50 years ago by the founding fathers of the Republic." The report added, this is slowly impacting all aspects of higher science education and research. There is all-round lack of qualified people for specialized jobs, in particular teaching in institutions. The latter is bound to have a serious cascading effect in the years to come.

This malady as the NKC reiterated, is the result of a process initiated in the 1950s "to create stand-alone research institutions, pampered with resources, in the belief that research should be moved out of universities. In the process, we forgot as essential principle. There are synergies between teaching and research that enrich each other. And it is the universities which are the natural home for research.... It is time to reverse what happened in the past and make universities the hub of research once again". But the NKC also notes in a realistic vain "It is ... difficult if not impossible, to outline a prescription for our universities, Nevertheless, it is clear that a reform of existing institutions must be an integral part of our Endeavour to transform higher education. We recognize that this is easier said than done".

Expansion of the university system to about 1500 universities will call for large investment. But before that, the severe resource crunch that afflicts all universities, infact the entire higher education system, should be addressed to correct the years of neglect. As the Indian National Science Academy noted as a matter of serious concern a few years ago, the investment per student has nosedived from Rs. 850 a year in the 1960s to Rs. 350 a year at the turn of the century (at 1990 prices). The allocation to education has already declined in recent years to about three percent of the GDP instead of attaining the figure of six percent recommended by the national education policy. The share of higher educator and science education in particular has dropped to 0.7 percent and 0.2 percent respectively compare the latter with those of the U.S (1.6 percent) the U.K. (1.4 percent) and Japan (1.04 percent) The NKC has called for increasing the investment in higher education to 1.5 - 2 percent.

There are, of course, imaginative initiatives that have been mooted by agencies such as the Department of science and Technology (DST) and the MHRD to foster talent and creativity but these would only serve to create a few more small pockets of excellence of islands of talent in an ocean of mediocrity. What is required is perhaps a radical overhaul of the system and a complete change in the outlook vis-à-vis education among the bureaucracy and the executive.

9

The Utilitarian View of Universities

(Alison Richard, Vice Chancellor of the University of Cambridge)

Cambridge's first full time woman vice-challenger had some misgivings about accepting what must surely be on of the most prestigious jobs in academic. She told me: "When Cambridge asked me to throw my hat into the ring. I was extremely reluctant to do so. I had already been working as an academic administrator for eight and a half years at Yale and I am a committed anthropologist with a great passion for teaching and research," But four and a half years into her term as Vice Chancellor of Cambridge she was what can only be called infectious enthusiasm for her job. Certainly her enthusiasm infected me.

"I miss my research", She tells me, "but I have the extraordinary interesting opportunity of sitting in the midst of one of the world's great universities surrounded by outstanding people of enormous talent thinking about all manner of fascinating things". But each year she does drop the role of Vice Chancellor and returns to Madagascar for two weeks where she has done some of her most exciting research into the behavior of primates. She is more than willing to share this enthusiasm for them with me, explaining that more than two-thirds of mammals live solitary lives, which raises two questions – what are the advantages of sociality and how do societies configure themselves. Those questions have led Alison Richard to the study of our nearest relations, the primates, and there is a wide variety of them in Madagascar. Her husband is an archaeologist but neither of their daughters has chosen to be an academic.

For all enthusiasm, Alison Richard did not have a burning ambition to be an academic and even more strangely doesn't seem certain whether she has chosen the right career. The daughter of a businessman who married at the late age of sixty, she was the first member of her family to go to university. She tells me: 'I'd love to say I had a concrete ambition but it's not true. I am still deciding what I want to do when I grow up, I think. One think just led to another". But she goes on to say: "At every step I have been totally consumed and interested by what I have been doing".

As Vice Chancellor, she is Cambridge's principal academic and administrative officer but Alison Richard prefers to be called an academic leader rather than an administrator, she is leading Cambridge towards the celebration of the eight hundredth anniversary of its foundation next year, having launched a campaign to raise one billon pounds by then. One of her ambitions is to ensure that the university increases its endowment sufficiently to insure that all students who have the ability to come to Cambridge can do so regardless of their family background.

What about the criticism often made that Cambridge and Oxford do take family background into account by taking a disproportionate number of students from private fee-paying schools? The Vice-Chancellor maintains that is a misunderstanding of the problem. She blames the inadequacy of many of the state schools for not producing students who can come up to the Cambridge entrance level. At the same time, she feels there are very good state school students who fear they might not be able to cope with Cambridge's academic standards. She believes the university needs to "get those students to raise their own self confidence and aspirations".

Alison Richard wants Cambridge's student body to be diverse and cosmopolitan, and this is one reason for what is only her second visit to India, and her first as Vice Chancellor. "We live in a world which is increasingly interconnected", she explains "Most of our statements are going to live and work across cultures, so we must take increasingly cultures. So we must take increasingly seriously the educational responsibility for producing citizens who can lie and work like that, That means having a cosmopolitan and diverse student body so we are interested in attracting some of the most talented students from around the world, including of course, India where there is so much talent.

I tell the Vice-Chancellor that only last week I met students fro IITs all over India at a Festival in Mumbai and everyone. I talked to hoped to study as postgraduates in America. The most common reason they gave was that it is cheaper. But Alison Richard thinks this is often a misapprehension. She points out that the Cambridge Trust has assisted a thousand Indian

Students over the last twenty five years and one hundred and thirty are currently studying with bursaries. But the admits that Cambridge does not provides as much financial assistance as the major American Universities and one of the aims of the fund raising campaign is to match America. Nevertheless she feels the comparison between American universities and Cambridge is often exaggerated and that more needs to be done to get the word out about the scholarships which are available. She says: "I keep coming on circumstances where American universities have done a much better job of communicating a positive and upbeat message. We haven't communicated as well as we should and the message has not been as positive and upbeat as it should be."

It has always seemed to me that there is a danger that foreign universities attempting to attract Indian Students will appear patronizing or even condescending giving the impression that they offer a superior education to anything available in India. The Vice-chancellor vigorously denies that, "I have come to India to strengthen Cambridge's partnerships with Indian universities". She tells me firmly and goes on to point out: "More and more major challenges are not amenable to solutions or study by individual academics or even academics in a single community working in isolation. They require international collaboration. Energy sustainability, religious and cultural conflicts, work on these and other subjects has to cross cultural and national boundaries. So I am coming to India to celebrate the partnerships we have and to continue to build them. There is so much opportunity here and I think there is a great fit between Cambridge and India".

The Vice-chancellor has also come here to announce a major new link with India. In order to celebrate the centenary of Jawaharlal Nehru's arrival at Trinity College, Cambridge to study natural sciences, the university is launching the "Jawaharlal Nehru Professorship of Indian Business and Enterprise." This chair has been endowed by the Government of India and there is also to be a Cambridge Centre for Indian Business, established as a result of a contribution by the BP group.

So how does Alison Richard see the future of Cambridge and indeed of universities around the world? Well, first of all, she believes "The role of universities has never been more important than it is today". But she is worried about what she calls the utilitarian view of the universities – the view that they have to be useful for the creation of economic wealth. My own deep, deep, belief is that the creation of cultural wealth and cultural insights is every bit as important as contributions to economic wealth that we make. That utilitarian view of universities takes away from their deep role of creativity in society".

When I suggest that many students nowadays seem to have utilitarian view of universities opting for subjects that will bring them the fattest pay packets rather than the richest cultural reward, the Vice-chancellor is less worried. She points out that in 1974 half the students at Cambridge were studying arts, humanities, or social sciences and the percentage is the same today. And that she insists is not because Cambridge imposes a quota system to insure the balance of subjects or lowers its standards to admit students in those subjects. "We get extraordinarily strong applicants", she says.

But Alison Richard does believe there could be something of utilitarian problem with academic staff. "I am not suggesting that anyone should be encouraged to come into academia to become rich. They won't any how. But we should be able to make a decent living and if we don't ensure that, students will vote with their feet". She is particularly concerned about the remuneration of young academics that are at that stage in life when they are buying a house and brining up a family. It's the post graduates and the lecturers that Britain is losing to America but at the senior level Cambridge at least is gaining as many academic from America as it is losing.

When I left Cambridge at the end of the fifties, colleges made little effort to encourage us to remain in touch with them or to ask us to offer and financial support. Alison Richards thinks that was because I went to Cambridge in the days of the Welfare state when it was believed that everything, including higher education, would be provided by the sate. She tells me: "it was a loss to the University not to have taken advantage of the extraordinary community of students and I would like to think a loss to all of you not to have been more engaged with your university".

I assure the Vice Chancellor all that has changed now and my college certainly keeps in touch with me. She believes that relations with alumni are far more important for the university than just getting them to contribute to the fundraising Campaign, which she says is "just one thing alumni can do for us and probably not the most important. You are our best advocates; you connect us to the real world".

I wonder whether to ask the almost inevitable questions – whether being the first woman Vice Chancellor ahs caused any difficulties for her - but I decided against it. For someone so assured ant at home in her job, that is clearly an irrelevance, and I don't want to end the interview with a crushing reply, so I ask instead whether she has any regrets about coming back to university where she took her first degree after so many years in the lasher pastures of American academia. I get a gentle rebuke: I wouldn't have come back from profound belief in the greatness of this university and its capacity to be able to continue to play a vital and important role in the world. Noting in the last four and half years since I've been back has changed my mind".

The Vice Chancellor hopes her visit will strengthen the ties with India and build a partnership that will enlarge the role both Cambridge and its Indian partners play in the world.

CARE TO SHARE

Encouraging children in slums to dream big... and finding the resources for it, calls for some corporate wizardry. Parikrma, a Bangalore based NGO, appears adept at it. I want to be a soldier. But my father wants me to be a doctor" says 11 years old Selvakumar in his blue – and green uniform as he makes his way to the school fish pond where a blue lotus is in bloom. "When I'm older, I know what I really want to be".

The bright - eyed boy has been in school for about two years. His parents are cobblers in a slum. His self - confidence today stems form the fact that he's at one of Bangalore's three Parikrma Humanity Foundation Centres for Learning. Based at Koramangala, Jayangar and Sahakaranagar, these are abused on an e2e or end to end pragmatic business model.

Launched in April 2003 as a non profit NGO, Parikrma attempts to "unleash the potential of underserved children" among the 15 lakh populations in Bangalore's 800-plus slums. The city has an estimated 1.1 lakh street children. Parikrma partners with other NGOs in areas of healthcare, nutrition and family care, but its core competency is imparting quality education.

Currently surviving two orphanages and 26 slum communities, Parikrma's 305 girls and 315 boys between five and 14 are drawn from households with an average of five people and a monthly income of about Rs. 750. Preference is given to orphaned or abandoned children, especially those below six. Girl children are given priority, so are school – age siblings. At Parikrma, there is no discrimination on the basis of caste, creed, colour and religion.

"All our children are agents of social change. They will leave our ICSE schools empowered. We'll take them to college or professional course. We'll place them in jobs. We hope to break poverty cycles and transform communities through these children". Explains Parikrma's founder (CEO, Shukla Bose, Former Indian managing director of Resort condominiums International chosen as the national Woman Entrepreneur for 1995. "We'd like our children to look at their communities with love and respect, yet recognize that this is not necessarily the only way in life".

To begin with, Parikrma has encouraged its children to be unafraid to dream. Today Manipur bore Zamzei Thouthang. 11 has set his sights on emulating Ronaldo on the football field or becoming a software engineer Naveen Maniraju 10, could be a future, ecologist, for he insists that all food waste should be consigned to a compost pit. Mohita Gunasheker, 5 would love to write children's stories once she's old enough. Jancy Mary Davil, 7 Hopes to teach English one day.

As for Karthik Selvamani, 10, the STD 4 Student dazzled the crossword audience during a Parikrma enacted story at a recent book launch. For his fox pundit was both quickly and brilliant. During holidays, he works at cycle repair shop to earn enough for food. Within a year, he has progressed from introducing himself in English to addressing a group of journalists on Indian Unity. His dream? To confirm for himself media report of live on mars!

Parikrma marketing head Vivek Raju says, "Our teachers are, in many ways, surrogate parents. They know details about every child in class".

Drawing on their corporate background the Parikrma business model makes sound sense. On how levi's agreed to a tow year MoU on the Sahakaranagar centre. Raju says, "We are one of the two social programmes they fund, the larger grantee. Like us, Levi's was interested in the community, Youth and women's empowerment. We got them to extend their interest to education. They liked the holistic way we affected a child's life, besides the school, they now fund development across the 26 Bangalore communities we work with."

UK - based Royal resorts thought likewise, when it sponsored the Koramangala centre, where the children have rendered their dreams pictorially on the outer walls. Dell pitched in with state - of the - art computer labs for the Koramangala and Jayanagar schools.

The software company Technology Learning Information, Sponsors a classroom, while its staff volunteers time to mentor the children.

Yahoo! is sponsoring another school at Nandini Layout, slated to open next year. Until then, its 39 first time learners are being schooled at Jayanagar. Sindhoor Pangal, voicing why the Yahoo! Employee, Foundation India (YEFI) choose this option, says,, "While YEFI has the passion and the means to help, Parikrma has the experience and the expertise to do so. We want to empower these children with the quality of education that will one day make them our co-workers".

To Kalpana Singh, Parikrma's academic head, education is about widening horizons. So at least Rs. 15000 will be spent on each child annually. Including visits to the theatre and concerts, to museums and scientific centres, even participation in inter-school sports meets. Regular heath checkups and psychological aid are assured. De-addition of select parents, Vocational training for older sibling, and three nutritious meals a day are programmed in.

In October 2003, Parikma signed an MoU with the Bangalore Mahanagara Palike to help 12 of the corporation's poorest performing schools. Alter five months of intensive. Post schools class 10 tutorials by retired government teachers, who were set new goals, the pass percentage among 875 students zoomed from nine to 31 percent. In 2004-05, a similar MoU impacted 4,783 students from classes 8-10.

Says Raju, "Those who invest in Parikrma are actually investing in a child's future. As a sustainable model, we'd like to create a franchise. ING Vysya has given us a fund with which to market our programme. Last year at a free concept they sponsored, 7,000 executives attended and over 4000 committed half a day's salary to us. This year, the funds will allow us to reach 5,000 more. Thus we're creating a sustainable flow of inputs".

Star TV has offered free screening of two powerful Parikrma shorts, funded by an anonymous donor. A Shukla points out, "In organizations we think big and long-term. Why can't we do the same in the social sector?"

10

Initiatives to Power the Knowledge Economy

(The author is NASSCOM president and these are his personal views)—Kiran Karnik

India cannot achieve it real potential unless. We have large numbers of people at the highest level of research in the universities.

The future of India is linked to the knowledge industries, and our success in these depends upon how were we nurture and grow our human resources. "Knowledge industries" is used here to include not only the trees "Os" - technologies related to info, bio and nano-but also knowledge based manufacturing and knowledge-based agriculture. The last includes transgenic crops, new seeds, new fertilizers, advanced technologies for agro-processing and food storage, value-addition and value extraction from farm produce. All these-and the conventional high tech areas of nuclear energy, space technology materials science, etc-Will require human resources of the highest capabilities, in large numbers.

In fact, India's biggest potential strength is the scalability of skills, and especially of high level skills. In the area of information technology (IT), we are already seeing an increasing recognition of this. Thus whether it is a massive ramping up simpler skills (e.g. for call centres) or deploying large numbers of doctorates (e.g. in R& D off-shoring), India has proven its competitive edge over rivals. However, to retain this advantage and hope fully further widen the gap, it is essential that we produce ever-greater-numbers of even better qualified professionals.

Demographics are in our side: we are a young country, with a majority of young people and projections indicate that both the number and proportion of working age people in the population will continue to rise for a couple of decades. In contrast, all the developed countries and – surprisingly - China too will face substantial shortages of working-age people. Whereas India is estimated to have a surplus of 47 million. while immigration may reduce the shortage, clearly it cannot bridge such a huge shortfall. This means that off shorting will not just continue, but gain greater momentum in the years to come. To take full advantage of these demographic trends, we need to ensure the availability of a skilled, education workforce.

Present selection rations, combined with past growth rates in the expansion of tertiary education, indicate possible shortage in the needs for both the IT and Business process outsourcing (BPO) sectors. Other knowledge sectors will similarly face shortages. The problem is not so much the availability of graduates, as the very low selection ratios – indicating inadequacy of skills. This reflects poorly on the general quality of education. While the top 10-15 percent of graduates is near world-class, a substantial proportion is below average. Therefore, the challenge is raise the floor. This is true not only for engineering, but even for non-technical graduates. The selection ratio for jobs in the booming ITES BPO sector (below 10 percent) illustrates this rather starkly, since the requirement for skill sets here is comparatively simpler.

The problems are many - fold and inter related. The quality of teaching and faculty is a major problem, and one that is of serious long-term concern. This affects multiple batches of graduating students, with a major impact on the quality of future faculty training and faculty development programmes.

Ensuring that the curriculum is up-to-date and relevant is another issue. Industry cans playa a major role in this by sharing trends. Likely future developments and the requirement of skill-sets. However, it is important not to convert professional education into polytechnic training: the former must focus on building a strong conceptual foundation, so that in a world a rapidly changing technology, the graduate can master new developments. The ability of learning how to learn is an essential part of good education.

Infrastructure especially for science and technology education needs to be upgraded and continuously updated. Laboratory equipment, libraries computers with high-speed connectivity, well-equipped classrooms: all these need to be at least adequate, if not world-class.

As we do more work of greater sophistication, the need for qualified researchers- those who have done a masters or a doctorate – is going to grow. India cannot achieve its real potentials as a country or fully tap the potential as a country or fully tap the potential of talented individuals, unless we have large numbers of people at the highest level of research in the universities. At present, the numbers are truly dismal; one estimate includes less than 500 PhDs in technology each year. Equally worrying is the quality: much research tends to be repetitive and irrelevant. Attracting more people into MTech and PhD programmes is an urgent necessity, as is the need to ensure that the research they do is relevant.

Infact, the inter-relatedness of these problems indicates a solution. If the research done is relevant, industry will value it. Mtech and doctorates will then be in demand in industry and will command a good compensation. In turn, this will attract more and better graduates to join an MTech progamme rather than take up a job. Possibly even those who take up a job immediately after graduating may choose to return to university for an advanced degree after a few years of work.

The greater number of MTech and PhDs, in turn will help reduce the problem of faculty shortages as well as quality. However to do this teaching needs to be made a more attractive profession. Today not only are teachers poorly paid, even their social status has suffered a decline. this is a tough problem. While raising the salaries of teachers is a very desirable step, it is obviously a difficult one, even while this is pursued, industry could help by providing funding for research, for facilities, and sponsor faculty travel to conferences. This will certainly enthuse teachers and permit them to pursue their research interests more fully. It will make the profession more attractive and may help in getting more people to join it.

In the non-technology area, it is essential to make education more relevant to today's needs. Even while a strong theoretical and conceptual foundation is laid, the three years of a degree education must include skills that industry needs. An overwhelming majority of students go into the employment market armed with only BA/BSc/BCom degrees. Ensuring their employ ability is responsibility academics and industry need to address together. Given the low load on students in most under graduate course, a series of optional, parallel, skill building courses may be considered. "Soft Skills" such as communication and teamwork must be an essential part of the curriculum in all streams.

Ensuring Quality

Quantity is not a serious problem today: the number of engineering seats is around 450,000 and the number of all graduates is around 3 million a year. However, as mentioned earlier, projections of needs as also the potential demand a substantial expansion. While doing so, it improved with privatization; market forces will hopefully play a role in ensuring quality. It may, however be necessary to go beyond market forces. This may be one area where the state can set the highest standards, creating a benchmark for private institutions. Already the IIMs and IITs are doing this. The Government must seek to create half a dozen such institutions of world quality each year, in all disciplines.

To stimulate private sector investment in truly high-quality education, the Government should create, on an experimental basis, special education zones, Modeled on the special Economic Zones: basically, areas where bureaucratic and other regulatory constraints are removed, with complete freedom of recruitment, compensation import equipment and students from all over the world. "This may help make India a major global education centre, even as standards are set for other institutions in India.

India also needs to foster innovation, an area in which we have a unique advantage. This requires that we celebrate our diversity, reduce rote-learning in schools, change our examination system, and bring openness into out higher education system. We need to inculcate the habit of questioning answers, rather than answering questions.

A final critical element for the future of the knowledge industry is the need to attract more of the brightest students into science, the foundation for all technology. Better science and mathematics teaching in schools, better laboratory facilities and an up-to-date curriculum are all necessary, as many more top-quality-institutions like the IISc

Much of this needs a private-public partnership, and close industry academia interaction. Much mutual benefit can flow from this, and the IT industry, for one, has been working to promote this, the national Association of Software and Service companies (NASSCOM) has been spearheading this effort and it is a major theme underlying its HR summit in Chennai on July 19-20. One of the failings of the Indian knowledge eco-system has been the lack of industry academic collaboration. It is time to correct this, urgently. Only through this can the dreams of India as a global knowledge power is realized.

11

An Optimistic March Through History

Sunil Khilnani,

(Sunil Khilanani is the author of the idea of India, and teaches at the Johns Hopkins school of Advanced International studies in Washington D.C)

Contention over our history, our culture and our identity has over the past decade and a half, acquired a new and sometimes disturbing intensity and passion. Everyone, it seems has a view a theory, a solution to our predicament. In a truly open society, it is right it should be this way-a democracy needs its bloggers. But our debates also need certain touchstones, and for many Indians Committed to sustaining our political heritage of pluralism, the recent writings of Professor Amartya Sen (henceforth Sen) have come to serve just this role.

Sen's Own reputation was made within the discipline of economics, that technical and culturally unallocated social science, given to abstract formulations which all things being equal, as economists like to say – leaves particular human beings out of the picture It has been made, too in the West. And yet his preoccupations have always been rooted in specific, India grounded concerns. His most publicly influential work, a counter intuitive argument about the causes of famines (he showed that they are not generally the result of a decline in absolute levels in food stocks, but of a collapse in the buying capacities of the poor), emerged out of his childhood memories of the Great Bengal famine of 1943. Similarly, his sensitivity to taxonomies – how we classify the world, and how classification can constrain options – is rooted in his Sanskrit education. (His grandfather was Kshiti Mohan

Sen, the great scholar of India's religious and popular mystical traditions, the author of the classic *Hinduism* which Sen as a young man helped to render into English, and which will shortly be reissued) Sen has now collected his essays and writings on India's culture wars and identity crises into a handsome volume. The collection is a bracing sweep through aspects of Indian history and cultures, and gives a tempered analysis of the highly charged disputes surrounding these subjects the nature of Hindu traditions, Indian identity, the country's huge social and economic disparities, and its current place in the world.

Sen deploys his philosophical energies to examine questions of identify and choice, gender and inequality, reason and dialogue, all of which arise out of a feel for their daily presence in his own country. Yet the pieces collected here are anything but parochial. Indeed they reveal his capacity to draw out the larger and universalistic implications of his Indian concerts a deftness that has made Sen a remarkably cosmopolitan individual. Former Master of Trinity, Cambridge, holder of not just one but two professorships at Harvard winner of the Nobel Prize and a staple of the "honorary degree" season: if ever there was a global intellectual, it is Sen. He was educated at Rabindranth Tagore's school, Shantiketan, and Radical thinkers like Joan Robinson, Maurice Dobb, and Pierro Sraffa.

In his later career, he engaged with his generation's best philosophical minds – Bernard Williams, John Rawls, Robert Nozick and Kenneth Arrow. Yet I think his true distinctiveness becomes clear when seen against the background of two still richer historical traditions, both reaching back to the 18th century, to the Scotland of Adam smith and the Bengal of Rammohun Roy. These are the traditions of classical political economy, and of social criticism and reform; the call and response of British liberal imperialism and Indian cosmopolitan nationalism.

The aspect of human existence that seems to fascinate Sen most is choice, both at the individual and social levels. Perhaps uniquely among al creatures, human make reflective choices, how are we enabled to choose? What are the bases of choices? What impediments stand in the way of making them? Above all, he is interested in the rationality of our choices – both in the since of what kinds of reasons we give for our choices, and to what extent our individual choices could yield collectively rational outcomes.

While Sen is partial to a dry, removed style, his work conveys a strong sense of intellectual personality. The 16 essays in Sen's new volume, several of them unpublished, express his anxieties as a self-confessed 'unreformed secularist' at the choice of narrow conceptions of Indian Identity by religious nationalists and at how their efforts to make India a 'Hindu' nation – state may affect India's future choices. In fact, India continues to be constitutionally secular state, with one of the largest Muslim populations the world and with millions of citizens who are Sikh, Jain, Christians, Animists, and atheists a fact outsiders are all too wont to forget when they facilely describe India as a 'Hindu nation'. This India one chosen by its founders, is what Sen believes in and defends.

One group of essays, "voice and Heterodoxy" shows the range and depth of India's traditions of skepticism dissent and irreverent questioning. Recalling this history matters, Sen indicts, because it is a living resource for social criticisms: Voice gives us more choice in techniques for the removal of social harms. Among the harms he is alert to are "The cultivated Western images of Indian historical traditions, which are typically taken to be pontifically serious and uncompromising spiritual" – not least because these images continually return to haunt Indian Self conceptions. Thus the favorite Harvard professor of the BJP is Samuel Huntington – his 'clash of civilizations' thesis a regular refrain of Lal Krishna Advani and his colleagues.

Against such views of hermetic and antagonistic cultures, Sen reminds us of India's manifold historical interconnections with the rest of the world-through such creative individuals as Tagore and the filmmaker Satyajit Ray and through India's centuries old relationship with China and the West. Sen wants us to notice the strong individuality of a culture such as India's as well as its openness to other influences and ideas. But his view of India is also critical. His essays take unsparing measures of our social and economic problems gender inequality literacy and poverty – areas where independent India's performance has been decidedly less impressive than its democratic achievements. In what is perhaps a self-conscious leap of hope, Sen asserts his belief in what he calls the "Sovereignty of reason," and exemplifies this in his arguments. He puts great faith in pubic deliberation and reasoning, and when the full flare of his own mind is on display, problems do seem to burn away. Yet the arena of politics is shaped by power (a concept that figures lightly in his work), in ways that can all too often leave reason disarmed. His is an essentially optimistic march through history.

Although Sen is free with his judgments, his writing always keeps to a coolly embattled tone, as well as an unfailing, old-style courtesy. There are a few minor slips in the next (the first woman president of the Congress was Annie Besant, not Sarojini Naidu; the original language of the Ashokan edicts was Magadhi, not Sanskrit), but Sen is otherwise scrupulous with the facts and always fair in its past history many qualities of reasoning and skepticism that often are denied in favour of exotic, spiritualist images which ironically, are usually recycled from the West's own view of India. Yet, in rebuff tot determinisms of either the cultural of historical kind, he points out that even if India's past did not have such reservoirs of dissent, this would not preclude it now from acquiring them; He also subjects to critical scrutiny the thicket of affirmative action policies (known as Reservations) that have grown since independence. He argues that the choice of such policies, intended to reduce certain inequalities, may in fact cause other kinds-a policy phenomenon he terms "friendly fire".

In short Sen is a distinguished inheritor of the Indian tradition of public philosophy and reasoning – Roy, Tagore, Gandhi, Nehru Social critics all, cosmopolitans who could hold their won anywhere, each was profoundly rooted in India. Sen's book opens by invoking Krishna Menon, a great arguer and a man of monsoon like wordage (he holds the record for the longest Speech at the UN: Nine hours). In the early 1960s Prime minister Jawaharlal Nehru wrote asking Menon to identify bright young economists who might be induced into Government. Menon, in his reply, mentioned a "Mr. A.K.Sen," a 29 year old who had just been appointed to a three year position at Cambridge. Menon considered him "by far the ablest economist" But he advised Nehru that such talents would be wasted if inducted into government as an economic advisor. Had Sen indeed been offered and taken such a position, perhaps India's economy would have been richer, or at least failure. But the discipline of economics, and more important, the world of pubic argument, would certainly have been poorer.

RELENTLESS HORROR STORY

The U.P. an estimated 40,000/- women die each year from complications during pregnancy. While under age and under weight mothers are more vulnerable, an additional factor is unsafe abortions. According to me study, the highest rate of abortion in the country is in this state over 20 lakh each year. Around 15 to 300 percent of the maternal deaths in U.P are the result of unsafe abortions. Women bleed to death, die of infections and injuries and no me in held responsible / accountable for these deaths.

The case studies gathered by women's health groups in U.P. including sahyog, expose the hollowness of the claims our government makes internationally that it is committed to women's reproductive health and rights.

If that were the case, women would not be forced to have abortions as they would have known the choices they have to prevent pregnancy. If their health and rights were a genuine concern, they would not have been abandoned after batched abortions and hurried sterilizations.

In theory, women are supposed to be given a choice in contraception methods. In reality, the only choice before them in sterilization through tubetomies of the total number of sterilizations performed in U.P. 97 percent are done on women. Just over half of them face post operative complications and can rarely access treatment. And the failure rate of sterilization in 4.7 percent. In other words, even after having these operations, women become pregnant, and if in desperation they seek an abortion, they literally risk death.

A study conducted by the group Health watch UP in Bihar and Utter Pradesh in 2002-2003 exposed the gaping chasm between the standards the Government of India sets for female and male sterilization and the reality on the ground.

To give just one or two instances: the standards lay down that sterilizations must be carried out under antiseptic conditions. The study found that internal examinations were being conducted on women with used gloves. The standards day down that the maximum number of sterilizations in mobile services should not exceed 20 a day. Instead, the study found that in one location, a surgeon had done 75 sterilizations in just two and half hours an average of only two minutes per case.

Utter Indifference

Most of three studies tell a similar tale of desperation on the part of the women and of utter indifference on the parts of the medical system. “No choice between sterilization and death” is the heading given to one such case study. This is of a woman from Taktakpur, Varansi District, who went through four child births in six years, she agreed to a sterilization operation four months after her last delivery.

During the operation, she collapsed when the doctor pulled her intestines by mistake. By the time her family managed to take her to the nearest District hospital she was dead. The family was given no explanation of how she died. Her husband finally did get compensation of Rs.10,000/- when a non – Governmental organization intervened and failed a case.

Stories like this are abundant not just in U.P. but also in other parts of India. These are poor woman. They are paying the price for a mindset that believes that in the ‘war’ against a burgeoning population, there are bound to be some causalities, collateral damage.

As long as we have a medical fraternity which refuses to acknowledge that the real problem lies in the lack of development of health case, of education – women in U.P. and else where will continue to die in obscurity away from the gage of the media and policy makers.

MOTIVATING STUDENTS

Any college or higher education course seems to be hard and boring. Though it is different to motivate students to invest the time and effort necessary to succeed in the course, have to meet the challenge. Many simple but empirical rules for keeping students focused and motivated have been assembled. The rules or these time honored suggestions apply to any course the students feel hard and boring. These rules are broadly applicable.

Emphasis on Concept

When a teacher has to introduce and teach a concept emphasis on the concept is important. If the concepts are critical emphasize them continuously. To repeat and reiterate these concepts in lectures and assignments throughout the course is a more welcome feature. The teacher should prepare and include questions relating to these critical subjects on every examination. These questions are definitely rewarding students for learning, retaining and applying this knowledge in a variety of contexts.

Visual aid

It will be more interesting if the teacher provides students with or set of 'visual aid' whenever possible to explain abstract concepts. A significant proportion of present day students are accustomed visual learners. For these students, a simple diagram or flow chart can certainly be more valuable than volume of words in a text or lecture.

Reply on Logic

Course materials are a mixture of information's, facts, findings, inferences and results. The teacher must rely on logic when applicable. He should point out to students which information is merely 'fact' that has to be memorized and which part of the course material is bared upon 'logic' He Must show the students how to employ logical thinking to learn and retain new information.

In Class assignment

It is always advisable to use in-class activities to reinforce newly presented material. Soon after a new concept or subject has been presented by text reading or lecture, the students are allowed to put the concept into action by completing an in-class assignment. There assignments may conveniently be shot but they must be developed to ensure that the students understand the critical concepts under laying the new material. The most learning takes place when the students work in small groups and are allowed to refer to their text and notes and to ask questions while completing the assignment. If these in-class assignments form part of the course grading scheme, class attendance also improves.

Linking

The teacher is expected to help students create a link, when teaching something new. If the student can ling or associate the new material to what is already learned or acquired, the order of learning the new material are greatly increase. Examples of possible 'links' include, prior material learned in a particular course, material learned in pre-requisite courses and "Real life" experiences of the students outside the class room to present "real world" definition and alternative terminology, in addition to text book definitions one way to help students assimilate the course vocabulary is to create a 'living' glossary on the instructor website where new terminology is added explained and illustrated throughout the course.

Vocabulary

For any course, through any medium of instructions vocabulary is more important students must realize and recognize the importance of vocabulary in a course. It is widely accepted that students often struggle with new vocabulary in many courses especially introductory ones. To become successful in there courses, Students must become comfortable with the new terminology. As subjects are presented, either confusing or quite new terms should be identified and introduced to the students. It is always desirable.

Respect

The present generation of students wants or demands a decent treatment from the educators. Patronizing behaviour may be expected in primary school teachers, and 'drill sergeant' strategies may be effective in military camps. However most college students will not respond will to these techniques. It is better to give students their dignity and make them give the teacher their best efforts.

High Standard

A proficient teacher holds students to a high standard. If students are not required to maintain a specified level of learning and performance, only the most highly motivated students will devote the time and effort necessary to learn. In contrast maintaining high standards not only will motivate student learning, it will also be the source of student feelings of accomplishment when those standards are met.

Each of these rules or guide lines can help motivate eve the most lethargy student, But the rule 8 and 9 are more important. If the students are not treated with respect and held to a high standard, scrupulously following the first six rules will have much less impact and might end up being an exercise in futility.

IMPORTANCE OF INVESTING IN TECHNOLOGY

The new dream in let China becomes a factory of the world, India the office of the world, and the two together conquer the world! This new slogan is an improvement on the old one, it is also plausible and however, one should not get carried away.

Undoubtedly, both, particularly China, are enjoying global success. Future prospects are even more alluring. At the same time, strictly speaking, neither country is in the driving seat, the success of either depends on the patronage of the west/

China has no doubt become a remarkable factory but it can manufacture only what the west has devised and is willing to out source. India's situation in even less autonomous, what business the V.S. and Europe have transferred today to India, they can shift tomorrow to Nigeria or Egypt or wherever. We are a dependent nation, not an economically independent one.

Manufacturing productivity is increasing so rapidly that the time will soon come when manufacturing employment may shirk to an insignificant figure the way it already has in agriculture. When that happens, western countries may not consider it necessary to outsource their manufactures to China. China too is still in the woods.

It is yet possible that China will become the factory of the world, India the office and the two together conquer the world. It is also possible that the moment either tends to get too powerful; the west will cut off oxygen supply, and leave it breathless. To day's dreams can turn into tomorrow's nightmares.

The future of china and India is at risk because neither owns the technology it operates, the intellectual property continues to remain in the west, any moment, the US and Europe decide to turn off the technology tap, both countries will be in serious trouble. Hence in the final analysis both countries are still at the mercy of the west, the short answer to this problem is that are should develop our own technology, we should acquire so much intellectual property that the west will be as much dependent on us as we are on them. That leads to the related affection of national self-interest in a globalize economy.

The labour force is always supreme, but the owners may or may not be even if they are citizens, the corporation is profoundly less relevant to.., economic future than the skills, the training and knowledge commanded by..... Workers (Rober B.Rich).

The control and ownership of corporation is not important, what is crucial is how much corporations invest in the future capability of the workers, and how far they employ local scientists, engineers and technicians in R & D. (Research and development) A corporation which invests in the training and upgrading of human capital is 'Ours' even if it is owned by foreigners, a corporation which does not invest in human capital is not 'ours' even if owned by our own citizens.

So, Rich's emphasis is on human capital, as distinct from financial capital. As the explains, the international capital movements are for simpler and easier than international movements of human capital. For that reason, human capital is reliable, financial capital is ephemeral and untrustworthy, hence, development based on human capital is dependable, and that based on financial capital is undependable.

Well trained workers attract global corporations, which invest and give the workers good jobs, the good jobs, in turn generate additional training and experience as stalls move upward and skill accumulates, nation's citizens add more and more value to the world and command greater and grater compensation from the world, improving the country's standard of living.

An Indian owned firm, even if it is a public sector undertaking is not one of "Ours" if it is wedded to imported technology, many public sector firms that have depended on imported know-how-the Indian telephone Industries and the Hindustan machine tools for instance are now critically ill.

Neither firm invested in Human capital, both remained, technologically a colonial appendage rather than a truly national asset. That has happened not because qualified manpower was not locally available, but because such talents were not patronized nor encouraged.

The IT, remained an independent player with a life of its own so long as it backed the design team of C-DOT. Once it gave up C-DOT, its life started ebbisy away. Any firm, irrespective of ownership, which invests in R & D employing Indian scientist's engineers and technicians to develop world-class technology, is truly one of 'ours'. All other firms, including those that are 100 percent owned by the Indian government are agents of foreign firms, not ours!.

Addressing the National manufacturing competitiveness council, the Prime Minister said that industrialization is the driving force behind India, whose manufacturing sector has stagnated at around 17 percent for nearly 15 years, has prematurely migrated to the service sector. In his view the present growth is creating a rural – urban divide which in neither viable nor sustainable.

There are important words of caution; an economic divide by which the west produces Intellectual property, China undertakes contract manufacture and India provides the back-up services, does not provide us enough, bargaining power to make our growth sustainable. It will not let us pursue our national welfare; our future will be constrained by the self interest of the nations that control technology.

The world is all praise for India's technical man power. Country after country is going out of its way to woo our engineers and scientists. Our government has no such interest. There is no move in India, to exploit efficiently and effectively the technical man power the country produces.

Private industries are no different. The patronize ITI graduates only after they have migrated to management and not as engineers. They ITI talent not to produce better technology but to produce better looking balance sheets, neither the Indian Government nor Indian industry is concerned why Indian engineers are not with in India. It appears that the Indian Government is more interested in subjugating talent (including that in the IAS) than in courting it the way other countries are doing).

Of late we have started worshipping 'Laxmi' assiduously. In the process we have consigned 'Saraswathi' to the dust bin. The future of our country which is treating teachers, scientists, engineers like domestic servants, with the later in turn succumbing to the mother – in- law / daughter – in - law syndrome to subjugate younger talent.

12

A Place For Every One

(Sache ramalingam, Vision rehabilitation specialist of Head of the department Dr. Shroffs charity eye hospital, New Delhi)

Policy makers should consult people who have successfully implemented inclusion instead of focusing on people who doubt it. Ever since the government announced a policy of inclusive education for all via Sarva Shiksha Abhiyan, the implementation and deliberation have begun, unfortunately the entire focus has been on the 'not - prepared - for it' syndrome.

If inclusive education was so simple, how does one explain the number of persons who are products inclusive education (including me) that exist in India. It simply shows that inclusion is merely a new vocabulary added to the existing system that we have been able to swim through.

I vividly remember that throughout my school life I had never come across a special educator or resource teacher or even introduced to Braille. I realized for the first time that I had a disability when I asked to take political science / history in class XI, despite getting 83 percent in matriculation examinations, one had wanted the Maths, physics, chemistry and Biology stream that were considered the best then; I sought and got admission in the town's best school for the stream I wanted. How?

Simply because the class XI teacher believed I could do well despite my low vision. She dared to tread the less trodden path. She also believed in her ability to take along the light other teachers who would be handling classes for us. I was in that school for two years. The principal confessed on the last day of the school that he had never realized that my vision impairment was so server, as he did not face a single problem because of me. why?

Simply because my nine teachers, believed that it was not an issue to have a visually impaired girl in their class (Co-ed), and also because they had a practical outlook.

Second, at no points did I ask for favours because of my vision problem. Advocacy was not a popular strategy then. Neither my teacher nor I knew of the existing policy granting extra time for disabled persons to complete on examination. How ever, I was given 15 minutes extra whenever needed. I scored 80 percent.

It all happened because the teachers were spontaneous human beings dealing with a fellow human being from their heart.

It was at college, when I choose rehabilitation science as my career, that I fumbled upon the facts that according to the legal definition of visual impairment, I was supposed to be a blind person. I never would have imagined myself being blind.

Even today, despite many rules and policies, the system at large behaves as if it is most unlikely than a disabled person may take an examination, they are usually unprepared to provide a writer or a reader. They believe that it would happen to somebody else and some other examination centre. After the initial chaos, there always emerge one or two spontaneous people who ensure that the best outcome in obtained despite the oversight, or lack of preparation.

It is note worthy that inclusion has been practiced least in the metros but best in smaller districts, where special residential schools do not exist. In Tamil Nadu for example, inclusion is best practiced in districts such as Madurai, Coimbatore, Tiruchi and least in Chennai During my school days the nearest special school was at least 350 km away. So the three different schools that handled me had put their best foot forward, experimented and, when principals asked the teachers concerned “Could you manage this child?” They had said: Yes’.

Because of pre existing special residential schools concentrated in the metrics parents find it craziest to take the secure path of special schools rather than tread a difficult, uncertain path of inclusion, Delhi is the capital city where all policies are formed for persons with disabilities, However on moving to Delhi form Tamil Nadu one was surprised to find that what Tamil Nadu had been in 1978, Delhi was in 2001 in terms of facilities for persons with disabilities.

A few suggestions to help improve the current scenario:

If teachers are adequately equipped, inclusion would become a naturalistic process. No principal would then dare to refuse admission to a disabled child.

Think from a grass roots level: what do the masses need?

The disabled child should be prepared emotionally and physically with stalls that could be useful in an inclusive environment. A disabled person should be taught not to use disability as a certificate to obtain favours or special exemptions, especially when he or she has been provide an inclusive environment, strive hard, your teacher will complements you.

Parents empowerment in intrinsic for successful inclusion

For persons with disabilities the self motivation 'mantra' should be 'be prepared to work harder than your peers' "I had to run twice harder than my white counter parts to win the race" said E.R. Braithwaite".

Police makers should consult people who have successfully implemented inclusion instead of focusing on people who do not like or doubt it. Reach out to the teacher's goodness. There are hundreds who have taken up the responsibility of educating children with disabilities even without any formal training, by incorporating relevant experiences and pedagogy in the B.Ed., or M.Ed., courses. We will have an enlightened generation of teaching force in the country. For existing teachers, a refresher training programme will help greatly.

There will soon be a day when the whole of India, will stand united as a role model to the rest of the world as pioneers in inclusive education

MANMOHAN LAUNCHES NATIONAL RURAL HEALTH MISSION

Government have "grievously erred" in designing the country's health programmes. "We have created a delivery model that fragments resources and dissipates energies. Most importantly we have paid in adequate attention to public health issues and the possibilities of social and preventive medicines". the Prime Minister Manmohan Singh, said here today.

Launching the ambitions National Rural Health Mission here today, he stressed upon the need to bridge, the income, education and the health gap of the people. The were inter connected in their causes and their solution were mutually reinforcing.

The NRHM, that will get Rs.6,713 cores for 2005-06, attempts a major shift in the governance of public health by giving leadership to panchayati Raj institutions in all matters related to health at the district and sub district levels. It aims to increase the out reach of the health system to village and even house hold levels through the provision of a voluntary trained female community health activist called ASHA. The mission will cover all the states in the country with special focus on 18 states which have a weak heath infrastructure and demographic indicators.

"Over the years, governments had addressed this issue with some success. However, the experience was somewhat run ever. some states had recorded impressive achievements on the health care front", the Prime Minister said while calling upon the less developed states to learn from the experience of the southern and western states in dealing with the challenge of affordable health care.

There had been a fatal flaw in the approach that had gradually abandoned a comprehensive health care and a public health perspective for focused attention on selective diseases. The Indian health system was perhaps, guilty of many sins of omission and commission.

He highlighted the need for a decentralized, district based management to provide an operational platform to harmonies all services and mobilize collective action on health goals through the opportunities provided by the panchayati Raj institutions. He hoped that the architectural correction that the architectural correction that the mission proposed by empowering district-level institutions, would offer a new ay out for effective rural health care.

The strengthening of the primary or community health care would be the key step to empowering public health infra structure. A significant step was the setting up of Indian public Health standards that would specify personal management and equipment norms including those for community control based on which these Hospitals would need to be built up.

The Prime Minister said in Government was committed to raising health spending from 0.9 percent of the GDP at preset to two percent in the coming years. The Government would adhere to the commitment and call upon the state Government to ensure their timely utilization after the architectural corrections were immediately effected.

The public health infrastructure would be strengthened under the Mission through the constructions of sub-centre buildings and the upgrading of public health centers and community health centers.

An united fund of Rs.10,000/- would be provided to every sub centre to cater to the unmet needs reflected in the village health focused on the promotion of alternative systems of medicine.

DEATH IN A BOOMING ECONOMY

It is conical that in the era of high economic growth rates, an unconscionably large number of women and children are dying in India for want of adequate health care and nutrition, earning for the country an enviable place among nations making 'slow progress' in reducing maternal and infant mortality, A few states, above all Kerala, have reduced the loss of life among women, giving birth and among children in the first year of life through socially progressive policies. The national record, however in appalling, the MMR and the mortality rate of children in the first four weeks and before they reach ages one and five continue to mock the health care system. The world Health Report 2005 provides another occasion to review the health indicators. It does little credit to an aspiring global power that 10 percent of its 27 million children born in a year will punish before they are five years old.

The literature available on key development indicators offers strong pointers to poverty and inequities in health care delivery as primary reasons for high death rates among women and infants. It is widely acknowledged that the major factors that influence the health out comes of pregnant women and new born children are nutrition levels access to institutional deliveries, emergency posterities, facilities and immunization. The National Family Health Surveys and other studies point to significant variations in the health status of pregnant women in different Indian states and social settings, and rural poor, and people living in the least developed states generally getting the lowest levels of care.

There can be little doubt that health policy and practice in some of the bigger states are in need and of a radical transformation if they are to meet national and millennium development goals by 2015. Medical science has progressed to such a level that virtually every death is maternity can be viewed medically as one too many. The world Health Organisation recommends that governments must provide at least me emergency posterity and neonatal care facility for every half million population. But even progressive states such as Tamil Nadu, which is implementing a World Bank funded Heath project, cannot hope to achieve such a ratio in the short term. There is a strong case for a national action plan to help the least developed states identified all too clearly by the world Health Report, to upgrade their obstetric and new rattail facilities with central funding as much as it takes. For decades, many states have failed to make the most basic life-saving interventions in reproductive and child health, with calamitous human and social consequences. Making up for past deficiencies and failures cannot be contingent on international grants and loans. It must be pursued with rigor and full budgetary support.

GUIDE TO GOOD PARENTING

The Archbishop of Canterbury challenged us in a speech this week to look hard at the moral growth of our children, and to ask ourselves if we like what we see, his challenge in central to our moral landscape. And it is one that secular liberal left finds it peculiarly difficult to respond to

Shooting down the moral child case prescriptions of others has long been a favorite field sport of progressives, but ask us, as Rowan Williams did, to describe "What a human adult might be like" and to clarify our role in guiding children to become such adults, and all you're likely to see from the left in players departing the pitch.

For a text book example of this, look no further than last month's report on anti social behaviour from the British Parliament. The report criticized child welfare and health agencies in the limited kingdom for failing picture of difficult damaged children being bounced between the dictatorial dad of the crime – prevention agencies and the molly coddling mum of the social welfare sector. We've all read enough parenting manuals and watched enough reality TV shows about dysfunctional families to know where that leads.

Dr. Williams was brave enough to offer some core elements of human morality. They included emotional intelligence, a concern for the consequences of our actions, respect for self and others and awareness of our fallibility and limitations.

A moments reflection on our own childhood will reveal two crucial insights, that many of our most powerful and formative moral experiences happened out of sight of adults, and that much of what went on wasn't very pretty. One reason why children's bad behavours is more trouble some to us than it used to be in because children's lives are more constrained and watched over by adults than at any time in recent history.

This gives children a double whammy; it frustrates their natural urge to explore and push boundaries, and it exposes their resultant behaviour to the ever more judgmental gaze of adults. The combined forces over anxious parents, over zealous institutions and hostile communities are leaving children deprived of the raw material they need to make sense of their growing moral and social engagement with the people and world around them.

It is not simply backing one stock liberal response to bad behaviour, "They are just being kids" There is a real problem, Solving it involves understanding more fully the journey that children need to go through if they are to become autonomous adults with self respect and respect for the rights and entitlement of others. This means giving more license and freedom to make mistakes and learn from them. It also means confronting children. Children with the consequences of their actions through proportional sanctions and incentives that nurture a sense of human agency, rather than behaviouristic and materialistic systems of punishment and reward.

The left's problem with the idea of intervening in the moral growth of children is partly a justified response to tendency to a moral relativism that tries to assume a position from which to declare it also reflects some confused ideas about what childhood is. The process by which a child grows into his or her moral slim is a mysterious one. It needs from adults a subtle blend of firmness, understanding and benign neglect.

It needs an appreciation of both the extent and the limitations of children's competences and how they evolve through child hood. And as the archbishop reminds us, it needs clarity about the directions of travel of all our moral journeys.

NEW STANDARDS FOR COMMUNITY HEALTH CENTRES

The union Health and family welfare Ministry today launched the Indian Public Health Standards (IPHS) for the community Health centers to provide expert care and maintain an acceptable standard of quality of care. The aim in also to make the services more responsive and sensitive to the needs of the community.

The mission aimed at strengthening referred hospital care for every one lakh persons as per the new standards, As of now, the health standards were under the purview of the Bureau of Indian standards.

The services assured in community health centers such as routine and emergency care in surgery, medicine, posterities, gynecology and pediatrics are to be made available under the IPHS.As regards man power two specialists' anesthetics and public would be provided on a contractual basis in addition to the available specialists. The support man power will include a pubic health nurse and an auxiliary nurse and midwife (ANH) in addition to the exiting staff.

An ophthalmic assistant will be provided at the centers where there is none at present. The routine and emergency services that the community health centers must provide include incision and drainage, hernia, appendicitis hemorrhoids and fistula.

They should be able to handle emergencies such as intestinal obstructions and hemorrhage Besides 24 hour delivery services including normal and assisted services, the centers should have a full range of family planning services, safe abortion services and newborn care.

The programmes that will be implemented through the community health centers at the District level include the revised National TB control programme, HIV/AIDS control programme, National Vector Borne Disease control programme including malaria, filarial, dingus, encephalitis and kala-azar, national leprosy eradication programme, National programme for control of blindness and the integrated disease surveillance project.

The centers will also have a blood storage facility, essential laboratory services and referral (transport) services.

HIGHER EDUCATION

Higher Education has undergone quite a lot of transformation over the years. After the Kothari commission report in 1966, discussions on college autonomy started and a few colleges because antonymous since 1978 and a few of them have completed 25 years of such freedom Academic freedom, under autonomy, helped many colleges to innovate new curricula, design relevant curves, frame new syllabi and introduce new evaluation methods. But the required flexibility for the students to have a greater choice of courses appropriate to their interests, needs and long-term goals is not available even in autonomous colleges, rather a rigid and compartmentalized system in perpetuated.

Choice based credit system (CBSC) or a cafeteria like system in the solution for this of transformation from the traditional teacher oriented education to a student - centered education. Taking responsibility for their own education in this way, students can benefit the most from all the available resources. Academic commissions and committees such as UGC, TANSCHE and NAAC recommend CBCS for Higher education.

Though a few institutions claim to have introduced this system, in reality not much of freedom in given to the students. Every one agrees that intellectual depth and breadth characterize higher education. But in allowing the students to choose their favorite courses, certain questions arise. The rules regarding the number of students in each class and the number of hours per week for the students or for the teachers have not changed from the old affiliated system.

There is a strong resistance to change from every quarter of the academic world. Students are compelled to take two years of language course of their mother Tongue. They are not encouraged to take courses according to their abilities and pace and there is no freedom for the first year student to take an advanced course or a third year student to take an introductory course students are compelled to be inside the classroom for the entire five hours a day schedule leaving no scope for independent study.

Why not a student earns a few credits from one college and transfers the credits to some other college? Why not a student who is working on a part-time basis earns a few credits and stretches his studies to four or five years according to his convenience? Why is there a kind of compulsion to complete a degree programme in three years? Why is there no provision to change to change the college after earning a few credits CBCS has the facility to transfer the credits from one institution to another there are provisions in the rules of the autonomous colleges and the universities to accept transfer of credits.

The academicians often talk about university and the industry collaborations. Why root a few credits earned in a related industry be considered with in the curriculum? As creative and performing arts are becoming popular in campuses, credits can be thought of for such activities too. Through the students will choose courses of inter disciplinary nature, the required courses for majoring in a subject will ensure depth. Professionalism and quality consciousness are the basis for every charge. With faculty advising, CBSC can offer a very flexible and open system for quality up gradation of higher education

13

Qualified Teachers - A Rare Tribe

(Prof. Sirohi, V.C.,Barkatullah university. Formerly Director of IT,Delhi. Graduation day address, Kumaraguru College of Technology)

India can become the 'Skill Capital" of the world but qualified teachers is hard to come by and there are not enough students in the educational institutions.

Professor R.S. Sirohi, Vice Chancellor Barkatullah University said, "We have a gigantic task before us, to provide education professional and vocational – to a large number of people so that India becomes a developed nation by the year 2020 a dream we all wish".

Prof. Sirohi was formerly the Director of the Indian Institute of technology in New Delhi. He said while delivering the graduation day address at the Kumara guru College of Technology", There are over 600 million people below the age of 24 and of this 320 million are between the ages of six and 16. This relatively large 'young population suggests that are have all the potential to be the 'stall capital' of the world, provided these young people are empowered; by quality education and vocational training".

Over 90 lakh persons were doing degree programmes at the universities through out the country, of which 8.5 percent where in technical institutions leading to certificates, diplomas and degrees.

If all the 1360 engineering colleges were full, a total of 3.8 lakh students would be studying in them. Astounding task "Thus there is an astounding task before us to provide quality education to such a large number.

The task becomes even move difficult due to shortage of qualified teachers. The problem is acute in some critical and strategic disciplines" he said Prof. Sirohi observed that India is considered the Third largest science and technology resources in the world.

POVERTY ON THE WANE?

The one significant impression from two recent 24-hour journeys in second – class trains? I was simply stunned at the number and variety of people who streamed through asking for coins or who did so at the stations. Or who were obviously destitute even if they did not beg. Blind couples; man on his behind with leg dropped around his neck and bag of grapes hanging from his toes; young girls signing tunelessly, boys and men and women sweeping the compartment, some with the shirts of their backs; filthy mothers with a seemingly lifeless kid lolling in their arms, a silent bearded midget; men without me or more limbs, on crutches, eunuchs, lean after who picked up watermelon rinds from under the train and ate them; a smiling old man who asked for money in Tamil, then English, them Tamil again., From early in the morning all through the day well into the night, On and on.

Through largely ignored by the international media, a little piece of Islamic history was created in Newyork recently with a woman leading a mixed gathering of men and women for Friday prayers. In an unprecedented lead Dr. Amina Wadud associate Professor of Islamic studies at Virginia common wealth university. Led a congregation of more than 100 men and women, drawing extreme reactions from the orthodox schools and those who would interpret Islam in the light of the west.

Interestingly, even as Islam forbids free intermingling of men and women one exception being the Hajj pilgrim – there was no separate entry for women at the site as is the practice in mosques across the would including the prophet's mosque in Medina. Nor was there a curtain or a screen to divide the men and women at the prayer. And in another first of sorts, another women with her hair flowing freely off her shoulders pronounced the call for prayer, Adhan. The prayer was conducted largely in English with verses from Qurun in Arabic.

Creating History

A little before leading the prayers, Dr. Wadud emphasized the equality of men and women asking for the removal of "inconvenient restrictions" on Muslim women. But for all her tough talk, Dr. Wadud is in unenviable company. She gets little support either from religion / tradition or her contemporaries. The grand Mufti of Al Azhar, an authority of Maters of

Islamic jurisprudence, has denounced her action. Throughout Islamic history no woman has ever led a mixed gathering of the devout, None of the four schools of Islamic through has any such precedence nor in there is an approval, tacit or explicit from the jurists of Medina, The prophet himself is reported to have said "Establish prayers the way you have seen me" And never did in his life time or that of the caliphs who followed, a woman lead prayers for men.

Infact, the Friday prayers or even prayers in a mosque are not compulsory for any women – importantly, they have been exempted, not prevented from coming to mosques for regular prayers. Islam has provided equality of status and rights to women. A woman has similar rights to a man with regard to her life, hounour, dignity and freedom. She is free to create and control property as a man does, she is as respectable in the eyes of God as a man and equally shares the responsibility of being the vicegerent of God. Her position is not inferior or subservient to that of man. At the same time Islam recognizes and provides for the biological, psychological and functional differences between the two sexes.

Look with in

The need of the hour is to follow the teaching of the faith in their spirit and not just letter. There is a need to look within because, in countries across the world, religion has become subservient to local tradition and women have been victimized in a patriarchal society. The Quran states, "They have same rights unto you as you have unto them".

The question of Dr.Wadud leady the prayers should not be seen as a dash of gender upsurge of feminism among the faithful. Intead one has to take recourse to history and tradition and learn from them. After all believing men and women have been declared by Allah to be the friends and supporters of each other and the faithful have been instructed to" Givt to man what in his and render to woman what belongs to her"

14

Higher Education in India

(Phipli G Altback, professor of higher education and director of the center for International higher education at Boston college)

India is rushing head long towards economic success and modernization, countering on high – tech industries such as information technology and biotechnology to proper the nation to prosperity. India's recent announcement that it would do no longer produce unlicensed inexpressive genetic pharmaceuticals bowed to the realities of the World Trade organization while at the same time challenging the domestic drug industry to complete with the multinational firms. Unfortunately, its weak higher education in recent years has yielded neither world – class research nor very many highly trained scholars, scientists or managers to sustain high-tech development.

India's main competitors- especially China but also Singapore, Taiwan and south Korea are investing in large and differentiated higher Education systems. They are providing access to large numbers of students at the bottom of the academic system while at the same time building some research based universities that are able to complete with the world's best institutions. The recent London times Higher Education supplements ranking of the world's top 200 universities included three in China, three in Hong Kong, three in South Korea, one in Taiwan, and one in India (as Indian Institute of Technology at Number 41 The specific campus was not specified) These countries are positioning themselves for leadership in the knowledge based economic of the coming era.

There was time when countries would achieve economic success, with cheap labour and low-tech manufacturing. Low wages still help, but contemporary large scale development requires a sophisticated and at least partly knowledge based economy. India has chosen that path, but will find a major stumbling block in its university system.

India has significant advantages in the 21st century knowledge race. It has a larger higher education sector- the third largest in the world in student numbers, after china and the United States. It uses English as the primary languages of higher education and research. It has a long academic tradition. Academic freedom is respected. There are a small number of high quality institutions, departments, and centers that can form the basis of quality sector in higher education. The fact that the states, rather than the central Government, exercise major responsibility for create a rather cumbersome structure, but the system allows for a variety of polices, and approaches.

Yet the weaknesses far outweigh the strengths. India educates approximately 10 percent of its young people in higher education compared with more than half in the major industrialized countries and 15 percent in China. Almost all of the world's academic systems resemble a pyramid, with a small high quality tier at the top and massive sector at the bottom. India has a tiny top tier. None of its universities occupies a solid position at the top. A few of the best universities have some excellent departments and centers and there in small number of outstanding undergraduate colleges.

The university grants commission's recent major support of five universities to build on their recognized strength in a step toward recognizing a differentiated academic system and fostering excellence. At present, the world class institutions are mainly limited to the Indian Institutions are mainly limited to the Indian Institutes of Technology (IITS), The Indian Institutes of Management (IIMS) and perhaps a few others such as the all India Institute of Medical Sciences and the Tata Institute of Fundamental Research. These institutions, combined, enroll well under 1 percent of the student population.

India's colleges and universities, with just a few exceptions have becomes large, under-funded, ungovernable institutions. At many of them, politics has intruded into campus life influencing academic appointments and decisions across levels. Under investment in libraries, information technology, laboratories and class rooms make it very difficult to provide top-quality instructions or engage in cutting – edge research.

The rise in number of part time teachers and the freeze on new full time appointments in many places have affected morale in the academic profession. The lack of accountability means that teaching and research performance in seldom perform, Bureaucratic inertia hampers change. Student unrest and occasional faculty agitation disrupt operations. Nevertheless, with a semblance of normality, faculty administrators are ablc to provide teaching, co-ordinate examinations, and award degrees.

Even the small top tier of higher education faces serious problems many IIT graduates, well trained in technology have chosen not to contribute their stalls to the burgeoning technology sector in India. Perhaps half leave the country immediately upon graduation to a stunning 86 percent of students in science and technology fields from India who obtain degrees in the United States do not return home immediately following their study. Another significant group, of about 30 percent, decides to earn MBAs, in India because local salaries are higher and are lost to science and technology. A corps of dedicated and able teacher's works at the IITs and ITMs but the job aboard and in the private sector makes it increasingly difficult to lure the best and brightest to the academic profession.

Few in India are thinking creatively about higher education. There is no field of higher education research. Those in government as well as academic leaders seem content to do the 'same old thing' Academic institutions and systems have become large and complex. They need good data, careful analysis, and creative ideas. In China, more than two dozen higher education research centers, and several government agencies are involved in higher education policy.

India has survived with an increasingly mediocre higher education system for decades. Now as India strives to complete in globalize economy in areas that require highly trained professionals, the quality of higher Indian large educated population bare and its reservoir of at least moderately well-trained university graduates have permitted the country to move ahead. But, the competition in fierce. China in particular is heavily investing in improving its best universities them world class in the coming alidade, and making a larger number internationally competitive research universities other Asian countries are also upgrading higher education with the aim of building world-class universities Taiwan, which in major designer and producer of IT hardware, in considering merging several of its top technological universities to create an "Asian MIT".

To compete successfully in the knowledge based economy of 21st century, India needs enough universities that not only produce bright graduates for export but can also support sophisticated research in a number of scientific and scholarly fields and produce at least some of the knowledge and technology needed for an expanding economy.

How can India build a higher education system that will permit it to join developed economies? The newly emerging private sector in higher education cannot spearhead academic growth. Several of the well endowed and effectively managed private institutions maintain reasonably high standards, although it is not clear that these institutions will be able to sustain themselves in the long run. They can help produce well-qualified graduates in such fields as management, but they can not form the basis for comprehensive research universities. This sector lacks the resources to build the facilities required for quality instruction and research in the sciences. Nor can enough money be earned by providing instruction in the main stream arts and sciences disciplines. Most of the private institutions do not focus on advanced training in the sciences.

Only public universities have the potential to be truly world class institutions. Institutions and programmes of national prominence have already been identified by the Government. But these institutions have not been adequately or consistently supported. The top institutions require sustained funding from public sources. Academic salaries must be high enough to attract excellent scientists and scholars, fellowships and other grants should be available for bright students. An academic culture that is based on merit based norms and competition for advancement and research funds is a necessary component as is a judicious mix of autonomy to do creative research and accountability to ensure productivity. World calls universities require world class professors and students and a culture to sustain and stimulate them.

A clearly differentiated academic system has not been created in India – a system where there are some clearly identified institutions that receive significantly greater resources than other universities. One of the main reasons that the university of California at Berkeley is so good is that other California universities receive much less support India's best universities require sustained state support they require the recognition that they are indeed top institutions and deserve commensurate support. But they also require effective management and an ethos of an academic meritocracy. At present, the structures are not in place to permit building and sustaining top quality programs even if resources are provided. A combination of specific conditions and resources are needed to create outstanding universities.

Sustained financial support with an appropriate mix of accountability and autonomy. The development of a clearly differentiated academic system – including private institutions in which academic institutions have different missions, resources and purposes. Managerial reforms and introduction of effective administrations.

Truly merit based hiring and promotion policies for the academic profession and similarly rigorous and honest recruitment, selection and instruction of students.

India can not build internationally recognized research – oriented universities over night, but the country has the key elements in place to begin and sustain the process. India will need to create a dozen or more universities that can compete internationally to fully participate in the new world economy without these universities, India is distained to remain a scientific backwater.

SCHOOLS FOR ALL

"Will you do our house work and look after the younger children if we send the older girl to school?" Parents ask the teachers, the teachers have no solution to offer.

The 86th constitutional Amendment passed in 2002, made elementary education a fundamental right. But there are no laws implement it to. One draft of a Bill to actualize the 86th C.A. Spoke of persuading parents by school developments committee and gram panchayats. But the law also needs to say what is to be done if persuasion fails. The central child labour (Prohibition and regulation) Act does not ban household labour of children during schools ours, through that is the most request cause of child labour.

The indicative law on child labour drafted by the second national labour commission and several state compulsory education laws too – speak only of punishment of parents (usually with a fine) for a child's non attendance of school without a valid reason,. But this is never invoked even incases where it could be done, as in (Reruka's case) worse the does not say the states must if a parent pays the fine but still does not send his child to school. It is also silent on the state's role in cases where the family or child genuinely needs assistance as in the case of (Anjali) there are no penalties on officials for failing to ensure. The right to education of any child. The Karnataka High Court in 1997 had given the enlightened ruling that "The state being the guardian of a minor" it should take charge of the child and ensure its rights when parents are unable to fulfill them. This too has never been implemented.

Yet, ministers and officials may be jet setting, attending international conference on child labour and (Renuka) will continue to blow into the stove all her life, and peer helplessly through the smoke of ignorance enveloping her, and (Anjali)will trudge around with (Saab Reddy) at her waist, cripped and disempowered by illiteracy for the rest of her life.

U.G.C. Sponsored study – Project

Using information provided by psychologists and experts in vocational skills, the researchers would strive to improve the health of the street children and help them learn vocational skills.

They will also decide on the type of educational programmes that will suit the children who now live in groups of 60 to 100 at various centers.

Educational Programmes

Educational programmes for the children would high light the importance of eating nutritious food, leading a healthy life, being clean and neat, and keeping away from substances such as tobacco, alcohol and drugs.

They would learn about sexual reproductive health, understand the advantages of managing emotions, listen to advice on overcoming anxiety through positive active activities and gain knowledge abut conquering physical and emotion stresses that might build up in the course of their everyday lives.

Valuable to Abuse

With no family support to fall back on, street children were often vulnerable to abuse by unscrupulous people and could be exploited in a variety of ways without being able to effectively resist their tormentors.

Hence the programme would motivate the children to be assertive when dealing with others, learn how to make decisions, solve problems and set goals.

By learning how to make use of their leisure time in a positive manner, they would not only refresh themselves, but also prevent themselves being led astray or exploited. For the projects they intend to take children from the rehabilitation homes for street children at Don Bosco Anbu Illum at Vkkadam, Mariyalaya at Ganapthi and NEST Tirupur.

Control Group

To compare the result of the life enrichment education programme the researchers would use a "Control Group" of street children who would not come under the project. Prof Jayapoorni said that her interest in street children had begun seven years ago.

The researcher / the principal investigator had co-authored two research articles on the subject. One was on the health status and efficacy of health education provided to street children and the other was on "Non-formal education provided to street children"

Over the last ten years, research had indicated that education could serve the needs of street children growing up in "A disadvantaged environment that lacked opportunities to develop several essential life enriching activities.

Enabling rural folk to over come Poverty

The Beijing +10 meeting, held to assess the progress of commitments to improve the lives of women, shows that India in making strides in addressing gender equality issues. This is also the year of Microcredit, and India, through its numerous, self-help groups and innovations in financial services to poor people, serves as an inspiration to other developing nations.

Since 1979 the International Fund for Agricultural Development (IFAD) has been working with the Government of India to help reduce poverty in some of the country's most remote and fragile areas, targeting the poorest and most marginalized people. Mutual learning and information exchange has been an important features of IFAD's work with India.

India's commitment to reducing poverty is reflected in the numerous initiatives it has taken, leading to the progress made over the last decades, but the country still faces a major challenge to reduce poverty on a larger scale. Millions of poor people in rural areas will continue to suffer under the weight of extreme poverty unless progress in made in addressing the plight of vulnerable groups, Three fourths of India's poor population, or 193 million people live in rural areas scheduled Tribes and Scheduled castes are among the poorest in India and constitute 40 percent of the internally displaced population. These groups, and especially women, suffer a higher incidence of poverty, grater vulnerability and lower social status than others. Targeting rural poverty, particularly among scheduled Tribes and scheduled castes and women will better enable India to reach its full development potential in a sustainable manner.

IFAD has provided India with more funding than it has to any other country. IFAD in dedicated to working closely with the Government of India to improve the lives of women and other vulnerable groups.

IFAD places empowerment at the heart of its projects and programmes in India. The main goal of IFAD's work is to empower people with the skills and assets they need to lift themselves out of poverty.

IFAD supports investment projects and programmes in the popular states of central India where levels of rural poverty are some of the highest in the country. Programmes in Orissa, Jharkhand and Chhattisgarh are benefiting 608000 tribal poor people by helping them improve their lively hood opportunities. IFAD is supporting the small Industry Development

Bank of India through the National Micro finance support programme. This programme will reach 1.3 million poor people in underserved areas, helping them to develop an extensive, national microfinance sector which will provide technical assistance so rural poor people can start, expand, or diversify income-generating activities.

PROMISE THEM THEIR CHILDHOOD

There is no shortage of words on the need for reform, when it comes to policies and issues related to children or even ideas on what those reforms should be. Some times within a few years of launch, reform programmes themselves become the targets of a new reform movement. This cyclical approach to change does make some children's lives better, but never do there reforms bring about wide spread or long term transformation.

The recast Juvenile Justice (JJ) System a creation of well intentioned child rights activates, legal experts and administrators is a classic example. The experience ever since the JJ Act was passed in 2000 has led to disillusionment. Many institutions set up under the Act are perceived as part of the problem, rather than the solution, Now, there are calls for a review.

Areas of Governance

Primarily, reform movements for children have focused on four areas of governance. Socio – economic, even demographic change. The need for new and additional resources – financial, human and institutional.

The role of the private sector

The inter relatedness of the problems children face and the need for holistic solutions. CRY's (Child Relieve of you) 25 years experience shows that every reform initiative selects one or two areas as particular challenges and evolves strategies aimed at closing the gap. Each reform effort strives to be inclusive, comprehensive and persuasive. And many a time policy shifts happen quickly short term and partial successes follows being perceived as pro children is also good for the inroads of a government. Since good policy making for children is a win-win situation politically, why is it that to dates, policies have failed to make enough impacts.

The ground reality is that the situations of children cannot be bettered without addressing the problems of the adults without addressing the problem; of the adults in their lives. So provision of food supplements, for instance would be of no value if the child is forced to become a migrant owing to its parents unemployment.

This means that a child's right to food can be ensured, only when the parents have the right to employment. The Government's refusal to assure every adult an annual income, adequate to provide for a family ends up hurting children, Thus providing quality services for children is of little consequence if the parents and guardians are unable to ensure access to them.

Uniformly India's policies for children fail to locate their interests within the wider social context. Instead of understanding the reality and evolving relevant. Policy responses, policy influencers select potions of a complex problem and merely address these. The failure to place children's interests within their home and social milieu, in turn, produces flawed policies in adequately designed programmes and increasing frustrations in the field.

So, what would a policy revolution for children involve? Policies that acknowledge the connections between the children and the adults in their lives. This would mean, for instance, linking the guarantee of elementary education for all with adult employment, day-care facilities, quality heath care and adequate nutritious food for both children and adults.

At a children's day ceremony last year, president Dr. A.P.J. Abdul Kalam made, he gathered children to promise, "I will pursue my education and do my work sincerely. I will plan at least five saplings. I will try to alleviate the sufferings of poor people and those in distress. I will never discriminate against any one on the basis of caste, creed or religion. I will remain honest and try to weed out, corruption from society".

If the children promise, to link their education with transforming India for the better, should it be so different for adults to think less of piece meal reform and more of a holistic solution? one that links bettering their childhood with improving the quality of life of the adults in their lives. As children and communities voice aspiration, demand their rights and together with other aware citizens, hold government and society accountable to each child transformation will surely happen.

A forceful Message but will it end poverty?

Flexibility in Plans

A National development strategy must be open to revision. A country, like a person, does best by revising its plans in light of new information. National and international plans for poverty reduction must incorporate flexibility, so that they can reflect the different conditions prevailing in different countries.

However, allowing for flexibility is not enough. A practical approach for reducing human deprivations must activity foster learning about the best strategies, rather than presuming that there strategies are known in advance. It in likely that new information will emerge over time about the best strategies. Human beings learn from the results of their own and other's practical experiments. A sound strategy for reducing global poverty must enable and encourage countries to undertake experiments and to learn from one another.

Impact of Mid-day meals

A telling example of the importance of arriving at sound policies through learning is provided by the mid day meals introduced in schools in southern Indian States in the early 1980s. This measure was initially indicated as populism and in effective. Many Indianan Economists feared that the programme would add little to child nutrition, as poor parents would react to availability of school meals by spending less on child nutrition themselves.

Only a few analysis's foresaw the real reason that these schemes would be an effective developmental tool, they encouraged parents to send their children to school in larger numbers than ever before, learning form this success, the central Government introduced subsidies for all states to implement such schemes and supreme court has mandated them in every state. The Supreme Court has rightly recognized that India's states are laboratories for experimentation which should be encouraged to learn from one another.

India's experience has give rise to many successful experiments from which other developing countries, have learnt. Every development intervention and institutional reform that is now the focus of attention around the world, from educating mothers about the use of 'oral dehydration therapy' to reduce child mortality from diarrloca, to creating a right to public information so as to increase state and local Government accountability – is ultimately the product of such learning from experiments.

Peer and Partner review

How can the world best reduce poverty?

A practical approach to reducing poverty must guarantee to countries the resources they need and it must allow for experimentation and learning a system called "Peer and partner review' offers a practical solution. Countries would at a regular interval (perhaps three years) voluntarily submit their plans to reduce poverty to scrutiny by their peers – others countries in similar circumstances and their partners – those from whom they receive or to whom they give development assistance. Each review committee would consist of representatives of governments independent experts and civil society organizations and would be empowered to collect and analyses information and hold hearings

The End of Poverty

The just published book by professor Jettrey Sachs, the end of poverty, rightly insists on the shared responsibilities of rich and poor countries alike to bring about global poverty reduction. Professor sachs, who is also an adviser to VNs secretary General Kofi Annan, Prescribes a set of interventions specific investments in health education and infrastructure, through which to substantially reduce poverty in developing countries.

He calls on developing countries to implement this intervention and calls on developed countries to triple aid from its current level of around $ 65 billion a year. Aid ferns are now relatively unimportant to many developing countries which have limited, internal resources, especially smaller countries and those in sub-Saharan Africa, Prof. Sachs emphasizes the role that aid can play in improving conditions in these countries. These recommendations carry great weight as they are likely to play a prominent role in this years' gathering of head of stales (2005) to assess how best to achieve the VNs "Millennium development goals".

The review committee would assess a nations' plan in the light of what has worked in the past and based on an examination of the country's present opportunities and constraints. The analysis and recommendations of a peer and partner review committee would be broadly distributed within and outside the country. Thereby encouraging pubic education and debate. A poor country's 'needs and gaps- the resources it requires in order to achieve poverty reduction goals and any short fall that remains after taking account of the country's own capacity to raise resources –would be identified Genuine 'Gaps" would then be filled through international assistance.

Fostering experiments and learning

Peer and partner review would be voluntary. Large countries such as India with unique circumstances and little need or desire for external resources rare unlikely to wish to participles. Other smaller and poorer countries would fund participation attractive. The approach would foster experiment and learning, avoid laying down conditions heavy-handedly and enhance mutual respect and accountability. It would not lay down one size fits all prescriptions but rather would look for solutions that work in local conditions.

India's example shows, empowering countries to find their own solutions offers the best hop of real progress.

Sanjai Reddy is Lawrence Rocks faller visiting Fellow, university center for Human values Princeton University and Asst. Prof. Department of economics, Barnard college, Columbia University, Antonia Hearty is an independent development consultant.

The Word Mantra

"What is the single most important thing that can be done to improve the world?" It's the kind of question that tends to bring out the bureaucrat in the most direct of communicators, as me feels obliged to explain how complex are the challenges confronting humanity, how no one task alone can be singled out over the other goals; how the struggle for peace, the fight against poverty, the battle to eradicate disease, must all be waged side by side and so mind numbingly on. But casting all cantions to winds sushi Tharoor (United Nations under-secretary General for communications and public Information) Ventured an answer to this most impossible questions; "Educate girls".

It really is that simple, there is no action proven to do more for the human race than the education of the female child. Scholarly studies and research projects have established what common sense might already have told us, that if you educate a boy, you educate a person, if you educate a girl; you educate a family and benefit an entire community.

The evidence is striking. Increased schooling of mothers has a measurable impact on the health of their children, on the future schooling of the child, and on the child's adult productivity. The children of educated mothers consistently out-perform children with educated fathers and illiterate mothers. Given that they spend most of their time with their mothers, this is hardly surprising.

A girl who has had more than six years, of education is better equipped to seek and use medical and health care advice to immunize her children, to be aware of sanitary practices from boiling water to the importance of washing hands. A World Bank project in Africa established that the children of women with just five years of school had a 40 percent better survival rate than the children of women who had less than five years in class. A Yale university study showed that the heights and weights for new born children of women with a basic education were consistently higher than those of babies born to uneducated women. A UNESCO project demonstrated that giving women just a primary school education decreases child mortality by five percent to 10 percent.

The health advantages of education extend beyond child birth. The dreaded disease AIDS spreads twice as fast, a Zambian study shows among uneducated girls than among those who have been to school. Educated girls marry later, and are less susceptible to abuse by older man. And educated women tend to have fewer children, space them more wisely and so look after them better; women with seven year's education, according to one study had two or fewer children than women with no schoolıng. 'The World Bank, with the mathematical precision for which they are so famous, has estimated that for every four years of education, fertility is reduced by about me birth per mother. The reason Kerala's fertility rate is 1.7 per couple while Bihar's is over four in that Kerala's women are educated and most of Bihar's are not.

The more girls go to secondary school, the Bank adds, the higher the country's per capita income growth. And when girls work in the fields, as so many have to do across the developing world, their schooling translates directly to increased agricultural productivity, the marvelous thing about women is that they like to learn from other women, so the success educated women is usually quickly emulated by their uneducated sisters. And women spend increased income on their families, which men do not necessarily do. (Rural toddy shops in Indian after all thrive on the self-indulgent spending habits of men) In many studies, the education of girls has been shown to lead to more productive farming and in turn to a decline in malnutrition. Educate a girl, and you benefit a community QED.

Catherine Bertini was this year's world food prize laureate for her tireless and effective work an head of the united Nations' World Food Programme. As she put in her acceptance speech for that prestigious prize. "If someone told you that, with just 12 years of investment of about $1 billion a year, you could, across the developing world, increase economic growth, decrease infant mortality, increase agricultural yields, improve maternal health, improve children's health and nutrition increase the number of children – girls and boys – in school, slow down population growth, increase the number of men and women who can read and write, decrease the spread of AIDS, add new people to the work force and be able to improve their wages without pushing be able to improve their wages without pushing others out of the work force – what would you say? Such a deal! hat is it? How can I sign up?"

Sadly, the world is not yet rushing to "Sign up" to the challenge of educating girls, who lag consistently behind boys in access to education throughout the developing world. Some 65 million girls around the world never see the inside of a class room and yet not educating them costs the world more than putting them through school.

UNICEF's energetic head carol Bellany, releasing, her flagship 'State of the world's children's report said bluntly. "The failure to invest in girls' education puts in jeopardy more development goals than any other single action". In our own country, we have a long way to go and we boast one state, Bihar which has enthroned an illiterate woman as chief Minister – as if to showcase its abysmal figure of a 23 percent female literacy rate, one of the worst on the planet.

Certainly, there is no better answer V.N. Secretary – General Kofi Annan put it simply" "No other policy is as likely to raise economic productivity, lower infant and maternal mortality, improve nutrition, promote health, including the prevention of HIV /AIDS, and increase the chances of education for the next generation. Le we invest in women and girls".

15

Values

INTRODUCTION

The values present a true perspective of the development of any society or nation. They tell us to what extent a society or nation has developed itself. Values are virtues, ideals and qualities on which actions and beliefs are based. Values are guiding principles that shape our world outlook, attitudes and conduct. Values however are either innate or acquired. Innate values are our inborn divine virtues such as love, peace, happiness, mercy and compassion as well as the positive moral qualities such as respect, humility, tolerance, responsibility, cooperation, honesty and simplicity.

DEFINITION OF VALUES

According to Cambridge dictionary of philosophy, the value is the worth of something that philosophers discerned these main forms of intrinsic, instrumental, inherent and contributory value.

Values are described as the socially defined desires and goals that are internalized through the process of condition, learning and socialization.

Values are goals set for achievement and they motivate, define and colour all our activities cognitive, affective and co-native. When education builds up true values in the life of our student, it has equipped the ship of students with RADAR and compass to sail clear on the stormy sea of life.

Values reflect different philosophical positions. The concepts of values are closely associated with the concept of man.

According to Jules Henry in "Culture against Man" (1963), values are something that we consider good such as love, kindness, quietness, contentment, fun, honesty, decency, relaxation and simplicity.

According to Carl Rogers in "Freedom to Learn" (1969), valuing is the tendency of a person to show preference.

According to Louis Raths, Merril and Harmin and Sidney B. Simon (1966) in "Values and Teaching", values are due to the out of experiences may come certain and guides to behaviour. These tend to give direction to life.

According to Shepard B. Clough (1960) in "Basic Values of Western Civilization", in a summary states that values have been variously viewed as preferences, criteria, objects and possessions, personality and status characteristics and states of mind that are absolutes, inherent in objects present in man and stages of mind and identical with his behaviour.

According to John Dewey "the value means primarily to prize, to esteem, to appraise, to estimate; it means the act of cherishing something, holding it dear and also the act of passing judgment upon the nature and amounts of values as compared with something else".

According to Parker, "values belong wholly to the inner world of mind. The satisfaction of desire is the real value; the thing that serves is only an instrument. A value is always an experience never a thing or an object".

According to Mukerjee "values are socially approved drives and goals that are internalized through the process of conditioning, learning or socialization and that becomes subjective preferences, standards and aspirations".

According to Alloport's "the term value means the relative prominence of the subject's interest or the dominant interest in personality".

According to Derek Rowntree's (1960), "Dictionary of Education" that the moral and aesthetics, principles, believes and standards that give coherence and direction to persons' decisions and actions. Where such values are held by or are imposed upon the majority of people in a society they may be known as social values.

In statistics, the different quantitative and qualitative in which an entity can be with respect to some variable that is different categories and measurement.

Values simply stated, are the determiners in the man that influence his choices in life and that decide his behaviour.

Values as indicated are inherent, in individual man but they are additionally inherent although perhaps less definably so, in collective man in a given culture that is or in a combination of cultures. Whatever the exact nature of human society, values exist in some form. In a primitive society, they reside in developed society they reside in written documents as well as in the intangible of social mores and expectances.

IMPORTANCE OF VALUES

In today's multi-cultural and multi-racial society, with its changing social norms and expectations, it can be difficult for a young person to know what is right. To enable young people to appreciate themselves and others, and to take greater responsibility for their actions and for the world around them. Sri Sugunendra Tirtha Swamiji of Puthige Math has said that it is necessary to give importance to human values in the present era of globalization.

Values are usually influenced by the changing philosophical ideologies, cultural and religious perspectives, social, political and geographical conditions. In modern emerging society, there has been a revolutionary change in the field of values due to many factors in addition to the influence of modern culture, industrialization, modernization, urbanization, globalization and multinationals.

Values are the guiding principles, decisive in day to day behaviors as also is critical life situations. Values are a set of principles or standards of behavior. Values are regarded desirable, important and held in high esteem by a particular society in which a person lives.

Every action and thought of ours leaves an impression in our mind. These impressions determine in our behavior at a given moment and our responses to a given situation. The sum total of all our impressions is what determines our character. The past has determined the present and even so our present thoughts and actions will shape our future. This is a key principle governing personality development. The human values are resolved having lasting impact necessary for bringing about change in thought and conduct, in the 21st century.

If there is righteousness in the heart there will be beauty in character. If there is beauty in character there will be harmony in the home. When there is harmony in the home there will be order in the nation. When there is order in the nation there will be peace in the world.

At the boyhood state, individual physical development is concerned, during manhood and old age intellectual and spiritual values start dominating the corporal values. Therefore while imparting moral education, educators must keep in minds that the young must be educated.

Prizes may be given to the deserving persons for showing honesty, bravery, truth etc. The award should be given during school gathering. Contests may be organized on values of life.

According to Father of Indian Nation Gandhi

"If wealth is lost nothing is lost
If health is lost something is lost
If character is lost everything is lost"

So, best of all things is character.

CLASSIFICATION OF VALUES

Thinking with love is truth
Feeling with love is peace
Acting with love is right conduct
Understanding with love is non-violence
— Sathya Sai Baba

In generally, values may be classified as;

- Personal Values
- Social Values
- Moral Values
- Spiritual Values and
- Behavioural values.

All these values are necessary for all types of persons in the society.

According the Sathya Sai Baba the following five values are necessary for students.

- RIGHT CONDUCT
- PEACE
- TRUTH
- LOVE
- NON-VIOLENCE

These values are specific because they are in line with a human being's make up. They are also heavily interrelated (e.g. right conduct is action with love and according to conscience).These five values are inter-related and inherent in human beings, raising them above the level of the animal kingdom.

RIGHT CONDUCT

Information is received through the five senses i.e. smell, taste sight, touch and hearing. When this information is referred to the conscience, the resulting action will be beneficial. Every action is preceded by thought. If the thought is consciously seen and noted, aims to help and is unselfish, the action will be good for oneself and others. If our mind is busy, or we are daydreaming, the action may be useless, clumsy or harmful to ourselves or others.

Right conduct is also concerned with how we look after and use our bodies. The body needs to careful maintenance to be strong, healthy and well co-coordinated to serve us in performing the tasks of life. Students need to understand the importance of exercise, such as gymnastics, yoga and sports combined with good rest. Good thoughts and good company (which includes everything imbibed by the five senses) are essential for healthy and well balanced development. Right conduct is taught through: Silent Sitting, Storytelling and Group Activities.

Values Relate to Right Conduct

Self-help Skills

- Care of Possessions
- Diet
- Hygiene
- Modesty
- Posture
- Self-reliance
- Tidy appearance

Social Skills

- Good behaviour
- Good manners
- Good relationships
- Helpfulness
- Not wasting

Ethical Skills

- Code of conduct
- Courage
- Dependability
- Duty
- Efficiency
- Ingenuity
- Initiative

- Perseverance
- Punctuality
- Resourcefulness
- Respect for all
- Responsibility

PEACE

We smile when we are happy and contented. Contentment is gained when we cease to want for us all the apparent 'good' things conveyed to us through our five senses. When our willpower is sufficiently strong to enable us to discern the difference between real needs and superfluous desires, we cease to be driven by the urge to own more and more things.

Inner agitation stops and we are left feeling peaceful. When there is peace in the individual, there will be peace in the family. When there is peace in the family, there will be peace in the community. In order to learn, self-esteem, calmness and freedom from anxiety are necessary.

These qualities are fostered by two of the Programmes components, namely silent sitting and the self-reflective exercises in some of the group activity sessions.

Values Related to Peace

- Attention
- Calm
- Concentration
- Contentment
- Dignity
- Discipline
- Equality
- Equanimity
- Faithfulness
- Focus
- Gratitude
- Happiness
- Harmony
- Humility
- Inner silence
- Optimism
- Reflection
- Satisfaction
- self-acceptance

- Self-confidence
- Self-control
- Self-discipline
- Self-esteem
- Self respect
- Sense control
- Surrender
- Understanding
- Virtue

TRUTH

The desire to know truth has prompted mankind to ask some of the great questions such as: Who am I? What is the purpose of life? How can I know my inner self/ God/ the Creator of the universe? How can I live fully in the present moment?

Learning to speak the truth is a first and vital step in the formation of a strong character. Voicing an untruth is an anti-social act and causes confusion in the mind of both the speaker and listener and leads to anti-social behaviour. Telling lies hurts us as well as others in a subtle, but very real way.

One great distinction between humankind and the rest of the animal kingdom is the ability to choose how to behave, rather than just to follow the lower instincts (the law of the jungle). A human being is also able to recognize past, present and future and to take note of changes occurring over time.

A quotation used in the lesson to stimulate thought and questions may later come to mind to provide guidance and choice in a life situation. Short Term Pain for Long Term Gain: Choosing to refer to this higher level of awareness and to consciously exercise moderation in our behaviour leads to better health and greater contentment. The value of truth can also be taught through story telling which promotes curiosity, optimism, fairness to all and noble ideals. It also aids the understanding of the value of honest speech and self-analysis.

Values Related to Truth

- Accuracy
- Curiosity
- Discernment
- Fairness
- Fearlessness
- Honesty

- Integrity
- Intuition
- Justice
- Optimism
- Purity
- Quest for knowledge
- Reason
- Self Analysis
- Self Awareness
- Sincerity
- Spirit of enquiry
- Synthesis
- Trust
- Truthfulness
- Determination
- Unity of thought
- Word and deed

LOVE

Love is not an emotion, affected by the sub-conscious mind, but is a spontaneous, pure reaction from the heart.

It is the power of love which causes one person to wish happiness for another and take pleasure in their well-being. A beneficial energy (love) is directed towards the other person. As this energy flows through our own body first, it also enhances our own health.

It is the power of love which causes one person to wish happiness for another and take pleasure in their well-being. A beneficial energy (love) is directed towards the other person. As this energy flows through our own body first, it also enhances our own health. Love is unconditional, positive regard for the good of another. It is giving and unselfish. Love is essential if children are to grow up healthy in mind and body. Love is the unseen undercurrent binding all the four values.

When the mind is turned away from selfishness, the 'heart' opens, and love flows. Love is energy, not an emotion, and is inherent in every breath. It is the motive force of the physical body and is enhanced through breathing exercises. The component of group singing in the Programme promotes harmony, co-operation and joyfulness. In singing a child may experience the sweetness of love. Love may also be fostered through storytelling and activities which provide young people with the opportunity to care for other people, animals, plants and objects.

Values Related to Love

- Acceptance
- Affection
- Care
- Compassions
- Consideration
- Dedication
- Devotion
- Empathy
- Forgiveness
- Friendship
- Generosity
- Gentleness
- Humanness
- Interdependence
- Kindness
- Patience
- Patriotism
- Reverence
- Sacrifice
- Selflessness
- Service sharing
- Sympathy
- Thoughtfulness
- Tolerance
- Trust

NON-VIOLENCE

For the non-violent person, the whole world is his family When the former four values are practiced (i.e. the conscious mind is keenly aware, love is flowing, there is peace and actions are right) life is lived without harming or violating anything else. It is the highest achievement of human living encompassing respect for all life -living in harmony with nature, not hurting by thought, word or deed.

Non-violence can be described as universal love. When truth is glimpsed through intuition, love is activated. Love is giving, rather than grasping and in allowing our stream of desires to subside, inner peace develops and right conduct is practiced. This results in nonviolence i.e. the non-violation of the natural laws which create harmony with the environment.

Non-violence is taught through quotations, storytelling and group activities. True knowledge is that which establishes harmony and synthesis between science on the one hand and spirituality and ethics on the other.

Values Related to Non-Violence

Psychological:

- Benevolence
- Compassion
- Concern for others
- Consideration
- Forbearance
- Forgiveness
- Good Manners
- Happiness
- Loyalty
- Morality
- Universal Love

Social

- Appreciation of other cultures & religions
- Bother/Sisterhood
- Care of Environment
- Citizenship
- Equality
- Harmlessness
- National Awareness
- Perseverance
- Respect for Property
- Social Justice

Spiritual knowledge is also very importance for students and people in the society. Living in a way which causes as little harm as possible to oneself, other people, animals, plants and the planet, is a sign of a well-integrated, well-balanced personality. Such a person is well tuned to the spiritual aspect of humanity and is in touch with an inner happiness which is permanent and part of one's real nature.

It is through our universal or spiritual aspect that we may experience:

- A feeling of awe and wonder for the universe
- A feeling of the unity of all
- The desire to improve the quality of life for everyone

- A sense of being part of a larger whole
- A feeling of oneness of the planet and love for everything on it
- An awareness of an underlying order to Creation
- Love and respect for the diversity of the human family

Learning takes place through lesson plans based on practical, meaningful and fun activities using the five **components** of:

- **Stories** - about life, identity & relationships;
- **Quotations, poems and prayers**;
- **Songs and music**;
- **Silent sitting** - exercises leading to inner calm and peace;
- **Activities** e.g. drama, discussion, games, role play, community service, etc.

In working through the lessons that comprise these components, the importance of the triple partnership (Student, Teacher and Parents) for education becomes apparent:

- Teachers will inspire children in their schools, if they are value conscious adults
- Parents' example affects the conduct of their children, and
- Children when reaching a certain age need self-discipline to balance their generally natural exuberance.

There are so many types/lists of values. Various authors classified different types of values. They are;

(a) 'A-Z' Values

1. Abundance
2. Acceptance
3. Accessibility
4. Accomplishment
5. Accuracy
6. Achievement
7. Acknowledgement
8. Activeness
9. Adaptability
10. Adoration
11. Adroitness
12. Adventure
13. Affection
14. Affluence
15. Aggressiveness
16. Agility
17. Alertness
18. Altruism
19. Ambition
20. Amusement
21. Anticipation
22. Appreciation
23. Approachability
24. Articulacy
25. Assertiveness
26. Assurance
27. Attentiveness
28. Attractiveness
29. Audacity
30. Availability
31. Awareness
32. Awe

33. Balance
34. Beauty
35. Being the best
36. Belonging
37. Benevolence
38. Bliss
39. Boldness
40. Bravery
41. Brilliance
42. Buoyancy
43. Calmness
44. Camaraderie
45. Candor
46. Capability
47. Care
48. Carefulness
49. Celebrity
50. Certainty
51. Challenge
52. Charity
53. Charm
54. Chastity
55. Cheerfulness
56. Clarity
57. Cleanliness
58. Clear-mindedness
59. Cleverness
60. Closeness
61. Comfort
62. Commitment
63. Compassion
64. Completion
65. Composure
66. Concentration
67. Confidence
68. Conformity
69. Congruency
70. Connection
71. Consciousness
72. Consistency
73. Contentment
74. Continuity
75. Contribution
76. Control
77. Conviction
78. Conviviality
79. Coolness
80. Cooperation
81. Cordiality
82. Correctness
83. Courage
84. Courtesy
85. Craftiness
86. Creativity
87. Credibility
88. Cunning
89. Curiosity
90. Daring
91. Decisiveness
92. Decorum
93. Deference
94. Delight
95. Dependability
96. Depth
97. Desire
98. Determination
99. Devotion
100. Devoutness
101. Dexterity
102. Dharma
103. Dignity
104. Diligence
105. Direction
106. Directness
107. Discipline
108. Discovery
109. Discretion
110. Diversity
111. Dominance
112. Dreaming

113. Drive
114. Duty
115. Dynamism
116. Eagerness
117. Economy
118. Ecstasy
119. Education
120. Effectiveness
121. Efficiency
122. Elation
123. Elegance
124. Empathy
125. Encouragement
126. Endurance
127. Energy
128. Enjoyment
129. Entertainment
130. Enthusiasm
131. Excellence
132. Excitement
133. Exhilaration
134. Expectancy
135. Expediency
136. Experience
137. Expertise
138. Exploration
139. Expressiveness
140. Extravagance
141. Extroversion
142. Exuberance
143. Fairness
144. Faith
145. Fame
146. Family
147. Fascination
148. Fashion
149. Fearlessness
150. Ferocity
151. Fidelity
152. Fierceness
153. Financial independence
154. Firmness
155. Fitness
156. Flexibility
157. Flow
158. Fluency
159. Focus
160. Fortitude
161. Frankness
162. Freedom
163. Friendliness
164. Frugality
165. Fun
166. Gallantry
167. Generosity
168. Gentility
169. Giving
170. Grace
171. Gratitude
172. Gregariousness
173. Growth
174. Guidance
175. Happiness
176. Harmony
177. Health
178. Heart
179. Helpfulness
180. Heroism
181. Holiness
182. Honesty
183. Honor
184. Hopefulness
185. Hospitality
186. Humility
187. Humor
188. Hygiene
189. Imagination
190. Impact
191. Impartiality
192. Independence

193. Industry
194. Ingenuity
195. Inquisitiveness
196. Insightfulness
197. Inspiration
198. Integrity
199. Intelligence
200. Intensity
201. Intimacy
202. Intrepidness
203. Introversion
204. Intuition
205. Intuitiveness
206. Inventiveness
207. Investing
208. Joy
209. Judiciousness
210. Justice
211. Keenness
212. Kindness
213. Knowledge
214. Leadership
215. Learning
216. Liberation
217. Liberty
218. Liveliness
219. Logic
220. Longevity
221. Love
222. Loyalty
223. Majesty
224. Making a difference
225. Mastery
226. Maturity
227. Meekness
228. Mellowness
229. Meticulousness
230. Mindfulness
231. Modesty
232. Motivation
233. Mysteriousness
234. Neatness
235. Nerve
236. Non-violence
237. Obedience
238. Open-mindedness
239. Open-heartedness
240. Openness
241. Optimism
242. Order
243. Organization
244. Originality
245. Outlandishness
246. Outrageousness
247. Passion
248. Peace
249. Perceptiveness
250. Perfection
251. Perkiness
252. Perseverance
253. Persistence
254. Persuasiveness
255. Philanthropy
256. Piety
257. Playfulness
258. Pleasantness
259. Pleasure
260. Poise
261. Polish
262. Popularity
263. Potency
264. Power
265. Practicality
266. Pragmatism
267. Precision
268. Preparedness
269. Presence
270. Privacy
271. Proactivity
272. Professionalism

273. Prosperity
274. Prudence
275. Punctuality
276. Purity
277. Quality
278. Quiet
279. Realism
280. Reason
281. Reasonableness
282. Recognition
283. Recreation
284. Refinement
285. Reflection
286. Relaxation
287. Reliability
288. Religiousness
289. Resilience
290. Resolution
291. Resolve
292. Resourcefulness
293. Respect
294. Rest
295. Restraint
296. Reverence
297. Richness
298. Rigor
299. Sacredness
300. Sacrifice
301. Sagacity
302. Saintliness
303. Sanguinity
304. Satisfaction
305. Security
306. Self-control
307. Selflessness
308. Self-reliance
309. Sensitivity
310. Sensuality
311. Serenity
312. Service
313. Sexuality
314. Sharing
315. Shrewdness
316. Significance
317. Silence
318. Silliness
319. Simplicity
320. Sincerity
321. Skillfulness
322. Solidarity
323. Solitude
324. Soundness
325. Speed
326. Spirit
327. Spirituality
328. Spontaneity
329. Spunk
330. Stability
331. Stealth
332. Stillness
333. Strength
334. Structure
335. Success
336. Support
337. Supremacy
338. Surprise
339. Sympathy
340. Synergy
341. Teamwork
342. Temperance
343. Thankfulness
344. Thoroughness
345. Thoughtfulness
346. Thrift
347. Tidiness
348. Timeliness
349. Traditionalism
350. Tranquility
351. Transcendence
352. Trust

353. Trustworthiness
354. Truth
355. Understanding
356. Unflappability
357. Uniqueness
358. Unity
359. Usefulness
360. Utility
361. Valor
362. Variety
363. Victory
364. Vigor
365. Virtue
366. Vision
367. Vitality
368. Vivacity
369. Warmth
370. Watchfulness
371. Wealth
372. Willfulness
373. Willingness
374. Winning
375. Wisdom
376. Wittiness
377. Wonder
378. X-Value
379. Youthfulness
380. Zeal

(b) Values identified by NCERT

1. Abstinence
2. Appreciation of cultural values
3. Anti-Untouchability
4. Citizenship
5. Consideration for others
6. Concern for others
7. Co-operation
8. Cleanliness
9. Compassion
10. Common Cause
11. Common good
12. Courage
13. Courtesy
14. Curiosity
15. Democratic decision making
16. Devotion
17. Dignity of the individual
18. Dignity of manual work
19. Duty
20. Discipline
21. Endurance
22. Equality
23. Friendship
24. Faithfulness
25. Fellow-feeling
26. Freedom
27. Forward look
28. Good manners
29. Gratitude
30. Gentlemanliness
31. Honesty
32. Helpfulness .
33. Humanism
34. Hygienic living
35. Initiative
36. Integrity .
37. Justice
38. Kindness
39. Kindness to animals
40. Leadership
41. National Unity
42. Loyality to duty
43. National Consciousness
44. Non-Violence
45. National Integration
46. Obedience
47. Peace
48. Proper Utilisation of time

49. Punctuality
50. Patriotism
51. Quest for knowledge
52. Purity
53. Resourcefulness
54. Regularity
55. Respect for others
56. Reverence for old age
57. Sincerity
58. Simple living
59. Social justice
60. Self discipline
61. Self help
62. Self respect
63. Self Confidence
64. Self support
65. Self study
66. Self reliance
67. Self control
68. Self restraint
69. Social service
70. Solidarity of mankind
71. Sense of social responsibility
72. Sense of discrimination between good and bad
73. 'Socialism
74. Sympathy
75. Secularism and respect for all religions
76. Spirit of enquiry
77. Team work
78. Team spirit
79. Truthfulness
80. Tolerance
81. Universal truth
82. Universal love
83. Value for national and civic property

(c) Bill Gothard has informally specified a set of forty-nine virtues

I. Exhorting

1. Creativity vs. Underachievement
2. Discernment vs. Judgment
3. Discretion vs. Simple-mindedness
4. Enthusiasm vs. Apathy
5. Faith vs. Presumption
6. Love vs. Selfishness
7. Wisdom vs. Natural Inclinations

II. Giving

1. Cautiousness vs. Recklessness/Rashness
2. Frugality vs. Luxury
3. Fulfillment/Contentment vs. Covetousness
4. Gratitude/Gratefulness vs. Ungratefulness/Unthankfulness
5. Promptness/Punctuality vs. Tardiness
6. Resourcefulness vs. Wastefulness
7. Tolerance vs. Intolerance/Prejudice

III. Mercy

1. Attentiveness vs. Unconcern
2. Compassion vs. Indifference
3. Deference vs. Rudeness
4. Fairness vs. Partiality
5. Gentleness vs. Harshness
6. Meekness vs. Anger
7. Sensitivity vs. Callousness

IV. Organization

1. Ambition/Initiative vs. Unresponsiveness
2. Commitment vs. Untrustworthiness
3. Courage vs. Cowardice
4. Decisiveness vs. Vacillation/Double-mindedness
5. Determination vs. Faint-heartedness
6. Loyalty vs. Unfaithfulness
7. Orderliness vs. Confusion/Disorganization

V. Prophecy

1. Adventurousness/Boldness vs. Trepidation/Fearfulness
2. Compliance/Obedience vs. Obstinacy/Willfulness
3. Forgiveness vs. Disaffirmation/Rejection
4. Persuasiveness vs. Combativeness/Contentiousness
5. Sincerity vs. Two-facedness/Hypocrisy
6. Truthfulness vs. Duplicity/Deception
7. Uprightness vs. Impurity

VI. Serving

1. Alertness vs. Unawareness
2. Availability vs. Self-centeredness
3. Endurance vs. Quitting/Giving up
4. Flexibility vs. Resistance
5. Generosity vs. Stinginess
6. Hospitality vs. Loneliness
7. Joyfulness vs. Self-pity

VII. Teaching

1. Dependability vs. Inconsistency
2. Diligence vs. Slothfulness
3. Patience vs. Restlessness

4. Reverence vs. Disrespect
5. Security vs. Anxiety
6. Self-control vs. Self-indulgence
7. Thoroughness vs. Incompleteness

(d) Gandhi's Classification

In order to create new social order Gandhiji introduced Nai Talim in the year 1937, which is popularly known as Basic Education.

1. Truth
2. Non-violence
3. Freedom
4. Democracy
5. Sarva Dharma Samabhava
6. Equality
7. Self-realization
8. Purity of ends and means
9. Self-discipline
10. Suddhi

(e) Gail M. Inlaw Classification

1. Traditional and cultural values
2. Economic values
3. Political values
4. Values in science and technology
5. Philosophical values
6. Values of the new left
7. Values of the black community

(f) Plato's Classification

1. Truth
2. Beauty
3. Goodness

(g) Parker's Classification of Values

1. Biological values
2. Economic values
3. Affective values
4. Social values
5. Intellectual values
6. Aesthetic values

7. Moral Values
8. Religious values

(h) Spranger's Classification

1. Theoretical values
2. Economic values
3. Aesthetic values
4. Social values
5. Political values
6. Religious values

(i) General Classification

In general, values may be classified as personal, social, moral, spiritual and behavioural values.

i. Personal Values

They refer to those, which are desired and cherished by the individual irrespective of his social relationship. The individual determines his own standards of achievement and attains these targets without explicit interaction with any other persons.

ii. Social Values

Social values refer to those, which are oriented and concerning to society. These values are practiced because of our association with others. Unlike personal values the practice of social values necessitates the interaction of two or more persons.

iii. Moral Values

Moral Values related to individual's character and personality conforming to what is right and virtuous. They reveal a person's self-control.

iv. Spiritual Values

Spiritual values refer to ethical value. It arises from the inner depth dimension of man. It bestows the capacity to see the false as the false and the true as the true. It is like a key to the integration of man. The ultimate ethical value is called spiritual value. Spiritual value is the awareness of itself.

v. Behavioural Values

Behavioural values refer to all good manners that are needed to make our life successful and joyous. These are the values, which are exhibited by our conduct and behaviour in our daily life. Behavioural values will adorn our life and spread cordially friendliness.

CONCLUSIONS

Value is "something which pervades everything. It determines the meaning of the world as a whole, as well as the meaning of every person, every event, and every action. It can be said of everything that is either good or bad; it can be said whether it must not be, or that it ought not to exist, that its existence is right or wrong" (Lossky and Marshall, 1935).

Values are the desirable ends, goals or modes of action which makes human behaviour selective. Value not only orients but also determines human behaviour.

The epics, the Ramayana and the Mahabharata contain many morals, from which we can learn how to live and conduct ourselves in various situations. The epics are meant for the laymen, people who are serious about their religious duties and salvation, but not enough to make it the single most important thing in their lives and pursue it steadfastly. Since they are in narrative form, their messages, morals and lessons are easy to understand and remember. For the last several centuries, both the epics served people well by inculcating in them a deep sense of reverence, devotion, commitment to the path of righteousness and belief and interest in the life beyond.

Moral education is becoming an increasingly popular topic in the fields of psychology and education. Media reports of increased violent juvenile crime, teenage pregnancy, and suicide have caused many to declare a moral crisis in our nation. While not all of these social concerns are moral in nature, and most have complex origins, there is a growing trend towards linking the solutions to these and related social problems to the teaching of moral and social values in our schools and colleges.

16

Gandhi and Character Building

I believe that Gandhi's views were the most enlightened of all the political men in our time.
We should strive to do things in his spirit: not to use violence in fighting for our cause, but by non-participation in anything you believe is evil—***Albert Einstein***

INTRODUCTION

India has given birth to Lord Rama, Lord Krishna, Maharshi Valmiki, Maharshi Vyasa, Emperor Ashoka, Harishandra and Varthaman Mahaveera etc. Mohandas Karamchand Gandhi was also a great son of India. He had loved all the people without concerning caste, religion, region and colour. His mind, thought and action were unique. Truth and non-violence were his weapons. According to Gandhi; "*If wealth is lost nothing is lost; if health is lost something is lost; if character is lost everything is lost*". So, best of all things is character according to Gandhi. We are living in the high-tech society. The impact of media is very much on the individuals of the society. We are facing so many problems like; poverty, corruption, illiteracy, alcoholism, sexual harassment, teenage pregnancy and terrorism. Lack of ethics in politics is not good for any society. Education in general and moral education in particular is more important and necessary for present generation students. Today's children are tomorrow's citizens. It is our duty to take care of them. The thoughts of Gandhi on character and character building are more useful for all in the society.

GANDHI

Mohandas Karamchand Gandhi was born on October 2, 1869, at Porbandar, a small town on the western coast of India, which was then one of the many tiny states in Kathiawar. Gandhiji was born in middle class family of Vaishya caste. His father, Karamchand Gandhi, was a Dewan or Prime Minister of Porbandar. His mother, Putlibai, was a very religious lady and left a deep impression on Gandhiji's mind. Gandhiji was a mediocre student and was excessively shy and timid.

Gandhiji was truthful in his conduct right from the childhood. There is a very famous incident in this regard. A British school inspector once came to Gandhiji's school and set a spelling test. Gandhiji spelled all the words correctly except kettle. The class teacher noticed the mistake and gestured Gandhiji to copy the correct spelling from the boy sitting next to him. Gandhiji refused to take the hint and was later scolded for his "*stupidity*".

Gandhi became one of the most respected spiritual and political leaders of the 1990's. Gandhiji helped free the Indian people from British rule through non-violence, and is honored by Indians as the father of the Indian Nation.

The Indian people called Gandhiji 'Mahatma', meaning Great Soul. At the age of 13 Gandhi married Kasturba, a girl the same age. Their parents arranged the marriage. The Gandhi had for children. Gandhi studied law in London and returned to India in 1891 to practice. In 1893 he took on a one-year contract to do legal work in South Africa.

At the time the British controlled South Africa. When he attempted to claim his rights as a British subject he was abused, and soon saw that all Indians suffered similar treatment. Gandhi stayed in South Africa for 21 years working to secure rights for Indian people.

He developed a method of action based upon the principles of courage, non-violence and truth called Satyagraha. He believed that the way people behave is more important than what they achieve. Satyagraha promoted non-violence and civil disobedience as the most appropriate methods for obtaining political and social goals. In 1915 Gandhi returned to India. Within 15 years he became the leader of the Indian national movement.

Using the principles of Satyagraha he led the campaign for Indian independence from Britain. Gandhi was arrested may times by the British for his activities in South Africa and India. He believed it was honourable to go to jail for a just cause. Altogether he spent seven years in prison for his political activities.

Mora than once Gandhi used fasting to impress upon others the need to be nonviolent. India was granted independence in 1947, and partitioned into India and Pakistan. Rioting between Hindu and Muslims followed. Gandhi had been an advocate for a united India where Hindus and Muslims lived together in peace.

On January 13th, 1948, at the age of 78, he began a fast with the purpose of stopping the bloodshed. After 5 days the opposing leaders pledged to stop the fighting and Gandhi broke his fast. Twelve days later a Hindu fanatic, Nathuram Godse who opposed his program of tolerance for all creeds and religion assassinated him.

CHARACTER

Different shades of meaning are pertaining to the term in different contexts. In general we may say that character is the expression of the personality of a human being, and that it reveals itself in his conduct. In this sense every man has a character. At the same time only human beings, not animals have character: it implies rationality. But in addition to this usage, the term is also employed in a narrower sense, as when we speak of a man "of character". In this connotation character implies a certain unity of qualities with a recognizable degree of constancy or fixity in mode of action. It is the business of psychology to analyze the constituent elements of character, to trace the laws of its growth, to distinguish the chief agencies which contribute to the formation of different types of character, and to classify such types. If anything approaching a science of character is ever to be built up, it must be a special psychology.

Character – Definition

Character may be defined as:

1. The combination of qualities or features that distinguishes one person, group, or thing from another.
2. A distinguishing feature or attribute, as of an individual, group, or category.
3. Genetics A structure, function, or attribute determined by a gene or group of genes.
4. Moral or ethical strength.
5. A description of a person's attributes, traits, or abilities.
6. The stable and distinctive qualities built into an individual's life which determines his or her response regardless of circumstances.

Importance of Character

Today's world faces many difficult problems. Escalating crime, drug and alcohol abuse, workplace violence, gang activity, vandalism, school dropouts, deteriorating work ethics, domestic violence, juvenile delinquency, racial tensions, broken families ... The list seems endless.

At their root, all of these problems spring out of the lack, or misapplication, of good character qualities. If we are to find lasting solutions to the problems of our day, we must deal with these roots. We must work to improve our own character, teach good character to our children, and help those around us to improve their character. Character development is essential to the ongoing success of our society. That is why Character Education is so important. Character is the Key to Success.

Abraham Lincoln said, "Reputation is the shadow. Character is the tree." Our character is not just what we try to display for others to see, it is who we are even when no one is watching. Good character is doing the right thing because it is right to do what is right.

GANDHI'S VIEWS ON CHARACTER

Mahatma Gandhi expressed his views on character at different platforms. They are;

- A man of character will make himself worthy of any position he is given. ... Young India: September 9, 1920.
- Character, not brains, will count at the crucial moment. ... Young India: September 19, 1920.
- Character is any day more eloquent than speech. ...Young India: August 30, 1928.
- Character cannot be built with mortar and stone. It cannot be built by other hands than your own. The principal and professors cannot give you character from the pages of books. Character building comes from their very lives and really speaking, it must come from within yourselves. ...With Gandhi in Ceylon: p.85
- Literary training by itself adds not an inch to one's moral height and character-building is independent of literary training. ...Young India, June 1, 1921.
- A dissolute character is more dissolute in thought than in deed, and the same is true of violence.
- A language is an exact reflection of the character and growth of its speakers.
- A vow imparts stability, ballast and firmness to one's character.
- All your scholarship, all your study of Shakespeare and Wordsworth would be vain if at the same time you do not build your character and attain mastery over your thoughts and your actions.
- Character alone will have real effect on masses.

- If you have no character to lose, people will have no faith in you.
- If you will express the requisite purity of character in action, you cannot do it better than through the spinning wheel.
- In the times to come the people will not judge us by the creed we profess or the label we wear or the slogans we shout but by our work, industry, sacrifice, honesty and purity of character.
- Men of stainless character and self-purification will easily inspire confidence and automatically purity the atmosphere around them.
- Sorrow and suffering make for character if they are voluntarily borne, but not if they are imposed.
- Success is the certain result of suffering of the extremist character voluntarily undergone
- The real property that a parent can transmit to all equally is his or her character and educational facilities.
- The truest test of civilization, culture and dignity is character and not clothing.
- What we start receiving education through our own language, our relations in the home will take on a different character.
- What will tell in the end will be character and not a knowledge of letters.
- Whatever may be the pros and cons of going to the public theatre, it is a patent fact that it has undermined the morals and ruined the character of many a youth in this country.
- Your character must be above suspicion and you must be truthful and self-controlled.

GANDHI – CHARACTER BUILDING

I had always given the first place to the culture of the heart or the building of character, and as I felt confident that moral training could be given to all alike, no matter how different their ages and their upbringing, I decided to live amongst them all the twenty-four hours of the day as their father. I regarded character building as the proper foundation for their education and, if the foundation was firmly laid, I was sure that the children could learn all the other things themselves or with the assistance of friends. **...Mahatma Gandhi**

Character - building is the national mission. So a concerted effort towards character - building is the most vital activity that should be taken up in schools. It is the only means to make the students evoke as enlightened citizens. Since Independence, our nation has effected great social changes through successful revolutions like the Green Revolution and White Revolution. Today, to overcome the moral malnutrition of the students, let us give the call for a character revolution. The teaching community should not leave. Any stone unturned, to achieve the goal i.e. a character - revolution. Mahatma Gandhi rightly said "The end of all knowledge must be the building up of character".

Character Building – Object of Education

In character-building, which is the object of education, the relationship between the guru and his disciples is of utmost importance and where there is no gurubhakti in its pure form; there can be no character-building. ("Question of Education-I", Navajivan, 6-3-28).

Herbart, the great German educator declared, "The one and the whole work of education may be summed up in the concept of morality". Mahatma Gandhi fully endorsed this view. According to him education of heart or moral education is the prime most function of education. If we succeed in building the character of the individual, the society will take care of itself. Character formation as an aim is pursued by both eastern and occidental thought leaders.

Mahatma Gandhi said that seven things will destroy us. Notice that all of them have to do with social and political conditions. Note also that the antidote of each of these "deadly sins" is an explicit external standard or something that is based on natural principles and laws, not on social values.

Wealth without Work
Pleasure without Conscience
Knowledge without Character
Commerce without Morality
Science without Humanity
Religion without Sacrifice
Politics without Principle

Character Building – Value Education

I had not to spend a lifetime in England, I said to myself. What then was the use of learning elocution? And how could dancing make a gentleman of me? The violin I could learn even in India. I was a student and ought to go on with my studies. I should qualify myself to join the Inns of Court. If my character made a gentleman of me, so much the better, otherwise I should forego the ambition.... **Mahatma Gandhi**

The importance of providing value education is felt necessary today because the present system of education cannot contribute much to the individual and social development. Value-oriented education does not mean preaching of mere moral sciences or propagating particular religious tenets, but it is imparting knowledge of values considered functional for both individual as well as society.

Gandhi's philosophical, religious, economic and social approach and a number of contemporary Gandhian perspectives are relevant to an understanding of human values and social change today. By Gandhian ideals in the education policy, we will be able to inspire the whole world by his ideas of truth, nonviolence, peace and love.

Gandhi frequently asserted that mass illiteracy is a curse that hampers the development of a nation. He wrote: "*I am a firm believer in the principle of free and compulsory primary education for India*". Gandhi felt that education should not only increase knowledge but also develop culture in heart and hand. Another of Gandhi's interests lay in character building. Education without character building was not education according to him. He considered a strong character as the basic of a good citizen. So the issues of character building through value-based education on the one hand and that of integrating science and technology on the other hand have to go together.

So we, in the contemporary situation, have to draw a balanced evaluation of science because its progress has a great role to play in determining the directions of value education.

In order to bring about social change we have to channelize human values through education. Truth and nonviolence can generate human values. Declaring the importance of nonviolence, he said: "*Nonviolence is the first article of my faith. It is also the last article of my reed.*" He further added: "*Without Ahimsa it is not possible to seek and find truth, Ahimsa and truth are so intertwined that it is practically impossible to disintegrate and separate them. They are like the two sides of the same coin.*"

Development of peace and security through cooperation seems to be essential for the modern society's progress and prosperity. This is possible because values and improvement are intertwined.

Value education in the sense of gaining knowledge of values is not enough, but has to be realized and loved by selecting the values which are relevant and best suited to the needs of our country. Gandhi infused in us a hope through his ideals of love, tolerance, truth, nonviolence and service of mankind which are even more relevant today than they were in his own time and they will continue to exercise a lasting influence in our society.

It may be said that the foundations of an ideal civilization as conceived by Gandhi was based on Truth and Nonviolence as the integrally related means and ends. They are values central to any society because all human relations in the social, political as well as economic spheres are influenced by them in one way or the other. They are to be the standards and goals of our society. These can also become the foundations of a more peaceful and happy world order which is very much the need of mankind today.

SUGGESTIONS FOR GOOD CHARACTER BUILDING

Mahatma Gandhi was influenced my Lord Roma, Jesus, Buddha, Varthamana Mahaveera and Allah. According to Gandhi Geetha has given solutions for all types of problems in the society. He studied all the religious books and books of great authors. He believed that character building takes place through education in general and value education in particular.

A value is a relationship between a person and an environmental situation which evokes an appreciative response in the individual. Moral values are inseparably related to values in general. Frequently values are divided into types, such as bodily values, economic values, social values, aesthetic values, religious values etc., while there are values which are primarily economic, aesthetic and so on, any human values may also be a Moral Value. To the extent that any activity increases or diminishes the worth of human life, it takes on a moral significance. Values are thus both individual and social.

Durkheim has pointed out that the first element of morality is a spirit of discipline, the second element being, according to him, attachment to social groups. The former is concerned with the development of character of the individual and the latter with the relationship he must bear with others in the society. Both these depend upon the education and training that the individual receives during childhood and adolescence. Children brought up in laissez-faire can hardly be expected to develop morality to any desired extent.

Educational institutions have to work in a way that the whole child is taken care of and it is possible when the goal before them is to work with the children as how to learn to live.

Teacher plays an important role in the field of education. Today's education is child-centred. The teacher is the maker of the future of the child. The children of today are the citizens and leaders of tomorrow. So, it is necessary to take care about children.

The quality of a nation depends upon the quality of its citizens; the quality of citizens depends upon the quality of their education; the quality of education depends upon the quality of teachers and the quality of teachers depends upon the quality of teacher education. We want value-oriented teacher education (Manchala, 2007).

The home and the school with the influence of parents and teachers have a role to meet and decide how to lead the child from darkness to light, from untruth to truth and from mortality to immortality.

In the family the child is a group member in a clan/family and in the school, the teacher mentors his association in groups. Curricular programmes in the areas of social studies, language and science could help inculcating moral qualities like righteousness, love, self control and truthfulness. Poetry could develop finer sensitivities. Mathematics can help in rationality and logistics.

Types of Activities Schools/Colleges could pursue for value mutation:

- School/College Assembly
- Special Assembly
- Students Panchayat
- Classroom Activities
- Hobby clubs
- Cultural and Literary Activities
- Talks on Values
- Stories
- Celebration of Special Days
- Auxiliary Activities
- Classroom Projects

The above stated values and activities are not an end.

CONCLUSION

Gandhi is an unforgettable man in the whole world. Gandhian thoughts and actions are more relevant to the present day situations. All his thoughts are practicable. There is no doubt that, no other man in the world is as like as Gandhi, who has given importance for Truth and Non-violence in the world. The main thing of Gandhi for this recognition is only his character. The words of Einstein about Gandhi are as follows: "*Generations to come will scarce believe that such a one as this walked the earth in flesh and blood*". It shows the greatness of Mahatma Gandhi. We are so fortunate that we were born in the land where Mahatma Gandhi was born. It is our main duty to follow in the path of Gandhi. Value oriented education is important for today's children. Without good character it is not possible to face all the problems in the society including terrorism. We can observe the character of the individual through his activities. Best of all this is character. Good character building is necessary for all in the society for happy and wealthy life.

REFERENCES

1. Amareswaran, N. (2010): "*Moral Values of Intermediate Students*", Discovery Publication, New Delhi.
2. Anu Bandyopadhyaya. (1964): "*Bahuroope Gandhi*", New Delhi.
3. Arun Gandhi. "*The Seven Deadly Social Sins*".

4. *Epigrams from Gandhiji* (Quotations).
5. Gandhi, M.K. (1927): "*Autobiography: The Story of My Experiments with Truth*", Navajivan Mudranalaya, Ahemadabad-380014, India.
6. Manchala, C. (2009): "*Achievement of B.Ed. Students*", Discovery Publication, New Delhi.
7. Nirmal Kumar Bose. (1948): "*Selections from Gandhi*", Navajivan Mudranalaya, Ahemadabad-380014, India.
8. Prabhu, R.K., and Rao, U.R. (1945): "*The Mind of Mahatma Gandhi*", Navajivan Mudranalaya, Ahemadabad-380014, India.
9. Rajput, J.S. "*Education on Gandhi*".

17

Gandhi on Religion and Morality

INTRODUCTION

Mohandas Karamchand Gandhi (1869-1948), better known as Mahatma ("Great Soul/Self"), was arguably the most admired human being of the twentieth-century. Not an academic philosopher, Gandhi has never concerned with abstract philosophical analysis. When asked his philosophy, he typically responded, "My life is my message." And yet one could make a strong case that Gandhi is more philosophically interesting and significant than at least 90 per cent of what is produced by professional philosophers.

Mahatma Gandhi considered religion, spirituality, morality, and ethics, in fact, all activities of life, whether personal or public, to be integrated into the search for self-realization. He said in the introduction to his Autobiography; "What I want to achieve... what I have been striving and pining to achieve for 30 years is self-realization, to see God face to face, to attain Moksha."

According to Peters J. "The growth of morality and value is complex psycho-social phenomenon". Morality is not something to be taken lightly. It is a form of thought and action, parallel to other forms, such as science, history and the study of literature. One should understand that science alone cannot promote a country's progress and prosperity. Equal importance should be given to character formation education also. There is no antithesis between religion and science. This has been clearly defended in the statement of Einstein that "Science without religion is lame and religion without science is blind". Hence moral education deserves the status of a school subject in the curriculum. But, unfortunately the present system of education has not taken proper cognizance of this vital aspect of personality.

Modern mass society presents a sharp contrast, as the young grow up. They are faced with confusions, delays and discontinuities. Adolescents in particular are uncertain about themselves. Some are in conflict with themselves, bewildered an insecure.

Values are usually influenced by the changing philosophical ideologies, cultural and religious perspectives, social, political and geographical conditions. In modern emerging society, there has been a revolutionary change in the field of values due to many factors in addition to the influence of modern culture, industrialization, modernization, urbanization, globalization and multinationals.

MORALITY

Morality may be defined as "The quality of being in accord with standards of right or good conduct".

"Morality is a private and costly luxury."

- **Henry Brooks Adams**

"The only immorality is not to do what one has to do when one has to do it."

- **Jean Anouilh**

"Moral excellence comes about as a result of habit. We become just by doing just acts, temperate by doing temperate acts, brave by doing brave acts."

- **Aristotle**

"The moral virtues, then, are produced in us neither by nature nor against nature. Nature, indeed, prepares in us the ground for their reception, but their complete formation is the product of habit."

- **Aristotle**

"Never let your sense of morals get in the way of doing what's right."

- **Isaac Asimov**

"While moral rules may be propounded by authority the fact that these were so propounded would not validate them."

- **Sir Alfred Jules Ayer**

GANDHI ON MORALITY

Unlike most philosophers, Gandhi, like Levinas, emphasises the primacy of morality. Gandhi has little sympathy for detached epistemology that is not grounded in morality or for theology and metaphysics that pretend to transcend morality.

In his approach to morality in general and violence in particular, Gandhi is well known for his emphasis on the integral, mutually reinforcing relationship between means and ends. One cannot use impure or immoral means to achieve worthy goals. This is the major reason he rejects utilitarianism. Although there may be short-term desired results, violent immoral means inevitably lead to defective ends. We fuel and become trapped in endless escalating cycles of violence and mutual destruction.

Gandhi's approach expresses an activist philosophy, which he often relates to the action-oriented philosophy of karma yoga in the Bhagavad-Gita: Act to fulfill your ethical duties with an attitude of non-attachment to the results of your actions.

RELIGION

Defined portion of the earth's surface now especially as distinguished by certain natural features, climatic conditions a special fauna or flora, or the like. A separate part or division of the world or Universe, as the air, Heaven etc. - **Vivan Ridler (1961)**

Religion is a fundamental set of beliefs and practices generally agreed upon by a group of people. These set of beliefs concern the cause, nature, and purpose of the universe, and involve devotional and ritual observances. They also often contain a moral code governing the conduct of human affairs.

Ever since the world began, man has demonstrated a natural inclination towards faith and worship of anything he considered superior/difficult to understand. His religion consisted of trying to appease and get favors from the Supreme Being he feared. This resulted in performing rituals (some of them barbaric) and keeping traditions or laws to earn goodness and/or everlasting life.

GANDHI ON RELIGION

Mahatma Gandhi as a great leader has recognized the major religions of the world as historical and cultural phenomena. Beyond these particular forms there is the religion of humanity which is reflected as faith in the moral order. This religious belief, Gandhi held, is common to all particular religions. He said: "The soul of religions is one, but it is encased in a multitude of forms. For him, the moral order which governs the universe is Satya and the process by which life is continued is ahimsa. All religions are nothing but appropriations of Satya under the condition of cultural limitation and human finitude. Thus religions as cultural and historical phenomena are more or less true. They are equal in the sense that no single religion has the absolute or exclusive truth. He said: "Religions are different roads converging on the same point. What does it matter that we take different roads as long as we reach the same goal? In reality, there are as many religions as there are individuals".

According to Gandhi, true religion is not narrow dogma. It is not external observance. It is faith in God and living in the presence of God, it means faith in a future life, in truth and ahimsa. He understood the fact that religion is a binding force which ultimately calls "to accelerate the process of realization of fundamental unity. He gives a simile of a faithful husband who would love no other woman. Even her faithlessness would not wean him from his faith. The bond is more than blood relationship, so is the religious bond if it is worth anything. It is a matter of the heart.

The first two religious books that Gandhiji studied during his student days in London (1888–1891) were Sir Edwin Arnold's English translation of the Bhagavad Gita—*The Song Celestial* (1885)—and *The Light of Asia* (1879)—which depicted the life and philosophy of Gautama Buddha. He writes in his *Autobiography*; "I read it [*The Light of Asia*] with even greater interest than I did the Bhagavad Gita. Once I had begun it, I could not leave off... My young mind tried to unify the teaching of the Gita, *The Light of Asia*, and the Sermon on the Mount. That renunciation was the highest form of religion appealed to me greatly." Much later in India, while denying that his 'philosophy' was an indifferent mixture of Tolstoy and Buddha, he had written in 1925 that he owed much to Tolstoy and Buddha but he fancied that his philosophy represented the true meaning of the teaching of the Gita, and further that the source of his inspiration was of no consequence as long as he stood for unadulterated truth.

Traditional Understanding

In those days, people had a conservative outlook towards religion. There were people who believed in primitive religion which was ruled by nature. Primitive man worshipped the natural forces believing that there was something supernatural in them; of course it was not devoid of superstitions. Man is seen accepting his condition passively and adapting himself to them without much criticism. Gandhi went against the current and engaged in vigorous dialogue with the traditionalists and upheld a dynamic view of Indian institutions and values. He sought to awaken in the millions of Indians an elementary minimum of self-respect and feeling of dignity which he regarded as an absolutely necessary pre-condition for his nonviolent struggle. He reinterpreted the traditional religion which often proved to give a greater impetus to economic and social development.

In the past the attitude of Christian missionaries towards non-Christian religions was a narrow and hostile one. They regarded Hinduism as an evil and idolatrous religion. It is relevant to see how the traditional virtues of a personal ethic, viz., Satya, ahimsa, brahmacharya, asteya, and aparigraha were applied and what empirical content they acquired from Gandhi's own life. Gandhi added abhaya (fearlessness) to the list and did not agree to include humility. Thus he brought a radical change in the traditional understanding of religion. Until the advent of Western civilization in its glaringly urban and industrial form, these features of ancient outlook persisted in India without serious interruption. In this sense, Indian aesthetics represents interruption, represents a continuous tradition from Bharatha's Natyasastra to Tagore's "Religion of an artist". Gandhi is the spokesman of the sociological aspect of this tradition.

New Understanding of Religion and its Praxis

Gandhi's perspective of religion was entirely different from that of others. In the past, Dharma was considered as one of the societal values. In the words of J.B. Kripalani, "It is indeed Gandhi's creative and constructive genius which inextricably blended the two traditions, namely the Truth of Sanatana Dharma and Ahimsa of Jaina Dharma". He insisted on the praxis of religion to the extent of saying: "I have come to this fundamental conclusion that if you want something really important to be done, you must not merely satisfy reason, you must move the heart also. The appeal of reason is more to the head but the penetration of the heart comes from suffering. It opens up the inner understanding in man". For him, religion and morality are inseparable. Politics bereft of religion is absolute dirt, even to be shunned.

According to Gandhi, the whole gamut of man's activities constitutes an indivisible whole; it must be inspired by one's religious faith, a faith in God, and living in the presence of God, it means faith in a future life in Truth and Ahimsa. After a long study and experience he discovers and concludes that all religions are true. All religions have some error in them. All religions are almost as dear to me as one's own close relatives. He too believed that all religions are God-given, and therefore stressed the necessity of religion. He compares the atheist and agnostic to 'a man saying that he breathes but that he has no nose.' Vows and observances taken in his religion not only facilitate the spiritual progress of the individual but also harmonious community living on the basis of spirituality, mutual help, and collective salvation. Hence removal of the evils, inequalities, and injustices become part of one's own religious duties. Thus his entire view of religion is an integrated one.

GANDHI ON RELIGION AND MORALITY

Mahatma Gandhi's mission was not only to humanize religion but also to moralize it. He would reject any religious doctrine, which was in conflict with morality.

According to Gandhi religion and morality are inseparably bound up with each other. To Gandhi, "There is no religion higher than truth and Righteousness." Morality is prized by almost all the great religions of the world. The emphasis on morality, by Gandhi helped his ideas to acquire a universalistic outlook.

Gandhi's religion was a federation of different religious creeds, theological schools and sectarian faiths that have survived in India from ancient times. People belonging to different religions would go to him for his advice and blessings on different matters. All through his life Gandhi devoted much time and energy for the promotion of Hindu Muslim unity and also fasted for his cause on many occasions. In the wake of the partition of the country, hundreds and thousands of Hindus and Muslims were killed in Punjab, Bengal and Bihar. Gandhi threw himself into a struggle to heal the breach between the two communities. Gandhi wanted communal harmony and peace not only between the Hindus and the Muslims but between all sections of the people who believe India to be their home, no matter to what faith they may belong. Gandhi had the good fortune to have as his colleague's people belonging to different religions. Two important examples are those C.F. Andrews and Maulana Abul Kalam Azad. The Ashram prayers of Gandhi had passages from holy books like the Gita, the Bible and the Koran. This tradition still continues in India in most of the public meetings and prayers. Gandhi also maintained that a reverential study of the different religious tradition is necessary. He felt that it is the duty of every cultured man and woman to read sympathetically the scriptures of the world. To respect other religion, a study of their scriptures, is a sacred duty according to Gandhi. To understand the point of view of another faith requires tolerance, sympathy, broad mindedness, humility and willingness to recognize Truth wherever it is to be found. If we posses these qualities we can appreciate other's faith, traditions, customs, culture and way of life. The prophets and seers of different religions have brought to mankind the consciousness of the unity underlying the whole universe and a deep sense of brotherhood of man. Gandhi therefore felt a need of the comparative study of religions to pave the way for unity and brotherhood amongst the followers of different religions.

Mahatma Gandhi was a Sanatani Hindu. His love for Hinduism was not blind love. Gandhi spoke about the lofty ideals preached by Hinduism.

Hinduism, according to him is the most tolerant and liberal religion. He was deeply impressed by the ethical and spiritual outlook of Hinduism. Gandhi said, “The chief value of Hinduism lies in holding the actual belief that all life is one i.e. all life coming from one universal source; call it Allah, God or Parameshwara”. Gandhi was also very much impressed by the teachings of the Gita saying, “when one sees me everywhere and everything in me, I am never lost to him and he is never lost to me”. But Gandhi at the same time was very radical in his approach and he did not hesitate in criticizing those aspects of Hinduism which did not appeal to his reason. For example he was very much against the caste system that was prevalent in Hinduism. To quote Gandhi, “My religion is Hinduism ... I can no more describe my feelings for Hinduism than for my wife ... Even so I feel about Hinduism with all its fault and limitations ... I know that the vice that is going on today in all the Hindu shrines ... My zeal never takes me to the rejection of any of the essential things in Hinduism”. Hinduism according to Gandhi did not have one central book for reference, no particular God of worship or one particular way of God realization. Whether he is a theist or an atheist, he is a Hindu.

Whether he believes in one absolute or many Gods, he is a Hindu. Whether he believes in Vedas or not, he remains a Hindu. Gandhi was therefore liberal enough to take idol worship as a part of human nature, though he did not believe in idol worship as such. Gandhi, was, however, deadly against untouchability, the greatest plague of the Hindu society according to Gandhi, which is the duty of every true Hindu or combat. Gandhi was also against animal sacrifice though prescribed in the Vedas as it went against his concept of non-violence. Instead he advocated the sacrifice of animality in us in the form of lust, greed, anger, hatred, ill-will etc. Referring to Rama and Krisna, the most popular Gods of Hinduism, Gandhi said, “My Krisna is not the historical Krisna. I believe in the Krisna of my imagination as a perfect incarnation, spotless in every sense of the word, the inspirer of the Gita, and the inspirer of the lives of millions of human beings. But if it is proved to me ... that the Krisna of the Mahabharata actually did some of the acts attributed to Him, even at the risk of being banished from the Hindu fold, I should not hesitate to reject that Krisna as God incarnate.” Though deeply religious by nature, Gandhi did not believe in rituals, customs, traditions, dogmas and other formalities observed for the sake of religion. Like Swami Vivekananda and Rabindranath Tagore, Gandhi’s religion was not confined to Temples, Churches, books, rituals and other outer forms. Thus Gandhi’s concept of religion was not bound by any formalities. His God may be a personal God to those who needs his personal presence. He may be a law to those who concentrate their minds on the orderliness of the universe. He may be an embodied being to those who need his touch. According to Gandhi God may have a thousand names as Ishwara, Siva, Vishnu, Rama, Krisna, Jehovah, Christ, Allah etc. according to the traditions in which a man is brought up. In the words of Gandhi, "Is there one God for the Mussalmans and another for the Hindus, Parsis, and Christians? No, there is only one omnipresent God. He is named variously, and we remember him by the name which is most familiar to us".

Gandhi also advocated his views on Islam, another great world religion. Islam is a religion of strict monotheism and rigorous ethical discipline. Gandhi had a very high esteem for this religion and regarded it as a religion of peace, love, kindness and brotherhood of all men. It may be true that sometimes the followers of Islam often took to sword for the spread of their religion, but this was not in accordance with the teachings of Koran. As Gandhi himself said in this connection, "I do regard Islam to be a religion of peace in the same sense as Christianity, Buddhism and Hinduism are". The charges of fanaticism against Islam cannot be justified, according to Gandhi as there are several passages in the Koran which speak of religious toleration. Of course, there is a place for Jihad in Islam and this Jihad is generally interpreted as a holy war against those who are not the followers of Islam. But Gandhi justifies the true meaning of Jihad by saying that the conditions laid down for the Jihad are so strict that they are not capable of being fulfilled by everybody. To quote Gandhi, "where is the unerring general to order Jihad? Where are the suffering and love and purification that much precede the very idea of drawing the sword? We are too imperfect and impure and selfish to resort to an armed conflict in the name of God".

Gandhi was also impressed by the personal and social codes of behavior that Islam prescribes. In the Koran there are rules and regulations for virtues like obedience to parents, avoidance of adultery, cheating and lying, refraining from theft, murder etc. The five pillars of Islam, which prescribes prayer, fasting, alms giving and hospitality, are the duties that every Muslim has to perform. All these aspects of Islam influenced Gandhi, a great deal.

From the comparative study of religions, Gandhi was convinced that a mere doctrinaire approach in the field of religion does not help to create inter religious fellowship. Dogmatic religions do not help to promote creative dialogue. The religions dogmas directly or indirectly breed an attitude of dislike towards other religions. Such an attitude does not help to provide any meeting grounds for religions. Gandhi realized that true religion vitalizes and elevates the inner life of human beings. The progress of any religion depends on how effectively one has been able to realise the inner spirituality and convictions in his day to day life. The rituals, the symbols, the churches, the temples or the mosques are aids so long as they help to nourish and fertilize the inner spiritual life of their followers. In their true aspects all religions call for peace and brotherhood amongst man. The great religions of the world should strive, according to Gandhi, in promoting a life of self control, sacrifice, harmony, peace and understanding amongst its followers so as to create a heaven on earth. We may conclude here, in the words of Swami Vivekananda, one of the greatest champion of peace and understanding of religions, which Gandhi also supported: "If any one hopes that this unity will come by the triumph of any one religion and the destruction of the others, to him I say, 'Brother, yours is an impossible hope.' Do I wish that a Christian would become a Hindu? God forbid. Do I wish that a Hindu or Buddhist would become a Christian? God forbid ... The Christian is not to become a Hindu or a Buddhist, nor a Hindu or a Buddhist to become a Christian. But each must assimilate the spirit of the others and yet preserve his individuality and grow according to his own law of growth."

CONCLUSION

The development of any nation depends mainly on the standards of its' educational institutions. Today's children are tomorrows' citizens. It is important to take care about present generation. The thoughts of Gandhi are valuable for all citizens not only Indians but also for foreigners. Gandhi is a symbol of Peace and Non-violence. According to Gandhi -"Truth is God and God is Truth". Gandhi had given full details about morality with the help of all different holy books like Geetha.

According to Gandhi- the world does not need a new religion. What it does need are the people who, discovering the eternal and universal truths in their own religion are bold enough to live in accordance with those truths. When it is done, the dry outer forms of religions, which divide the entire human race into several groups, will crumble before the radiance and power of the mighty human spirit. The power of the human soul, knows no bounds, no limits and if religion is its vehicle then that vehicle will surely participate in transforming the human society on its journey towards the Divine Being. Gandhi has been killed. Physically he is no more with us. But his spirit lives amidst us and within us, with all its glory than ever before. It is the duty of all Indians to celebrate Gandhi's Birthday every year. Some more research on Gandhi is necessary for the well being of all persons in the world.

18

Nehru and Secularism

INTRODUCTION

India is a great county. *'Unity in diversity'* is the foremost greatness of our nation. We have thousands of years of tradition and culture since before Vedic period. Different types of rulers were rules India. Few of them showed their mark in the progress of the nation. And some others had taken negative decisions against the progress and unity of the country. The Britishers spread the communal virus all over India from very first day, which means, 1757, the unfortunate day when Sirajuddaulah, the Nawab of Bengal was defeated by Clive. If we look into the pages of history, we find how the East India Company started playing one community against the other. For a short period in 1857, the Britishers were overawed by the massive demonstration of Hindu-Muslim unity in 1857, during the First War of independence which the British historians, much to the chagrin of Indian revolutionaries and honest students of history depict as Sepoy Mutiny. The Viceroys, thereafter, watered the small plants of communal hatred which resulted in the partition of Bengal in 1905 on communal lines by Lord Curzon. But the great Lord had to swallow a humble pie soon thereafter and the united movement of Hindus and Muslims again got Bengal United unfortunately the final division came in 1947. India was divided on religious basis – Pakistan representing the Muslims and India, the Britishers felt, representing the Hindus. But his machinations of the Britishers could not succeed primarily because of the two great stalwarts of secularism – Mahatma Gandhi and Pandit Jawaharlal Nehru. They strongly felt the need for the establishment of a secular state where religion could not be allowed to creep in the matters of administration and running of the government.

NEHRU

There is no need for the introduction of Pandit Jawaharlal Nehru, the First Prime Minister of Independent India. Nehru, an Indian with Western education and Western liberal influence was the symbol of a new policy – liberal, progressive, humanist and egalitarian. Nehru with his charismatic personality and character of dominance was one among the few who was really committed to secularism, parliamentary democracy and democratic values. Few men of Nehru's caliber could have resisted the temptation to become an autocrat in free India. Moreover his strong faith in the ability of common man, human equality, free elections, freedom of speech, free press and parliamentary system implied that Nehru was a genuine democrat.

SECULARISM

The word 'secularism', according to dictionary meaning, is an ideal where politics is completely separated from religion. Secularism is commonly defined as the idea that religion should not interfere with or be integrated into the public affairs of a society. The view that the present well-being of mankind should predominate over religious considerations in civil or public affairs is termed secularism. In common usage, the term means indifference to or rejection of religious ideas. Secularism has increased in the 20th century as more people worldwide have exercised their right to choose whether to worship in an organized religion. It has seemed to coincide with "modernization" of societies through industrialization and urbanization; traditional, conservative, and rural societies have tended to resist secularism and remain bound to their religious affiliations. It has caused some traditions to change.

Secularism as a doctrine undoubtedly derives its central inspiration from the 'philosophy' of modern science when it demands the abandonment of any reference to God in our understanding of man and the world. In broad terms it advises the separation of church and religion from State confining the domain of the religious to the 'sacred' and making the State deal with the this-worldly aspects of individual and community life. On the other hand people who still believe in the Theo-centric understanding of man and the world must reject secularism as a moral doctrine or show that the adherents of the so-called secular morality are in reality genuine believers. But in our country the commitment to secularism in our Constitution has people of all kinds and faiths claiming belief in the truth of secularism. People who are stringent practitioners of any particular religion quite often swear by secularism. Also, a little more understandably, who vociferously reject the validity of the religious vision declare their total commitment to the pursuit of secular ideals. The situation becomes more confusing because we as a nation sincerely wish to give a "respectful" place to all religions.

NEHRU AND SECULARISM

Influence on Nehru

Nehru was an intellectual child of his own period. In fact, intellectual and social influence of the west largely shaped his liberal democratic ideas. Nehru read ideas of Locke, Rousseau, Montesquieu, Bentham, J.S. Mill and Karl Marx. He became a passionate lover of democracy and one of the pioneers of parliamentary democracy in India.

Nehru's Definition of Secularism

Nehru's concept of 'Indian Secularism' was largely negative. 'Keeping in view India's specific condition, he defined secularism in the dual sense to keep the state, politics and education separate from religion, making religion private matter for the individual. He developed this approach to act as a crusader against communalism, the most powerful contemporary Indian political leader.

Socialist Measures for Secularism

But Nehru as a socialist believed in socio-economic justice to be the real foundation for a secular state. Economic disparity is the main cause of communal disharmony. So every effort should be made to ensure economic justice removing disparities among the different sections of the society. He emphasized planning as the only way for balanced economic growth of all religious and social groups. That's why he introduced Five Year Plans for inclusive growth.

Secularism and Democracy

Nehru was a democrat who always opposed the tyranny of majority. Like J.S. Mill, Nehru said, democracy does not mean the stifling of the voice of minority by a majority through its sheer voting strength. According to him, democracy means tolerance not merely of those who agree with us but of those who do not agree with us. It implied Nehru's objective to establish a secular democracy in which Hindu majority would allow equal rights to Muslim and Christians minorities. He made provision in Indian Constitution for protecting cultural and religious rights of the minorities.

Secularism for Protection of Minority

In post-Independence era Nehru's secularism became minority oriented. Because while he piloted many reform measures in Hindu code, he hesitated to do so for the Muslims for which he had been severely criticized. But Nehru's argument was that while Hindu community had been intellectually prepared for changes in their personal law, Muslims were not so. He hoped that a result of education and propaganda, uniform civil code would be accepted by Muslims without resistance. Thereby he undoubtedly sounded partial, but he was determined to create a sense of confidence among the Muslims which was shaken as a result of the trauma of participation; the Christians were assured of full freedom for evangelical work so long as it did not undermine national unity and integrity of India. He gave special attention for Muslims and argued that Hindus were safe anyhow in India but minorities should be protected even if majority had to sacrifice something.

So far, for over 300 years, Islam had come peacefully as a religion and taken its place among the many religions of India without trouble or conflict. The new approach (Mahmud's attack) produced powerful psychological reactions among the people and filled them with bitterness. There was no objection to a new religion, but there was strong objection to anything, which forcibly interfered with and upset their way of life.

Article 370 of the Indian Constitution which gives a special status to Kashmir unlike any other constituent unit of the Indian Union was included on Nehru's insistence. Nehru's idea was to please the Kashmiri Muslims in general and Sheikh Abdulla in particular. Nehru believed that Muslims were an essential ingredient of secularism. He had always been very confident of his personal popularity with the Muslim masses.

Nehru's Views on Secularism

Nehru is acknowledged as the foremost advocate of modern Indian secularism. Critics have argued that as a secular, nationalist historian and politician, his views on Hindus and Muslims were balanced. Of all the nationalist thinkers and politicians, Nehru was the most pragmatic. On the question of Hindus and Muslims, he was certain that under no circumstances could Hindus exclude Muslims from the larger socio-economic, religious and political process of India. He was conscious of this fact from the time he joined the nationalist movement.

Nehru himself says, 'the need of the moment is to secularize the intelligentsia at least and to proceed on secular lines in politics... how long that will take I cannot say. But religion in India will kill the country and its people, if it is not subdued'. In another speech he asks, "What is communalism itself? You may well have described Hindu communalism as Hindu nationalism and you would have been correct they came into conflict with each other". He concludes, "It is a strong sight with a moral that none can miss to see the Christian rules of India pretending to become the bulwarks of Hinduism and Islam".

He had problems with understanding the word religion in the spirit of true secularism. The word religion he felt had lost all precise significance. "In the present times it almost invariably brings about a strong emotional response which makes dispassionate considerations impossible. It would be far better if the word religion was dropped altogether and other words with more limited meanings were used instead, such as theology, philosophy, morals....

"Personally, I am not interested in religious labels and I am sure that they will soon disappear, or at any rate, cease to have any political significance".

Elsewhere he claims, "Religion, as I saw it practiced and accepted even by thinking minds, whether it was Hinduism or Islam or Buddhism or Christianity, did not attract me. It seemed to be closely associated with superstitious practices and dogmatic beliefs, and behind it lay a method of approach to life's problems which were certainly not that of science".

Most would agree that Nehru shared with other modern scientific thinkers the conviction that with the spread of 'Scientific temper' all religions which deal with the unchartered regions of human experience are exercising some kind of hold on mankind but once the so-called invisible world is investigated by the scientific positive knowledge of the day, science will replace religion.

Nehru and like-minded thinkers who generated a very essential idea of 'secularism' that all religions are basically irrational. Of course some religions may be more irrational that others but since irrationality is, as it were, an essential part of the stuff of religion, the 'scientific mind' looks at them all with equal intellectual disfavor. They not only hoped but really worked for the spread of scientific spirit in the country with the target of exposing the fundamental irrationality of religion altogether. Nehru had great respect for men and women of religion as of the 'higher moral and spiritual type'. But by and large he left that the "religious outlook...hinders the moral and spiritual progress of a people, if morality is to be judged but this world's standards and not by the hereafter. Usually religion becomes a social quest for God or absolute and the religious man is concerned far more with his own salvation than with the Good of Society".

It is no wonder that he was not at all at peace with Gandhi's use and understanding of religion. Gandhi's famous comment in his autobiography that those who said that religion had nothing to do with politics did not know the meaning of religion, suggested a rejection of secularism in the sense acceptable to Nehru. A religious outlook in politics, however noble and sophisticated the concept of religion might be, could not but as Nehru saw, give the national movement a revivalist character as far as the masses were concerned. In any case Gandhi's attitude to religion remained an embarrassment to Nehru. When Gandhi decided to fast unto death in disapproval of the separate electorates given by Ramsey Macdonald's Communal Award to the depressed classes, Nehru was annoyed with him. "I felt angry with him at his religious and sentimental approach to a political question and his frequent reference to God in connection with it".

Nehru always held that there would be no official religion in free India. He emphasized that belief was a private matter for each individual. He wanted secularism to be the cement of a new social contract binding together the multi-religious inhabitants of India into one political community – the integrated Indian – with religious faith having no bearing on civil, political or administrative rights.

Nehru's aversion towards religion is well known. He is said to have 'always grimaced painfully whenever he had to go through even the most perfunctory religious observance. He once even angrily waved away a Hindu sadhu who tried to anoint him with holy water at a dam dedication. During the Independence Struggle, it was Nehru, Jinnah, and Subhash Chandra Bose who maintained that it was wrong for religion to interfere in politics. From 1920 onwards, Nehru's view that all human enterprise should be delivered from religious dominance because more apparent. As an agnostic, he believed in rationality, secularism, and a scientific approach as the true means of progress in India. He understood that the destruction of religious superstition by secularism was the only means to a peaceful India. In a country divided by religious differences, of fundamental nature, Nehru looked at secularism as a great cementing force of the diverse people of India. Secularism had to displace the religious outlook if people of India were to live and grow together in unity and fraternity.

His stand on secularism found expression officially for the first time in the resolution drafted by him on 'Fundamental Rights and Duties' which was adopted by the Karachi Congress in 1931(The State shall observe neutrality in regard to all religions). Every citizen would enjoy freedom of conscience and the right to freely profess and practice any religion or subject to public order and morality, all citizens for these reasons in regard to public employment and in the exercise of any trade or calling, and the state would observe neutrality in regard to all religions. He was convinced that a secular state along could maintain social stability in a country divided by diverse religions, creeds and faiths. Besides no modern state could be called a civilized state unless it was committed to the ideal of secularism, "any other ideal means encouragement of that fatal weakness in India separatism". Organized religion, he strongly felt, closes and limits the mind of man producing narrowness, intolerance, credulity and superstition. The champion of Hindu religion of his usually disgusted him. With the 'mind of a frog', they were bent upon keeping all doors shut to outside influences. Nor were they the seers of truth in line with the great ancient tradition.

When he became the Prime Minister of Independent India, he confessed that it had been extremely difficult for him as a Prime Minister to build a secular State out of a religion-dominated nation. It was the able leadership of a secular visionary such as Nehru that held India together throughout the early turbulent years of the country. In a country where the population in majority was Hindu (one reason behind the Muslim League's skepticism regarding the possibility of true secularism in India), it was the secular vision of Nehru that helped him maintain the 'rule of law' in a democracy which was continually in danger of falling into the 'rule of people'. India, therefore, owes a lot to Nehru for the development of a form of secularism in India that was constitutional and majoritarianist. To the chagrin of the Hindutvavadis, it is this form of secularism that makes possible for people of all religions to live together under legal protection and keeps any community in majority from violating the rights of the minority. Nehru's agnosticism and rationalism had no place for religious dictates in political matters. Therefore, he was able to see religion with a scientific eye and keep religious fundamentalism from sabotaging Indian politics.

Nehru laid a great emphasis on the secular aspect of the Government. Inside his' own party there were various leaders who had communal ideals and who spoke many a time on religious strains. Nehru was very much against them. He writes to Kidwai in 1951, "We have to think outside our narrow grooves of thought and action and face the situation squarely. History has cast a role upon us and we cannot escape from it". He writes, to Dr. B.C. Roy on August 17, 1951, "If any person raises his hand to strike down another on the ground of religion, I shall fight him till the last breath of my life, both as the head of the Government and from outside".

In his fight against communalism, in his tireless endeavour to build a real secular state, Nehru finds himself a lonely man after the death of Gandhi. The members the Congress High Command were largely and inherently communal in their outlook; through they would seldom come out in the open. There came a critical moment in 1951, it is not known to many – Nehru wanted to resign. He said, "I regret to say that the President attaches more importance to his astrologers than to the advice of his Cabinet on some matters. I have no intention of submitting to the astrologers", (Nehru to N.G. Iyenger, September 22, 1951). Nehru wanted to have the Hindu Code Bill passed and to see that a Code Bill for Muslims should also be passed. But he failed to get the second one passed and here is one instance where he capitulated to the Muslim fundamentalists. M.C. Chagla in his autobiography writes, "Jawaharlal showed great strength and courage in getting the Hindu Reform Bill passed, but he accepted the policy of Laissez faire where the Muslims and other minorities were concerned. Jawaharlal deeply sympathized with the unfortunate conditions and situations of Muslim women and always spoke to his intimate ones his failures to do something positive for them".

Nehru had unflinching faith in democratic institutions and constitutional methods. He wholeheartedly subscribed to the idea of welfare state accepted by Pigou. He was committed to the theory and practice of mixed economy. The concept has been operationalised by the Five Year Plans.

Nehru represented the Western form of secularism very well. While Gandhi stressed on the quality of all religions and religious pluralism, Nehru was more inclined towards the modernity of the Enlightenment. In fact, Kazi Anwarul Masud considers him to be the first in India to have accepted Western secularism. He writes: 'While Mahatma Gandhi and Maulana Azad spoke of secularism from the perspective of religion, Pandit Nehru was the first in the sub-continent to accept the western concept of secularism'.

History accords the highest place to Jawaharlal Nehru in supporting unstintingly the ideal of secular nationalism in India. "Men such as Jawaharlal Nehru subscribed to a secularist view of life and helped to produce growing temper of mind which relegated religions entirely to the individual's conscience".

Secularism in the sense Nehru understood it made popular the twin ideas of the (a) basic irrationality of religion and (b) the idea that religion is a private matter with no part in public life. These two were to be the basis for the building of the new national identity divorced from all religions, of the large majority, as well the minority groups.

Nehru was firmly committed to a vision of public life that was derived from the principles of Enlightenment rationality and saw the secular state as the primary agent of societal secularization. In the *Discovery of India* he states: "We have to get rid of that narrowing religious outlook, that obsession with the supernatural and metaphysical speculations, that loosening of the mind's discipline in religious, ceremonial and mystical emotionalism, which come in the way of our understanding ourselves and the world. We have to come to grips with the present, this life, this world, this nature which surrounds us in its infinite variety".

Secularism: An Unending Process

Secularism is a continuous process. It is unending. It must be a part of our national psyche. We not only have to live up to the ideals of secularism proclaimed in our constitution but make them a part of thinking and living; thus build up a really integrated nation. Secularism does not mean absence of religion. But it means cherishing the noble ideals of religions like love, sympathy, compassion, humanity etc.

Nehru was a committed secularist. Secularism was both a system and a way of life for him. Chester Bowel had said that one of the greatest achievements of Mr. Nehru was the creation of a state in which the forty five million Muslims who choose not to go to Pakistan may live peacefully and worship as they please.

CONCLUSION

Nehru's socialism which can be termed as 'Nehruist' will always provide the rest of the underdeveloped world with a pattern of development which will make communism or state socialism look both old fashioned and barbarian by comparison. It is rather a special form of socialism whose emphasis is on equality rather than on state ownership of the means of production, distribution and exchange. It attaches more importance to people's consent and cooperation than to anything else.

No words could have given a better illustration of Nehru's mind – the mind of a man who once observed: "I want work and work and work. I want achievement. I want men who work as crusaders...I want you to do big things. I want you to build India". We are proud to say 'we are Indians'. India is a land of holy souls like Nehru and Gandhi. It is our duty to respect Nehru's views. It is our primary duty to give support to the secular state of India for unity in diversity.

REFERENCES

1. Amalendu Misra (2004). "Identity and Religion-Foundations of Anti-Islamism in India", Sage Publications, New Delhi.
2. Bhave, Y.G. (1995). "The First Prime Minister of India", Northern Book Centre, New Delhi.
3. Das Gupta, N.B., et.al (1993). "Nehru and Planning in India", Concept Publishing Company, New Delhi.
4. Domenic Savio Marbaniang, R. (2005). "Perspectives on Indian Secularism".
5. Jawaharlal Nehru (1946): "Discovery of India".

6. Mehrotra, R.R., et.al (1990). “Nehru Man among Men”, Mittal Publications, New Delhi.
7. Mohanty, D.K. (2004). “Indian Political Tradition from Manu to Ambedkar”, Anmol Publications Pvt. Ltd., New Delhi.
8. Priya Kumar (2008). “Limiting Secularism: The Ethics of Coexistence in Indian Literature and Film”, Minnesota Press, United States of America.
9. Ranbit Vohra (2001). “The Making of India-A Historical Survey”, M.E. Sharpe, Inc., New York.

19

Attitude of Intermediate Students Towards Moral Values in Relation With Certain Psycho-sociological Variables

INTRODUCTION

- Be good, see good and do good. That is the way to God.
- Money comes and goes; but morality comes and grows!
- Good and bad, peace and agony, pain and pleasure, all these originate within man and not outside him.
- The past is beyond recovery. We are not sure of the future. The given moment is the right time. Do not delay; do right action ....***Sri Sathya Sai Baba***

We are living in the highly modernized, scientific and technological and globalized world. We have thousands of years of tradition and culture. We are transforming our values and tradition form one generation to other through Vedas, Upanyshads, Mahabharat, Ramayan, Bhagavad Gita and other literatures, monuments and sculptures. Vasudhaika Kutumbam (The whole earth as one family) is one of the main concept of Indian tradition.

Om Asato Maa Sadgamaya
Tamaso Maa Jyotir Gamaya
Mrityor Maa Amrtam Gamaya

Lead us from the unreal to the Real; from darkness to Light; from death to Immortality. These types of shanti mantras are necessary in the present day situation. It is more important to know about Mahatma Gandhi,

Sarvepalli Radhakrishnan, Swami Vivekananda, Swami Shankaracharya and Ramakrishna Paramahamsa etc. Unity in diversity and joint family system are the pillars of Indian culture. It is also important to know about good and greatness of other religions like Christianity, Islam, Buddhism and Jainism. Imbibe goodness from anywhere and avoid badness within and outside is the precursor for world peace and welfare of mankind. By inculcating love, goodness, beauty, honesty, mercy, co-operation and helping nature in the children, it is possible to create the concept Vasudhaika Kutumbam.

REVIEW OF LITERATURE

"Books are the carriers of civilization. Without books, history is silent, literature dumb, science crippled, thought and speculation at a standstill."— Barbara W. Tuchman

"Literature is not exhaustible, for the sufficient and simple reason that a single book is not. A book is not an isolated entity- it is a narration, an axis of innumerable narrations. One literature differs from another, either before or after it, not so much because of the text as for the manner in which it is read." **— Jorge Luis Borges**

"Practically all human knowledge can be found in books and libraries. Unlike other animals that must start anew with each generation, man builds upon the accumulated and recorded knowledge of the past" (Best, 1959).

For any worthwhile study in any field of knowledge, the research worker needs an adequate familiarity with the library and its many resources. Only then will an effective search for specialized knowledge be possible. The search for reference material is a time consuming, but very fruitful phase of a research programme. Every investigator must know what sources are available in his field of enquiry, which of them he is likely to use and where and how to find them (Sukhia, et al., 1980).

In the field of education, as in other fields too, the research worker needs to acquire up-to-date information about what has been thought and done in the particular area from which he intends to take up a problem for research. But it is found that generally the extent of important; up-to-date information regarding educational research and ideas possessed by educational workers is very limited (Sukhia, et al., 1980).

Survey of related literature, besides forming one of the early chapters in research report for orientating the researchers, serves some other purposes. Good, et. al., (1941) analyzed these purposes as given under:

1. To show whether the evidence already available solves the problem adequately without further investigation, and thus to

avoid the risk of duplication;

2. To provide ideas, theories, explanations or hypotheses valuable in formulating the problem;
3. To suggest methods of research appropriate to the problem;
4. To locate comparative data useful in the interpretation of results; and
5. To contribute to the general scholarship of the investigator.

There are number of studies relating to the Moral Values done in the past. However, only the literature pertaining to the independent variables (sex, locality, caste, religion, study habits, self-concepts and personality etc.) will be used in the present study.

The review of literature will be discussed into eight heads given below:

A. Moral values – Socio-demographic Variables

Boys and girls at the adolescent stage studying in urban and rural schools/colleges may be having different moral views. Because of the technological advancement in the urban environment may be more modern and sophisticated where as the rural environment may be more agriculture oriented. Therefore, this background itself might affect the Moral Values among the students. Not only locality but also other socio-demographic variables affect the Moral Values among the students. Hence, socio-demographic variables are treated as independent variables in the present study.

The term socio-demographic variables are broadly defined to include the social, educational, professional or occupational and economic status of the parents. The environment facilities also are taken into account.

Socio-economic status of the family plays an important role in boosting up the educational proficiency of children (Burt 1937, Jammur 1961, Chopra1966)

According to Mukharjee (1956), "values are socially approved desires and goals that are internalized through the process of conditioning, learning or socialization and that become subjective preferences, standards and aspirations".

According to Kane (1962), "values are the ideals, beliefs or norms which a society or the large majority members hold. They are responsible for the definition of a problem, they may help to create a problem and they may also interface with its solution.

According to Zale and Davig (1963), "values are the ideas in the minds of men comparable to norms in that they specify how people should behave.

Values also such attach degrees of goodness to activities and prescribe how people should behave in certain relationship etc. We are expected to behave respectfully towards other persons".

B. Moral values – Personality

Maslow (1938) considered "values as a psychological need".

Woodruff (1952) defines "values as an object, condition or activity which the individual feels, has an effect on his well being". According to him "values are conceptualized in terms of personal happiness, security and existence of behaving organism".

Hardold Falding (1965) says "a value is a generalized end that guides behaviour towards uniformity in the varieties of situation with the object of repeating a particular self-sufficient satisfaction. Thus, the values are organizing ends, organizing precisely because many other satisfaction and actions are subordinate to them".

Hall and Lindzey (1966) opine the amount of psychic energy invested in an element of the personality is called value of that element. Value is a measure of intensity. When we spear of placing a high value upon a particular idea as fouling be mean that the idea as fouling exerts a considerable force instigating and directing behaviour.

According to Jones and Gerad (1967), value is a motivation which sustains an individual's efforts to achieve a particular goal. "This suggests that the person makes his persistent efforts to achieve a goal because it is a value for him".

C. Moral Values – Self Concepts

Self-Concept refers to the experience or one's own being. It includes what people come to know about them through experience, reflection, and feed-back from others. The self-concept is an organized cognitive structure comprised of a set of attitudes, beliefs and values that cut across all facets of experience and action, organizing and typing together the variety of specific habits, abilities, out looks, ideas, and feelings that a person displays.

Self-concept is operationally defined as a measure of the evaluation, which the individual makes and customarily maintains with regards to himself; it expresses an attitude of approval or disapproval and indicates the extent to which the individual believes himself to be capable, significant, successful and worthy (Smith 1959, 1967). Despite controversy regarding the meaning of self as a unitary trait or an integrated system of situationally specific traits, all are agreed that self is a life space on life force for the individual and particularly for the adolescent (Gergen, 1971). The awareness of self comes through the gradual process of adaptation to the environment (Piaget, 1969). It begins when an individual becomes aware of being a separate entity. This is when the individual can differentiate those events emanating from or involving one knows just as other environmental events can be objects of one's knowledge (Turner 1973).

Manar (1981) compared the attitudes, values, and self-concepts of the professional college students with non-professional college students. Hypothesis was that there would be significant difference in self-concepts of professional and non professional college students. It was found that professional students perceived themselves as more confident and suffering from the feeling of emotional instability than the non-professional students.

D. Moral values - Study Habits

Every parent wants their child to do well in school and to learn as much as they possibly can. To be good students children need to develop good study habits at home and at school/college. The outcome of education determines the level of life, progress and status of the people, living anywhere in the world and it is the vital force for the development of human life and the society at large. No education is worth its name unless it helps the students to feel at home in the world of books. The best any one can do is to make the students cultivate a taste for reading and this can be done only helping students to build up study habits. Through these habits he gets good character and other values.

Onubugwu (1990) defines study habits as the techniques a student employ to go about his or her studies, which are consistent, and have become stereotyped as a result of long application or practice.

E. Studies related to moral instruction/activities in colleges

Sarangi (1944) studied the implications of moral education in schools. His objective was to study the extent of utilization of moral education and the interest of children in moral education.

Annamma (1984) in her "Values aspiration and adjustment of college students in Kerala" studied moral instruction and values of college students according to sex, age, curriculum, religion, residential background, family background, socio-economic status and academic achievement. She found moral instruction is beneficial and majority college students are conformists with a stable system without religious tendencies.

Kumari (1987), in her study, "Personality needs, moral judgment and value patterns of secondary school teachers – a correlational study", studied the impact of moral instruction and mean scores differences on value, personality needs and moral judgments according to sex, locality and generations and found that moral instruction had a good impact on male, urban and older generation and they had positive value patterns with the other groups.

Srivastava (2004) carried a study on 'A study of School Activities Promoting Values Inherent in Fundamental Duties mentioned in the Indian Constitution.

F. Studies related to theories of moral Development

Piaget's stages of Moral Judgement and Kohlberg's theory of Moral Development, Domain Theory: Distinguishing Morality and Convention and Carol Gilligan-Morality of Care.

G. Studies related to moral values

Vijayalakshmi (2006) studied on 'Prioritisation of Secondary School Children's Values by their Parents and Teachers'. She said that values are very important for all human beings, mainly for students and teachers. The main objectives of the study are: To find out the difference in prioritising values by the parents (whose children studying at secondary level) and teachers (who are handling the classes at the secondary level).

Chatterjee (2009) in his convocation address; 30th convocation, Acharya Nagarjuna University, Guntur, Andhra Pradesh; gave a call to the student community to be more vigilant against all declining values in all walks of life. "Criminalisation of politics has led to immense pressure on functioning of political institutions and there is considerable cynicism among citizens of the country", Mr. Somnath Chatterjee opined.

H. Studies related to concept of value oriented education

NCERT, document (1979) of social, moral and spiritual values in education has enlisted eighty-four values, which have neither inter-relationship nor hierarchy. Five basic values supported in all eight major religions of the world identified by Gokark and they are truth, right conduct, love, peace and non-violence.

Vivekananda said "Each soul is potentially divine. The goal (of human life) is to manifest this divinity within". This divinity within, the self, is the source of all perfection, power, bliss and glory. The purpose of our value education programme with therefore is to help people become aware of their innate divinity and how to make its perfection and happiness manifest in every movement of life

Sinha (1981) measured value oriented and value patterns of students and their parents and found some significant results in favour of parents.

Reddy (2004) made an attempt to study on 'Attitude towards Value-oriented Education in Primary School Children in Chittoor District'. The major objectives of the study were:

i) To find out the significant difference between urban and rural teachers on value-oriented education.
ii) To study the difference between government teachers and private teachers on value-oriented education.

TITLE OF THE PROBLEM

The title of the problem is "*Attitude of Intermediate Students towards Moral Values in Relation with Certain Psycho-Sociological Variables*".

IV. OBJECTIVES OF THE PROBLEM:

1. To elicit the attitude of Intermediate students towards moral values.
2. To study the influence of personality factors on the attitude of Intermediate students towards moral values.
3. To map the impact of Study Habits on the attitude of Intermediate students towards moral values.
4. To gauge the impact of Self Concepts on the attitude of Intermediate students towards moral values.
5. To probe into the influence of Socio-demographic variables on the attitude of Intermediate students towards moral values.

HYPOTHESES

Based on the above objectives, the following hypotheses are formulated for the purpose of the study.

1. There is no significant difference between the attitude of boys and girls towards moral values.
2. There is no significant influence of personality factors on the attitude of Intermediate students towards moral values.
3. There is no significant impact of self-concepts on the attitude of Intermediate students towards moral values.
4. There would not be significant influence of study habits on the attitude of Intermediate students towards moral values.
5. There is no significant influence of Socio-demographic variables on the attitude of Intermediate students towards moral values.

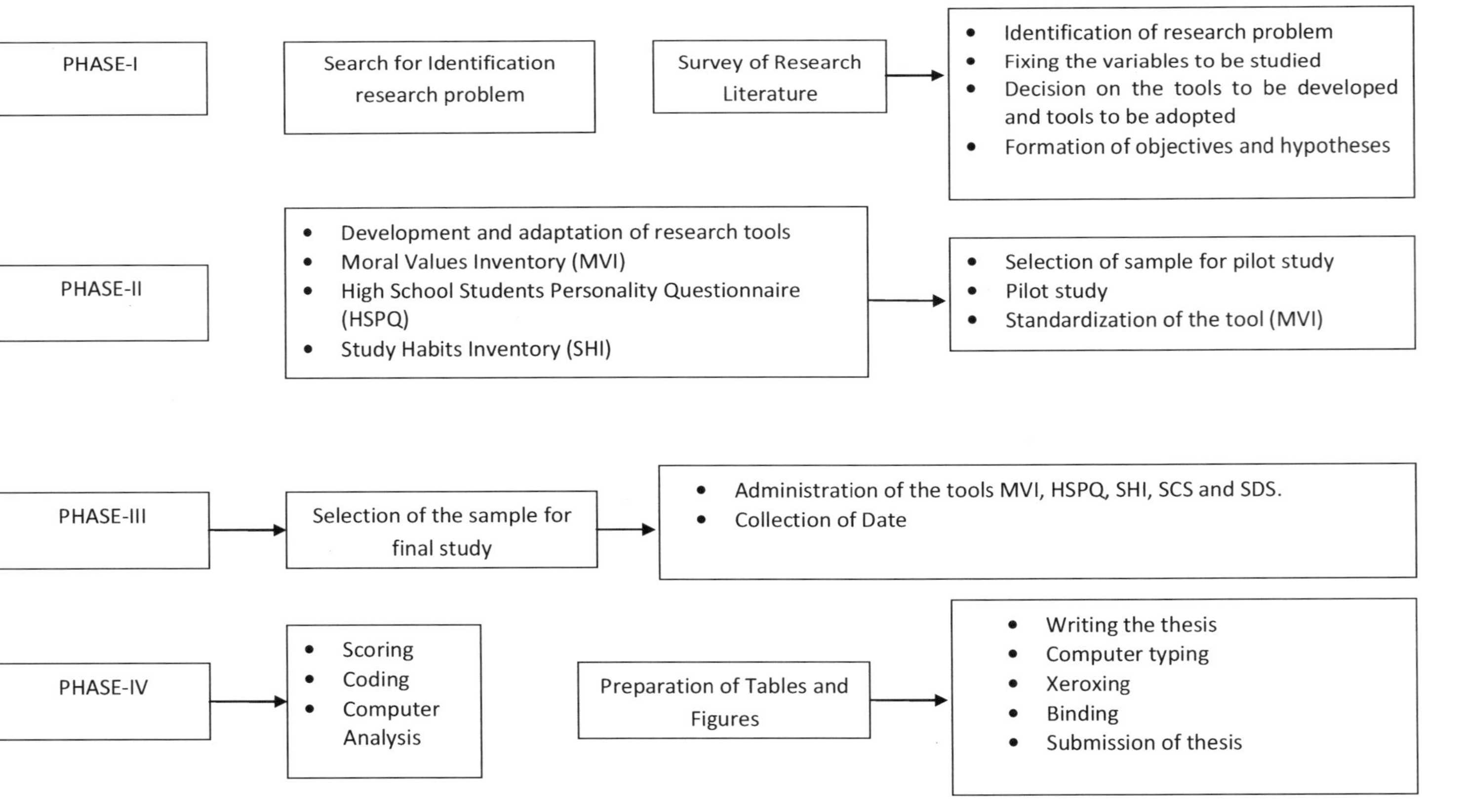

The flowchart showing the procedures followed in the present study is given in Figure-1.

RESEARCH DESIGN AND METHODOLOGY

Research design and methodology is discussed in six heads below.

a) Construction and adoption of tools
b) Sample selection
c) Collection of data
d) Scoring
e) Analysis
f) Findings of the study

a) Construction and adoption of tools

The investigator has developed and adopted the following tools for the present study.

1. Amareswaran and Reddy to test the attitude of Intermediate students towards moral values developed attitude towards Moral Values Inventory. (Full details were given in the column 'details of the tools'.)
2. The Cattell's HSPQ was adopted as a tool to assess personality of the Intermediate students.
3. For measuring the Study Habits of the Intermediate students, Study Habits Inventory developed by Patel was used.
4. Self Concept scale developed by Mukta Rani Rastogi (1974) was adopted to measure the Self Concept of the Intermediate students.
5. Socio-demographic Scale was developed by the investigator to obtain Socio-Demographic factors of the Intermediate students.
6. Statistical Package for Social Sciences (SPSS).

b) Sample selection

Based on the population, the investigator selected different types of Colleges namely Government Colleges, Private Colleges and Aided Colleges in Chittoor District covering all the revenue divisions. Out of the total students 600 students are boys and remaining 600 students are girls. Four groups of students were selected namely, M.P.C., Bi.P.C., H.E.C. and C.E.C. both Telugu and English Medium in the Rural, Urban and Municipal areas.

c) Collection of data

The investigator personally visited all the selected colleges for the study, and a good rapport was developed with the Heads of the Institutions and Teachers. With the help and cooperation of Teachers and Students in the colleges, all the data gathering instruments were administered to the sample subjects and all the required data were collected. The data were gathered at the end of the academic year.

d) Scoring

Attitude towards Moral Values Inventory was scored on a 5 point scale by giving weights 5,4,3,2 and 1 in the case of Positive Items and 1,2,3,4 and 5 in the case of Negative Items to the five alternative names; Strongly Agree, Agree, Doubtful, Disagree and Strongly Disagree. Much care was taken in scoring the responses. For HSPQ, Study Habits Inventory and Self Concept Scale, the scoring key prepared by the concerned authors was employed. The information furnished by the respondents on the Socio-Demographic scale was also coded numerically.

e) Analysis

The total scores obtained by each of 1200 students on all the variables were computed. The data were carefully analysed on the basis of Objectives of the study and Hypotheses formulated by employing appropriate statistical techniques.

To understand the nature of the distribution of attitude scores of Moral Values, all the descriptive statistics such as Mean, Median, Mode, Range, Quartile Deviation, Standard Deviation, Skewness and Kurtosis were calculated.

Frequency distribution tables were prepared for the total sample. The inferential statistical techniques such as 't' test (Critical ratio) and 'F' test were employed to test different hypotheses. Step wise regression analysis was employed to identify the contribution made by each one of the independent variables on the attitude of Intermediate students towards Moral Values. Necessary graphs were also used for presenting the data.

DETAILS OF THE TOOLS

The investigator has developed and adopted the following tools for the present study.

1. Moral values inventory:

On the basis of review of literature of moral values the investigator was developed moral values inventory with the help the mentor; consisting of more than seventy five items. Each item of the inventory will be arranged on a five point scale with responses: Strongly Agree (A), Agree (B), Doubtful (C), Disagree (D) and Strongly Disagree (E).

2. Cattell's HSPQ:

HSPQ consisting of 14 personality factors

1. Factor A (Reserved Vs Outgoing)
2. Factor B (Less Intelligent Vs More Intelligent)
3. Factor C (Emotionally less stable Vs More Intelligent)
4. Factor D (Phlegmatic Vs Excitable)
5. Factor E (Obedient Vs Assertivc)
6. Factor F (Sober Vs Happy go lucky)
7. Factor G (Moral Standards Vs Super ego strength)
8. Factor H (Shy Vs Venturesome)
9. Factor I (Though minded Vs Tense minded)
10. Factor J (Vigorous Vs Doubting)
11. Factor O (Placid Vs Apprehensive)
12. Factor Q_2 (Group Dependent Vs Controlled)
13. Factor Q_3 (Undisciplined Vs Controlled)
14. Factor Q_4 (Relaxed Vs Tense)

Study habits inventory:

Looking to the importance of good study habits for good moral values, study habits inventory constructed and standardized by B.V. Patel was adopted to assess the study habits of the sample for the present study. There are 7 items in area one, 9 items in area two, 5 items in area three, 4 items in area four, 6 items in area five, 8 items in area six and 6 items in area seven, a total of 45 items in the inventory. Among them 18 items are negative and 27 items are positive. Five alternative choices of options were given to get more exact responses from the students. The five points are: 1) Always; 2) Often; 3) Sometimes; 4) Seldom; and 5) never. The seven areas of study habits were given below.

a) Home environment and planning of work
b) Reading and note-taking
c) Planning of subject
d) Habits of concentration
e) Preparation for examinations
f) General habits and attitudes
g) School environment

3. Self concept scale:

The self-concepts scale was developed by Dr (Miss) Mukta Rani Rastogi (1974), was adopted for the purpose of the present study. This scale consists of 51 items with 10 areas. It is a five point attitude scale with the alternative answers viz., Strongly Agree, Agree, Undecided, Disagree and Strongly Disagree. The 10 areas are:

a) Health and Sex Appropriateness
b) Abilities
c) Self-confidence
d) Self-acceptance
e) Worthiness
f) Present, Past and Future
g) Beliefs and Convictions
h) Feeling of Shame and Guilt
i) Sociability
j) Emotional Maturity

4. Socio-demographic Scale:

Socio-demographic scale is defined as the ranking of an individual in terms of his/her material belongings and cultural possessions along with the degree of respect, power and influence she/he derives.

The investigator was prepared a Socio-demographic scale and be used in the present study.

5. Statistical Package for Social Sciences (SPSS):

With the help of SPSS, the investigator was computed the values of critical ratio ('t'-value), one way ANOVA ('F'-value), factorial design, multiple regression analysis etc. more easily.

ACADEMIC SIGNIFICANCE OF THE PROBLEM

The present study is about Intermediate students. We know today's children are tomorrow's citizens. It is necessary to take stock of moral values of Intermediate students because they are future teachers and administrators. We want good citizens for national development.

The development of any nation depends mainly on the standards of its educational institutions. Education is the most powerful and effective instrument for inducing radical changes in the behaviour of students. Education is the process through which an individual is developed socially, psychologically, morally, culturally, spiritually, which embodies one's good personality. Education should be individualized and personalized to the utmost and should constitute preparation for self-learning.

Education, according to Indian tradition, is not merely a means to earn a living, nor is it only a nursery of thought or a school for citizenship. It is an initiation into the life of spirit, a training of human soul in pursuit of truth and the practice of virtue. Aristotle, however, held that education exists exclusively to develop man's intellect in a world of reality, which men can know and understand. Value-oriented education is important.

Today there is lot of degradation of values in every walk of human life. Individuals are crazy for material wealth. Money making is the main motive of the majority of the individuals even through immoral ways. Proper foundation will be laid on Moral Values at the initial stages of the child. Schools and colleges are the institutions which can shoulder the responsibility of inculcating Moral Values among the people and students. Hence there is a need to take up research activities in the area of Moral Values.

RELEVANCE TO PRESENT-DAY PROBLEMS

"If there is righteousness in the heart, there will be beauty in character.

If there is beauty in character, there will be harmony in the home.

When there is harmony in the home, there will be order in the nation. When there is order in the nation, there will be peace in the world" ...***Sri Sathya Sai Baba***

Modern mass society presents a sharp contrast, as the young grow up. They are faced with confusions, delays and discontinuities. Adolescents in particular are uncertain about themselves. Some are in conflict with themselves, bewildered and insecure.

The world wide resurgence of interest in value education has been explained as the natural response of the modern industrialized societies to the fast erosion of Moral Values in all aspects of life and the crisis of values experienced in modern times. It is common place to say that sweeping political, economic and social changes have overtaken human civilization during the past few centuries and these have been largely responsible for the predicament of the modern man. In the case of India, however, the picture appears to be slightly different. While there is no doubt that technological development, however little it might be, compared to the western societies, and is one factor that has contributed to the value crisis that the Indian society is facing today. There are also other factors like personal greed, meanness, selfishness, indifference to others' interests and laziness that have brought about large scale corruption in almost all spheres of life-personal and public, economic and political, moral and religious. One can even say that our fall in moral standards is not so much due to industrialization as to the lack of it. Perhaps, we can achieve better moral standards in our democratic way of national life if we become more industrialized and thus overcome mass poverty and the general feeling of insecurity which gives rise to greed.

Moral Values are things held to be right or wrong or desirable or undesirable. While morality is sometimes described as 'innate' in humans, the scientific view is that a capacity for morality is genetically determined in us, but the set of Moral Values is acquired, through example, teaching, and imprinting from parents and society. Different cultures have very different moral value systems. Moral Values, along with traditions, laws, behaviour patterns, and beliefs, are the defining features of a culture.

Value education means inculcating in the children a sense of humanism, a deep concern for the well being of others and the nation. This can be accomplished only when we instill in the children a deep feeling of commitment to values that would build this country and bring back to the people pride in work that brings order, security and assured progress.

Value education refers to a programme of planned educational action aimed at the development of value and character. Every action and thought of ours leaves an impression in our mind. These impressions determine in our behavior at a given moment and our responses to a given situation. The sum total of all our impressions is what determines our character. The past has determined the present and even the present thoughts and actions will shape our future. This is a key principle governing personality development. The human values are resolved having lasting impact necessary for bringing about change in thought and conduct, in the 21st century.

At the boyhood state, individual physical development is important, during manhood and old age intellectual and spiritual values start dominating the corporal values. Therefore while imparting moral education educators must keep in minds that the young must be educated in the right perspective.

Today we are facing so many problems like poverty, malnutrition, environmental pollution, terrorism and corruption. Why these are all happening? The only one reason is lack of values and ethics. Lack of ethics is the main cause of present economic crisis of the world said by Dr. D. Subbarao, the incumbent governor of Reserve Bank in his speech on 'Ethics and Economic Crisis' in presence of Sai Baba in Andhra Pradesh. Inculcation of values in the Intermediate students is necessary. They are teachers for future generation. Value-oriented education is important. According to Sarvepalli Radhakrishnan, 'Teacher is a National Builder'. It is very easy to solve all the problems through education in general through value education in particular.

RELEVANCE TO NEEDS OF SOCIETY/COUNTRY

Education in general and value education in particular occupies a prestigious place in the modern context of the contemporary society.

Education is a powerful instrument of national development – social and economic. The highest priority should, therefore, be accorded to the development of national system of education which will accelerate transformation of the existing social system into a new one based on the principle of justicc, cquality, liberty and dignity of the individual, enshrined in the Constitution of India; provide adequate and equal opportunity to every child and help him to develop his personality to its fullest; make the coming generation conscious of the fundamental unity of the country in the midst of her rich diversity, proud of her cultural heritage and confident of her great future.

The essence of education lies in stimulating the growing generation with a consistent, compelling and creative system of values around which cultural heritage, both spiritual and material, of the community is transmitted to the tender souls so as to develop them into civilized, creative and productive members of a progressive society.

The present Indian society is infested with the social viruses like degradation of moral values in public, private, corporate and political sectors resulting in corruption, deceitfulness, violence, terrorism, rat race in academic and political circles. It is astonishing to see that violence and terrorism are sponsored clandestinely by government and some organizations floated for the purpose which receives tacit funding by international communities and vested interests. The young and the poor are attracted towards such nefarious activities by taking advantage of their poverty and un-employment by pumping pecuniary benefits for their luxurious living. If this trend is continued, there will be anti-social activities in every part of the country leading to running of parallel administrations (governments) pushing the common man back to the wall. Since the students in general and the Intermediate students in particular are the architects of future fabric of our society, one should take care that they should not fall prey to the machinations of anti-social elements. The study has ample relevance which dwells in to attitude of Intermediate students towards moral values. Since they are the future teachers and administrators, instilling moral values in them will do a world of good as they act as the messiahs or good Samaritans of moral legacy which is likely to percolate in to posterity.

Hence, a right man for a right job at right place is to be identified for governance in civil society as the succeeding Chinese proverb yells:

"If you wish to plan for a year, sow seeds;
If you wish to plan for ten years, plant a tree; and
If you wish to plan for lifetime, develop man."

...CHUNG Tzu (7th century BC)

MAJOR FINDINGS OF THE STUDY

The statistical treatment of the data reveals the following major findings of the study.

A. Distribution Characteristics of Moral Value Scores

1. The mean Moral Value score of the Intermediate Students is 339.68 out of maximum score of 395. The median is 341.622 and mode is 351. The gap among the Mean, Median and Mode is negligible. Hence, the distribution is very nearer to normal distribution.
2. The values of skewness and kurtosis for the Moral Value Scores are -0.631 and 0.958. Hence, the distribution of total Moral Value Scores for the whole group is slightly negative and lepto kurtic.
3. It is found that the mean total Moral Value Scores for female students is significantly higher (344.83) than the male students (334.53). Therefore female students have better Moral Values than male students. The skewness of male and female students is -0.401 and -0.957 respectively and kurtosis of male and female students are -0.022 and 2.40. skewness is slightly negative for both male and female students. Kurtosis for male and female students is less than 3.00. Hence, these two distributions are lepto-kurtic.
4. The mean Moral Value sore for the Christian students is 331.11, less than the Muslim (345.78) and the Hindu (339.89) students. It is found that the Muslim students have significantly better Moral Values than other two communities' viz., the Hindu and the Christian. Skewness is slightly negative for all the three communities and kurtosis is less than 3.00. Hence, these three distributions are lepto-kurtic.
5. It is found that the mean Moral Value Scores for BC (342.39) students is significantly better than SC/ST (337.22) and OC (341.4) students. It is concluded that BC students have better Moral Values than SC/ST and OC students. Skewness is slightly negative for all the three castes and kurtosis is less than 3.00. Hence, these three distributions are lepto-kurtic.

B. Factorial Designs

1. There is significant influence of sex at 0.01 level on Moral Values of the Intermediate Students (F=49.199). It is in favour of female students.
2. There is significant influence of college at 0.01 level on Moral Values of Intermediate Students (F=17.173). It is in favour of Government Colleges.

3. There is no significant interaction effect of college X sex on Moral Values of Intermediate Students (F=0.405).
4. There is significant influence of community at 0.05 level on Moral Values of Intermediate Students (F=4.037). It is in favour of Muslim community students.
5. There is significant influence of caste at 0.05 level on Moral Values of Intermediate Students (F=4.355). It is in favour of Backward Caste students.
6. There is no significant interaction effect of community X caste on Moral Values of Intermediate Students (0.841).

C. Influence of Socio-Demographic Variables on Moral Values

1. Residence has significant influence on Moral Values of Intermediate Students than hostlers. Day scholars have significantly better Moral Values than the hostellers.
2. Medium of Study has no significant influence on Moral Values of Intermediate Students.
3. Religious festivals have no significant influence on Moral Values of Intermediate Students.
4. Religious Discourses have no significant influence on Moral Values of Intermediate Students.
5. Type of family has no significant influence on Moral Values of Intermediate Students.
6. Age has significant influence at 0.01 level on Moral Values (F= 4.776). The mean value of Moral Value Scores of students whose age is 16 years (344.1612) have better Moral Values than the other two age groups viz., 17 years (338.8300) and 18 and above years (337.0987).
7. Family Annual Income has significant influence at 0.01 level on Moral Values (F= 5.180). The students whose family annual income is Rs. 25,001-50,000 (M=345.5455) have better Moral Values than the other three groups viz., up to Rs. 25,000 (M=339.8915), Rs. 50,001- 1 lakh (M=313.8333) and Rs. above 1 lakh (M=339.6858).
8. Educational Qualifications of Mother has no significant influence on Moral Values of Intermediate Students.
9. Educational Qualifications of Father has no significant influence on Moral Values of Intermediate Students (F=1.480).
10. Father occupation has no significant influence on Moral Value of Intermediate Students (F=0.400).
11. Mother occupation has no significant influence on Moral Value of Intermediate Students (F=2.650).

12. Birth order of the students has no significant influence on Moral Values of Intermediate Students (F=1.975).
13. Total members in the family have no significant influence on Moral Values of Intermediate Students (0.298).
14. Native Place has no significant influence on Moral Values of Intermediate Students (0.643).
15. Family Economic Position has significant influence on Moral Values of Intermediate Students (F=4.555). The mean value of Moral Values scores of students whose Economic position is medium (M=341.2261) have significantly better Moral Values than the other two groups viz., rich (M=325.0000) and poor (M=336.7675).
16. Visiting Temple has significant influence at 0.05 level on Moral Values of Intermediate Students (F=3.268). The students who are visiting temple occasionally (M=340.6489) have significantly better Moral Values than the other two groups viz., students never visiting temple (M=335.0417) and students visiting temple regularly (M=336.1026).
17. When you go wrong who corrects you has not significant influence on Moral Values of Intermediate Students (F=2.306).
18. Group Subjects has significant influence on Moral Values of Intermediate Students (F=23.059). M.P.C. group students (M=347.1071) have significantly better Moral Values than the other three groups viz., H.E.C. (M=333.1240), C.E.C. (M=344.4811) and Bi.P.C. (M=333.3274).

D. Influence of Psychological Variables

1) The Personality Factors viz., C, I, O, Q_2, Q_3 and Q_4 have significant influence at 0.01 level; Personality Factors-B and E have significant influence at 0.05 level and the Personality Factors-A, D, F, G and H have no significant influence on Moral Values of Intermediate Students.

It is observed from the mean values that the students with personality characteristics (1) High Intelligence; (2) Emotionally Stable, Mature, Faces Reality, Calm; (3) Obedient, Mild, Easily Led, Docile, Accommodating; (4) Tough-minded, Rejects Illusions; (5) Self-assured, Placid, Secure, Complacent, Serene; (6) Sociably Group Dependent, A Joiner and Sound Follower; (7) Uncontrolled, Lax, Follows Own Urges, Careless of Social Rules; (8) Relaxed, Tranquil, Torpid, Unfrustrated, Composed have significantly better Moral Values than the students with personality characteristics (1) Low Intelligence; (2) Affected by feelings, Emotionally Less Stable, Easily upset, Changeable; (3) Assertive, Aggressive, Competitive, Stubborn; (4)

Tender-minded, Sensitive, Dependent, Overprotected; (5) Apprehensive, Self-reproaching, Insecure, Worrying, Troubled; (6) Self-sufficient, Resourceful, Prefers Own Decisions; (7) Controlled, Exacting Will Power, Socially Precise, Compulsive, Following Self-image; and (8) Tense, Frustrated, Driven, Overwrought, Fretful. The 'T' values of remaining personality factors viz., A (Reserved Vs Outgoing), D (Phlegmatic Vs Excitable), F (Sober Vs Happy go lucky), G (Moral Standards Vs Super ego strength) and H (Shy Vs Venturesome) are not significant at 0.05 level. It is concluded that the personality factors A, D, F, G and H don't have significant influence on Moral Values of the Intermediate Students.

2) It is observed that the students who scored better on four areas of self-concepts viz., (i) Abilities, (ii) Self Acceptance, (iii) Worthiness, (iv) Present, Past and Future and on total self-concepts have significantly better Moral Values than others.

It is observed that the students who scored Q_3 and above in the self-concepts areas (1) Abilities, (2) Self-acceptance, (3) Worthiness, (4) Present, Past and Future, and (5) Self-concepts total score have significantly better Moral Values than the students who scored up to Q_1. It indicates that better self-concepts leads to better Moral Values.

3) It is observed that the students who scored better on all the seven areas of Study Habits Inventory (SHI) viz., (i) Home environment and Planning of work (SH_1), (ii) Reading and Note taking (SH_2), (iii) Planning of Subject (SH_3), (iv) Habits of concentration (SH_4), (v) Preparation for Examination (SH_5), (vi) General Habits & Attitudes (SH_6) and (vii) School Environment (SH_7) and Total Study Habits score (SHT) have significantly better Moral Values at 0.01 level. It shows that better study habits leads to better Moral Values.

E. Step-wise Multiple Regression Analysis

It is found that the best multiple regression equations for predicting Moral Values of Intermediate Students are:

1. With the help of 22 socio-demographic variables.
   MVS= 358.355+9.638 (S)-9.825 (C)-6.617 (R)-4.074 (A) +2.271 (Ca)
   The variance explained with the help of the above 5 variables is 9.3 %.
2. With the help of HSPQ (14 personality factors).
   MVS= 358.476 -3.965 (Q4) -3.887 (Q3) -2.798 (O) +2.258(G)
   The variance explained with the help of the above 4 variables is 5.2 %.
3. With the help of self-concepts (10 areas + Total self-concepts)

MVS= 321.351+ 6.093 (SC_2) +3.304 (SC_5)-2.725 (SC_9) +2.634 (SC_4)

The variance explained with the help of the above 4 variables is 6.1 %.

4. With the help of study habits (7 areas + Total study habits)

   MVS= 322.239 + 5.813 (SHT) + 3.090 (SH_5)

   The variance explained with the help of the above 2 variables is 4.3 %.

5. With the help of 55 independent variables (All the independent variables in the study)

   MVS= 351.500 + 3.797 (SC_2) + 8.736 (S) – 7.649 (C) – 8.037 (R) + 3.533 (SHT) – 3.658 (A) – 2.669 (HE) + 2.372 (SC_4) – 2.010 (SC_9).

   The variance explained with the help of the above 9 variables is 13.6 %.

CONCLUSIONS

In the light of the findings presented in the preceding pages, the following conclusions are drawn:

1. In general the Intermediate Students have better Moral Values.
2. The frequency distributions of Moral Values of Intermediate Students in sex, community and caste are very nearer to normal distribution.
3. All the Intermediate Students do not have same Moral Values.
4. Community has its own influence on Moral Values of Intermediate Students.
5. Caste has its own influence on Moral Values of Intermediate Students.
6. Medium of Study, Type of Family, College (management), Age of the Student, Family Annual Income, Family Economic Position, Visiting Temple and Group Subjects have its own significant influence on Moral Values of Intermediate Students.
7. Residence, Sex, Religious Festivals, Religious Discourses, Educational Qualifications of Mother, Educational Qualifications of Father, Father's Occupation, Mother's Occupation, Total Members in the Family, Native Place, When you go wrong who corrects you have no significant influence on Moral Values of Intermediate Students.
8. There is no significant interaction effect of college X sex on Moral Values of Intermediate Students.
9. There is no significant interaction effect of community X caste on Moral Values of Intermediate Students.
10. HSPQ factors B, C, E, I, O, Q_2, Q_3 and Q_4 have their significant influence on Moral Values of Intermediate Students. The remaining

facts A, D, F, G, H and J have no significant influence on Moral Values of Intermediate Students.

11. The Five areas of self-concepts viz., 'Abilities', 'Self Acceptance', 'Worthiness', 'Present, Past and Future', 'Sociability' and total score of self-concepts have significant influence on Moral Values of Intermediate Students. The areas 'Health and Sex Appropriateness', 'Self confidence', 'Beliefs and Convictions', 'Feeling of Shame and Guilt' and 'Emotional Maturity' have no significant influence on Moral Values of Intermediate Students.
12. All the 7 areas of study habits and total score of study habits have significant influence on Moral Values of Intermediate Students.
13. It is possible to predict the Moral Values of Intermediate Students with the help of different sets of independent variables.
14. It is possible to develop the regression equations for predicting the Moral Values of Intermediate Students with the help of all the independent variables in the study.

EDUCATIONAL IMPLICATIONS AND RECOMMENDATIONS

A value is a relationship between a person and an environmental situation which evokes an appreciative response in the individual. Moral values are inseparably related to values in general. Frequently values are divided into types, such as bodily values, economic values, social values, aesthetic values, religious values etc., while there are values which are primarily economic, aesthetic and so on, any human values may also be a Moral Value. To the extent that any activity increases or diminishes the worth of human life, it takes on a moral significance. Values are thus both individual and social.

Durkheim has pointed out that the first element of morality is a spirit of discipline, the second element being, according to him, attachment to social groups. The former is concerned with the development of character of the individual and the latter with the relationship he must bear with others in the society. Both these depend upon the education and training that the individual receives during childhood and adolescence. Children brought up in a laissez-faire can hardly be expected to develop morality to any desired extent.

Educational institutions have to work in a way that the whole child is taken care of and it is possible when the goal before them is to work with the children as how to learn to live.

Teacher plays an important role in the field of education. Today's education is child-centred. The teacher is the maker of the future of the child. The children of today are the citizens and leaders of tomorrow. So, it is necessary to take care about children.

The quality of a nation depends upon the quality of its citizens; the quality of citizens depends upon the quality of their education; the quality of education depends upon the quality of teachers and the quality of teachers depends upon the quality of teacher education. We want value-oriented teacher education (Manchala, 2007).

The home and the school with the influence of parents and teachers have a role to meet and decide how to lead the child from darkness to light, from untruth to truth and from mortality to immortality.

In the family the child is a group member in a clan/family and in the school, the teacher mentors his association in groups. Curricular programmes in the areas of social studies, language and science could help inculcating moral qualities like righteousness, love, self control and truthfulness. Poetry could develop finer sensitivities. Mathematics can help in rationality and logistics.

Types of Activities Schools/Colleges could pursue for value mutation:

- School/College Assembly
- Special Assembly
- Students Panchayat
- Classroom Activities
- Hobby clubs
- Cultural and Literary Activities
- Talks on Values
- Stories
- Celebration of Special Days
- Auxiliary Activities
- Classroom Projects

The above stated values and activities are not an end.

On the basis of the results of this investigation, the following recommendations are made.

1. Government College students have high Moral Values than Aided and Private College students. Aided and Private College should follow all the instructions given by the Government Colleges.
2. Lower age is positively related with Moral Values. Take necessary steps to minimize wastage and stagnation at lower classes.
3. Family Annual Income is positively related with Moral Values. Government should take special interest to increase annual income of the family by providing more job opportunities.

4. Caste and Community are positively related with Moral Values. Government should increase community development programmes with the help of NGOs.
5. Family Economic Position is positively related with Moral Values. Government should takc necessary steps to increase the status of economic position of the family.
6. Visiting Temple is positively related with Moral Values. Encourage students to visit temple at least twice in a week.
7. Group Subjects is positively related with Moral Values. Teacher should take some more care at the time of teaching. Special care may be taken with regard to arts group students. Inculcate more values whenever it is necessary.
8. Some of the Personality Characteristics are related to Moral Values and hence special care may be taken for developing such Personality Characteristics among students.
9. Self-concepts are related to Moral Values. Necessary self-concepts may be developed among students.
10. Study Habits are positively correlated with Moral Values. Better study habits may be developed among Intermediate Students.
11. Necessary infrastructure facilities and physical facilities may be created in Intermediate Colleges. Congenial atmosphere may be developed in Intermediate College. It inculcates sound health value.
12. Value-oriented teaching is necessary.
13. Special care may be taken for pre-primary, primary and upper primary students (the children have high grasping power below age 14 years).
14. Speeches of great persons (role models) may be provided at least once in a month.
15. Separate Moral Education subject may be introduced.
16. A common subject like Science & Civilization, Indian Heritage and Culture may be introduced to inculcate all types of social and human values.
17. Special classes may be provided for Telugu medium students to inculcate more values.
18. Highly qualified, committed and dedicated teachers may be recruited in the colleges.
19. The Intermediate Board should plan special training courses to the principals of Intermediate Colleges for making their administrative styles more acceptable, more effective, more dynamic and more humane.

20. Working with community has to be insisted upon. Appropriate areas have to be allocated. Surveys, interviews, observation, demonstration, exhibition etc. may be organized and reported back to the authorities. Credits and incentives should also be introduced.
21. Inter institute/District/State/Country visits may be arranged for exchange of ideas and sharing of experiences.
22. Special care/attention should be given to the educationally challenged personnel to inculcate values.
23. Stories, illustrations and events mainly from Indian nation and its literature from various religions that included in value oriented education leads to national integration.
24. The psychology of learning says that rewards motivate the students towards better learning and understanding, resulting greater achievement. It increases the confidence in the students. Teachers have to encourage the students to do a certain activity and praise them for their work.

LIMITATIONS OF THE STUDY AND SUGGESTIONS FOR FURTHER RESEARCH

The following limitations and suggestions are considered for further investigation.

1. The study is limited to the students of Senior Intermediate only. It is advised to extend it to Primary School, High School, DIET, Degree, B.Ed, Engineering, Medicine, P.G. students and Research Scholars.
2. The attitude of students is measured through the Moral Values Attitude Inventory constructed by the investigator. Use other scales of Moral Values.
3. Attitude of Moral Values of the students depend on Psychological, Sociological, Economic and Environmental factors. No factor can be studied in isolation.
4. Due to laborious calculations, only certain variables are studied in this investigation. It may be extend to other variables.
5. This is a presage study in the area of Moral Values. Studies of presage-process, presage-product, process-product and presage-process-product may be undertaken in the area of Moral Values.
6. The study is confined to 16 intermediate colleges in Chittoor District of Andhra Pradesh only. It may be extended to other districts of Andhra Pradesh and to the other states.
7. This study is confined to 1200 senior intermediate students. It is suggested that a more detailed study can be made covering more number of senior intermediate students.

8. Research studies may be conducted to see the relationship between students Moral Values and teacher behaviour in the class room.
9. Prediction of Moral Values in Intermediate Students may be attempted with some more independent variables like moral adjustment, social adjustment, interests, aptitudes etc., in order to get further insight into the problem.
10. This study has not included any institutional variables such as year of establishment, facilities available, results produced, titles and awards obtained etc. Institutional variables may help us to identify the variations between good and poor institutions. Studies in this direction may help us to improve the status of education.

Let there be an optimistic view on educational issues like these in the years to come.

"The cultivation of Human Values alone is Education".

"There is one religion; the religion of Love. There is one class; the class of Humanity. There is one language; the language of the Heart".

"If there is righteousness in the heart,
There will be beauty in character.
If there is beauty in character,
There will be harmony in the home.
When there is harmony in the home,
There will be order in the nation.
When there is order in the nation,
There will be peace in the world".

So, be righteous; avoid all prejudices against others on the basis of caste, creed, colour, mode of worship, status or degree of affluence. Do not look down on any one; look upon all as divine as you really are.- Sri Sathya Sai Baba

BIBLIOGRAPHY

1. Annamma, A.K. (1985): "*Values Aspirations and Adjustment of College Students*", in M.B. Buch (Ed.,) Fourth Survey of Research in Education, NCERT, New Delhi.
2. Best, J.W. (1959): "*Research in Education*", U.S.A., Prentice-Hall, Inc., Englewood Cliffs, Chapter 3, pp. 31-83.
3. Chatterjee (2009): "*Criminalization of politics cause of cynicism; Somnath*"; The Hindu, daily, Sunday, March 15, 2009, Andhra Pradesh edition, p.4 columns 5 to 8.
4. Garrett, H.E. (1973): "*Statistics in Psychology and Education*", a Textbook, Vakils, Feffer and Simons Pvt. Ltd., Bombay, India, pp.213-215, 337-370.

5. Good, C.V. Barr, A.S., and Scates, D.E., (1941): "Methodology of Educational Researc*h*", New York, Appleton Century Crofts, Inc., Chapter III, pp.104-184.
6. Manar, R.N. (1974): "*A study of Attitudes, Self-concepts and Values of Professional and Non-professional College Students and relation of these variables will then Achievement*", Ph.D. (Edu), Meerat University, Meerat, U.P., India.
7. Reddy, V.D. (2004): "*Attitude towards Value-oriented Education in Primary School children in Chittoor District*". Journal of Educational Research and Extension, Vol.41 (2), 42-47.
8. Sathya Sai Baba (1972): "*Sathay Sai Institute of Human Values*", Anantapuram.
9. Sukia, S.P., Mehrotra, P.V. and Mehrotra, R.N. (1980): "*Elements of Educational Research*", A textbook, Allied Publishers, Bombay, India, pp.101-102.

20

Jiddu Krishnamurti's Philosophy and the Future of Humanity

INTRODUCTION

The word '**philosophy**' is derived from the Greek words "**philos**' (loving) and 's**ophia**' (wisdom) and means '**love of knowledge and wisdom'**. However, as it is used today 'philosophy' means 'fundamental beliefs and convictions'. Accordingly, everyone has a philosophy of life whether he is aware of it or not and whether he is aware of it or not, and whether he would admit it or not. Thus etymologically the word 'philosophy' means '**love of wisdom'**. In ordinary usage the same word means 'fundamental beliefs and convictions'.

Titus (1964) points out that there are five different approaches to the meaning of philosophy as a professional activity. There are:

1. Philosophy as a personal attitude towards life and the universe;
2. Philosophy as a method of reflective thinking and reasoned inquiry;
3. Philosophy as an attempt to gain a view of the whole;
4. Philosophy as the logical analysis of language and the clarification meaning and,
5. Philosophy as a group of problems as well as theories about the solution of these problems.

DEFINITIONS OF PHILOSOPHY

There are as many different definitions of philosophy as there are philosophers.

1. **Lucas** (1969) defines philosophy as 'a response to that sense of bafflement about what we know but do not understand. Death and undeserved suffering are familiar to us. But we are unable to understand them'.

2. **Millard and Betrocci** (1958) define philosophy as 'the persistent, critical and systematic attempt to discover and consistently formulate in relation to each other the basic characteristics, meanings and values of our experience in its widest perspectives'.

The main divisions in philosophy are:

1. **Metaphysics**
2. Epistemology, and
3. Axiology

PHILOSOPHERS OF INDIA

Abhinavagupta, Acharya Hemachandra, *Acharya Nagarjuna,* Akka Mahadevi, Vyasa, Ramanuja, Mahatma Gandhi, Rabindranath Tagore, Aurabindo Gosh, Basava, Vinoba Bhave, Bodhidharma, Bodhiruci, Gautama Buddha, Sarvepalli Radhakrishnan and Jiddu Krishnamurthy are the some of Indian Philosophers. Among these Jiddu Krishnamurthy was a famous and well known philosopher throughout the world.

JIDDU KRISHNAMURTHY

Jiddu Krishnamurti was born on May 12, 1895 in a small town of Madanapalle, Chittoor District, Andhra Pradesh, India. J. Krishnamurti was raised within the Theosophical Society to be a vehicle for a prophesied World Teacher (Second Coming, Maitreya Buddha). But his life took a different turn.

In 1922, Krishnamurti established his lifelong home in California's Ojai Valley. Under an oak tree he would talk informally with people who were drawn by his ideas.

In 1929 Jiddu Krishnamurti made a dramatic break with the organization which had sponsored him and began to emerge as one of the 20th century's most iconoclastic and influential teachers. Krishnamurti repudiated not only all connections with organized religions and ideology, but denied his own spiritual authority as well. Travelling constantly, Krishnamurti also rejected ties to any country, nationality or culture. Although Jiddu Krishnamurti wrote and lectured widely, he accepted no fees for his talks, or royalties on his books and recordings. Jiddu Krishnamurti died on February 17, 1986.

The teachings of Jiddu Krishnamurti can be found in books, films, university courses, workshops and progressive schools that he started. As of 1990, his works have been translated into forty-seven languages, including Swahili; through them his influence is felt worldwide. His ideas, which revolved around the centrality of individual consciousness free from the programmed filters of religion and culture, attracted people as varied as George Bernard Shaw, Greta Garbo, Bertrand Russell, Aldous Huxley, Joseph Campbell, Albert Einstein, Alan Watts, Jackson Pollock, Anne Morrow Lindbergh, Christopher Isherwood and Charlie Chaplin. H e finally settled in Ojai, Calif., where from 1969 he headed the Krishnamurti Foundation. His writings include Commentaries on Living (1956-60), Freedom from the Known (1969), The First and Last Freedom (1975), Life in Freedom (1986), and Think on These Things (1989).

IMPORTANCE OF JIDDU KRISHNAMURTI'S PHILOSOPHY

Today we are living in the Scientific and Technological world. There are a lot of changes occurring in the day to day life of human beings. Because of busy life men and women and children can't give much importance for mental and physical health. Today we are suffering so many problems poverty, high-population and terrorism. Because of these and high stress and strain, the people control their psychological balance.

In the world, there is great disturbance, corruption; people are very disturbed. It is dangerous to walk on the streets. When we are talking about freedom from fear, we want outward freedom, freedom from chaos, anarchy, or dictatorship. But we never demand or enquire if there is an inner freedom at all: freedom of the mind. Is that freedom actual or theoretical? We regard the State as an impediment to freedom. Communists and other totalitarian people say there is no such thing as freedom; the State, the government, is the only authority. And they are suppressing every form of freedom. So what kind of freedom do we want? Out there? Outside of us? Or inward freedom? When we talk about freedom, is it the freedom of choice between this government and that, here and there, between outer and inward freedom? The inner psyche always conquers the outer. The psyche, that is, the inward structure of man - his thoughts, emotions, his ambitions, his actions, and his greed - always conquers the outer. So, where do we seek freedom? Could we discuss that? Can there be freedom from nationality which gives us a sense of security? Can there be freedom from all the superstitions, dogmas and religions? A new civilization can only come about through real religion, not through superstition, dogma or traditional religions.

HUMAITY

Humanity may refer to:

- The human species
- The total world population of humans
- Human nature
- Compassion, altruism, etc.
- One branch of the humanities, those academic disciplines which study the human condition using methods that are largely analytic, critical, or speculative.

Jiddu Krishnamurti's aim was to set humanity free. Krishnamurti maintained that the individual is freed by becoming aware of his/her own psychological conditioning, and that this awakening will enable him/her to give love to another. "If you want to spread these teachings", Krishnamurti went on to say, "live them, and by your life you will be spreading them".

Traditionally, the future of humanity has been a topic for theology. All the major religions have teachings about the ultimate destiny of humanity or the end of the world. In more recent times the literary genre of science fiction has continued the tradition. Very often, the future has served as a projection screen for our hopes and fears; or as a stage setting for dramatic entertainment, morality tales, or satire of tendencies in contemporary society; or as a banner for ideological mobilization. It is relatively rare for humanity's future to be taken seriously as a subject matter on which it is important to try to have factually correct beliefs. There is nothing wrong with exploiting the symbolic and literary affordances of an unknown future, just as there is nothing wrong with fantasizing about imaginary countries populated by dragons and wizards. Yet it is important to attempt (as best we can) to distinguish futuristic scenarios put forward for their symbolic significance or entertainment value from speculations that are meant to be evaluated on the basis of literal plausibility.

We need realistic pictures of what the future might bring in order to make sound decisions. Increasingly, we need realistic pictures not only of our personal or local near-term futures, but also of remoter global futures. Because of our expanded technological powers, some human activities now have significant global impacts. The scale of human social organization has also grown, creating new opportunities for coordination and action, and there are many institutions and individuals who either do consider, or claim to consider, or ought to consider, possible long-term global impacts of their actions. Climate change, national and international security, economic development, nuclear waste disposal, biodiversity, natural resource conservation, population policy, and scientific and

Technological research funding are examples of policy areas that involve long time-horizons. Arguments in these areas often rely on implicit assumptions about the future of humanity. By making these assumptions explicit, and subjecting them to critical analysis, it might be possible to address some of the big challenges for humanity in a more well-considered and thoughtful manner. The fact that we "need" realistic pictures of the future does not entail that we can have them. Predictions about future technical and social developments are notoriously unreliable – to an extent that have led some to propose that we do away with prediction altogether in our planning and preparation for the future. Yet while the methodological problems of such forecasting are certainly very significant, the extreme view that we can or should do away with prediction altogether is misguided. That view is expressed, to take one example, in a recent paper on the societal implications of nanotechnology by Michael Crow and Daniel Sarewitz, in which they argue that the issue of predictability is "irrelevant".

CONCLUSION

Jiddu Krishnamurthy was a world famous philosopher. It is necessary to read all his valuable speeches and books. According to Mahatma Gandhi "If wealth is lost nothing is lost, if health is lost something is lost, if character is lost everything is lost". So best of all things is character. Jiddu Krishnamurthy philosophy is necessary for present generation people. Jiddu Krishnamurti's aim was to set humanity free.

REFERENCES

1. Heilbroner, R. L. (1995) Visions of the future: the distant past, yesterday, today, and tomorrow (New York: Oxford University Press).
2. Rajaganeshan, Subramanyam, S. "Philosophical and Sociological Foundations of Education", DDE, Sri Venkateswara University, Tirupati.

21

Importance of Purusharthas

Now men and women including children are living happily with the help of science and technology. A lot of changes are occurring in the day to day life of human beings because of globalization, liberalization and privatization. At the same time we are facing so many problems like terrorism, poverty, high-population and poor-health. It is important to know what is goal of an individual. It is very important to know about purusharthas for the human wellbeing.

Purusha means either God or human being. Artha means an object or objective. Purusharthas means objectives of human being. Purusha does not mean male in the physical sense, but any soul in its differential aspect. So the purusharthas are applicable to both men and women.

The four chief purusharthas are:

1. Dharma (righteousness)
2. Artha (material wealth)
3. Kama (desire)
4. Moksha (salvation or liberation)

Every individual in a society is expected to achieve these four objectives and seek fulfillment in his life before departing from here. The concept of Purusharthas clearly establishes the fact that Hinduism does not advocate a life of self negation and hardship, but a life of balance, achievement and fulfillment.

1. DHARMA

Dharma is the way of the higher Truths. Dharma forms the basis for philosophies, beliefs and practices originating in India. The oldest of these, widely known as Hinduism, is Sanatana Dharma or Eternal Dharma. Buddhism, Ayyavazhi, Jainism and Sikhism also retain the centrality of Dharma. In these traditions, beings that live in harmony with Dharma proceed more quickly towards moksha, nirvana, or personal liberation.

Dharma is a very complicated word, for which there is no equivalent word in any other language, including English. Dharma actually means that which upholds this entire creation. It is a Divine law that is inherent and invisible, but responsible for all existence. Dharma exists in all planes, in all aspects and at all levels of creation. In the context of human life, dharma consists of all that an individual undertakes in harmony with Divine expectations and his own inner spiritual aspirations, actions that would ensure order and harmony with in him and in the environment in which he lives.

Since this world is deluded, a human being may not know what is right and what is wrong or what is dharma and what is adharma. Hence he should rely upon the scriptures and adhere to the injunctions contained therein. In short, dharma for a human being means developing divine virtues and performing actions that are in harmony with the divine laws.

Dharma is considered to be the first cardinal aim because it is at the root of everything and upholds everything. For example see what happens when a person amasses wealth without observing dharma or indulges in sexual passion against the social norms or established moral values. Any action performed without observing dharma is bound to bring misery and suffering and delay ones salvation. Hinduism therefore considers it rightly as the first cardinal aim of life.

In ancient India dharmashastras (law books) provided guidance to people in their day to day lives and helped them to adhere to dharma. These law books were written for a particular time frame and are no more relevant to the modern world. The best way to know what is dharma and what is adharma, is to follow the religious scriptures such as the Bhagavad Gita and the Upanishads or any other scripture that contains the words of God.

2. ARTHA

Artha means wealth. Hinduism recognizes the importance of material wealth for the overall happiness and well being of an individual. A house holder requires wealth, because he has to perform many duties to uphold dharma and ensure the welfare and progress of his family and society. A person may have the intention to uphold the dharma, but if he has no money he would not be able to perform his duties and fulfill his dharma. Hinduism therefore rightly places material wealth as the second most important objective in human life. In the modern days also we know that 'money makes many things'.

Lord Vishnu is the best example for any householder who wants to lead a life of luxury and still be on the side of God doing his duties. As the preserver of the universe, Lord Vishnu lives in Vaikunth amid pomp and glory, with the goddess of wealth herself by his side and yet helps the poor and the needy, protects the weak, upholds the dharma and sometimes leaving everything aside rushes to the earth as an incarnation to uphold dharma.

Hinduism believes that both spiritualism and materialism are important for the salvation of human beings. It is unfortunate that Hinduism came to be associated more with spiritualism, probably because of the influence of Buddhism, where as in truth Hinduism does not exclude either of them. As Swami Vivekananda rightly said religion is not for the empty stomachs. Religion is not for those whose main concern from morning till evening is how to make both ends meet. Poverty crushes the spirit of man and renders him an easy prey to wicked forces.

In ancient India Artha shastras (scriptures on wealth) provided necessary guidance to people on the finer aspects of managing their wealth. Kautilya's Artha Shastra, which is probably a compilation of many independent works, gives us a glimpse of how money matters were handled in ancient India.

3. KAMA

Kama in a wider sense means desire and in a narrow sense, sexual desire. Hinduism prescribes fulfillment of sexual passions for the householders and abstinence from it for the students and ascetics who are engaged in the study of the scriptures and in the pursuit of Brahman.

The Bhagavad Gita informs us that desire is an aspect of delusion and one has to be wary of its various movements and manifestations. The best way to deal with desires is to develop detachment and perform desireless actions without seeking the fruit of one's actions and making an offering of all the actions to God. This way our actions would not bind us to the cycle of births and deaths.

One of the important sects of Hinduism is Tantricism. It recognizes the importance of sexual freedom in the liberation of soul. The Tantrics accept sex as an important means to experience the blissful nature of God and the best way to experience God in physical form. They also refer to the concept of Purusharthas to justify their doctrines. They believe that sexual energy is divine energy and it can be transformed into spiritual energy through controlled expression of sex.

Just as the dharmashastras were written for the sake of dharma, and artha shastras for artha, kama shastras were composed in ancient India for providing guidance in matters of sex. We have lost many of them because of the extreme secrecy and social disapproval associated with the subject. What we have today is Vatsayana's Kamasutra, which like the Arthashastra seems to be a compilation of various independent works rather the work of a single individual.

4. MOKSHA

Human life is very precious because of all the beings in all the worlds, only human beings have the best opportunity to realize the higher self. It is also precious because it is attained after many hundreds and thousands of lives. Rightly, salvation should be its ultimate aim.

Moksha actually means absence of moha or delusion. Delusion is caused by the inter play of the triple gunas. When a person overcomes these gunas, he attains liberation. The gunas can be overcome by detachment, self control, surrender to god and offering ones actions to God.

If dharma guides the life of a human being from below acting as the earth, showing him the way from above like a star studded mysterious sky is moksha. Dharma constitutes the legs of a Purusha that walk upon the earth; both artha and kama constitute his two limbs active in the middle region; while moksha constitutes the head that rests in the heaven.

CONCLUSION

The four Purusharthas are like the four wheels of a chariot called human life. They collectively uphold it and lead it. Each influences the movement of the other three, and in the absence of any one of them, the chariot comes to a halt. So to attain all the four purusharthas we want the strength of God. Pray the Lord Vishnu to attain all the four purusharthas.

Vina Venkatesam na Naatho na Naatha:
Sadha Venkatesam smarAmi smarAmi
Hare! Venkatesa! Praseedha Praseedha
Priyam Venkatesa! Prayaccha Prayaccha!

22

Inclusive Education

INTRODUCTION

Education

The development of any nation depends mainly on the standards of its educational institutions. Education is the most powerful and effective instrument for inducing radical changes in the behaviour of students. Education is the process through which an individual is developed into individuality and a person into a personality. Education should be individualized and personalized to the utmost and should constitute preparation for self-learning.

Education, according to Indian tradition, is not merely a means to earn a living, nor is it only a nursery of thought or a school for citizenship. It is an initiation into the life of spirit, a training of human soul in pursuit of truth and the practice of virtue. Aristotle, however, held that education exists exclusively to develop man's intellect in a world of reality, which men can know and understand.

Importance of Education

Education is the process of instruction aimed at the all round development of boys and girls. Education dispels ignorance. It is the only wealth that cannot be robbed. Learning includes the Moral Values and the improvement of character and the methods to increase the strength of mind.

Education plays an important role in the progress of an individual's mind and country. Ignorance and poverty are major speed-breakers in the developing country and can be overcome easily through education.

INCLUSIVE EDUCATION

Inclusive education is gaining ground. Throughout the world, teachers and others involved in education are working to develop positive educational experiences that all children and young people can enjoy and benefit from, together. For disabled children and those experiencing difficulties in learning, this means inclusion in mainstream schools and classrooms alongside their non-disabled peers. For all children - and adults - it means a more enriching and rewarding educational experience.

Inclusive education has grown from the belief that education is a basic human right and that it provides the foundation for a more just society. All learners have a right to education, regardless of their individual characteristics or difficulties.

Inclusive education initiatives often have a particular focus on those groups, which, in the past, have been excluded from educational opportunities. These groups include children living in poverty, those from ethnic and linguistic minorities, girls (in some societies), children from remote areas and those with disabilities or other special educational needs. The latter are often the most marginalised, both within education and in society in general.

Traditionally, disabled children and those with other special educational needs have experienced exclusion, discrimination and segregation from mainstream education and their peers. Some are placed in separate classes or schools; many have been denied access to education of any sort.

Segregated educational provision separates children from their peers and families and may not be cost-effective. Establishing or extending separate provision does nothing to identify and remove the barriers preventing these children from learning in mainstream schools. Inclusive education is about helping mainstream schools to overcome the barriers so that they can meet the learning needs of all children.

Inclusive education is not only concerned with disabled children, or with finding an alternative to segregated special schooling. Inclusive education encourages policy-makers and managers to look at the barriers within the education system, how they arise and how they can be removed. These barriers usually include:

- Inappropriately-designed curricula

- Teachers who are not trained to work with children who have a wide range of needs
- Inappropriate media for teaching
- Inaccessible buildings.

INCLUSIVE EDUCATION IN INDIA

The Ministry of Human Resource Development is currently in the process of developing a Comprehensive Action Plan on the Inclusion in Education of Children and Youth with Disabilities. A statement spelling out the areas of action was made in the Rajya Sabha by Shri Arjun Singh, Minister for Human Resource Development on the 21st of March, 2005. Since then, the Ministry has been interacting and consulting with experts, NGOs, Disability Rights Groups, Parents Groups, and Government bodies etc.

The last decade has seen the passing of three major legislations on disability by the Government of India. The Rehabilitation Council of India Act(1992), Persons with Disability Act (1995), and the National Trust Act (1999) have been enacted and implemented at both the Central and State level.

- Education of children with disability has been part of the National Policy on Education (NPE), 1986 and the Programme of Action (1992)
- Currently education provisions for children with disabilities are covered by 'special schools' and integrated mainstream schools.
- Over 1.24 lakh children with disabilities have been integrated in over 20,000 mainstream schools under the Integrated Education for Disabled Children Scheme of the Ministry of HRD.
- At the elementary level, under the Sarva Shiksha Abhiyan programme, over 14 lakh children with disabilities have been enrolled.
- However despite efforts over the past three decades by the government and the non-government sector, educational facilities need to be made available to a substantial proportion of persons with disability need to be covered.
- Compared to a National literacy figure of around 65 percent the percentage of literacy levels of the disabled population is only 49 percent
- Literacy rates for the female disabled population is around 37 percent compared to national average of over 54 percent for the female population.
- Literacy rates for the male disabled population are 58.14 percent compared to 75.85 percent for males.

- According to NSSO 2002 figures, of the literate disabled population only 9 percent completed secondary and above education

Goal of Action Plan for Inclusion

Recognizing Education for All children as a fundamental right, to ensure the inclusion of children and youth with disabilities in all available mainstream educational settings, by providing them with a learning environment that is available, accessible, affordable and appropriate to help develop their learning and abilities.

Target Group

- Infants and children with special needs in the age group 0-6 yrs.
- Children with special needs in the age group 6-14yrs
- Young persons with disabilities in the age group 14 - to 21 yrs. who are part of the educational stream

Disability would refer to sensory, physical and intellectual impairments, communication, emotional and behavioral disorders, mental health difficulties and multiple disabilities. It would cover the disabilities as defined under the Persons with Disability Act (1995) and the National Trust Act (1999):

- Blindness
- Low vision
- Leprosy cured
- Hearing impairments
- Locomotor disabilities
- Mental retardation
- Mental Illness
- Autism
- Cerebral Palsy
- Multiple disabilities

In the 0-6 yrs, this may also cover all children indicating developmental delay, low birth weight, termed at risk and medical problems that may lead to disabling conditions.

The 6-14 yrs group may also be referred to as Children with Special Needs (CWSN) as under the Sarva Shiksha Abhiyan programme which guidelines may be taken as a reference point.

INCLUSIVE EDUCATION-WORLD WIDE

Internationally, the drive towards inclusion is fuelled by a number of initiatives and treaties, including the UN Convention on the Rights of the

Child (1989), the UN Standard Rules on the Equalisation of Opportunities for Persons with Disabilities (1993) and the UNESCO Salamanca Statement (1994). Together, these documents recognise the human right of all children to education which is inclusive. 193 countries have signed the Convention on the Rights of the Child, with Somalia being the most recent in May 2002. All but two countries (Somalia and the United States) have also agreed to be bound by the Convention by ratifying it.

Some countries have made significant advances towards promoting inclusive education in their national legislation. Examples include Canada, Cyprus, Denmark, Iceland, India, Luxembourg, Malta, the Netherlands, Norway, South Africa, Spain, Sweden, Uganda, the United Kingdom and the United States. Italian law has supported inclusive education since the 1970s.

As the 1999 report by the Organisation for Economic Co-operation and Development (OECD), Inclusive Education at Work: Students with Disabilities in Mainstream Schools, states: 'The rights of students with disabilities to be educated in their local mainstream school is becoming more and more accepted in most countries, and many reforms are being put in place to achieve this goal. Further, there is no reason to segregate disabled students in public education systems. Instead, education systems need to be reconsidered to meet the needs of all students.'

From rhetoric to reality

This drive towards inclusion is not only rhetoric. Rather, the reality of inclusive education is transforming the lives of millions of children - and teachers - in countries across the world. According to the OECD report, there is a decline in the proportion of students in 'special' schools in most countries. CSIE's Index for Inclusion, which helps ordinary schools break down barriers to learning and participation, is being taken up in a range of countries around the world.

Diversity in the mainstream is increasing in many countries. The vast majority of disabled children and young people in Iceland attend their local schools. In Italy, more than 99.9% of all children in the state sector are educated in ordinary schools. In the province of New Brunswick, in Canada, there are no 'special' schools - all children are educated in local mainstream schools.

A national study on inclusion in the United States in 1995, carried out by the National Center on Educational Restructuring and Inclusion, reported a huge growth in inclusive education for students with all levels of disability. A report from the Ontario School District in Oregon stated: 'The only criteria for a student to attend any of our six elementary schools, our middle school or our high school is they must be breathing.' In Uganda, the human rights of disabled people are enshrined in the Constitution and sign language is recognised as an official language. Deaf children now attend their local schools, with appropriate support to enable them to learn. One observer noted: 'Instead of sitting silently and unnoticed in their classrooms, they now have sign language interpreters provided.'

In the district of Douentza, in Mali, West Africa - one of the 'poorest' areas of the world - villagers worked together with outside agencies to set up a much needed local school, which disabled boys and girls attend together with every other child. One of the teachers said: 'To begin with we had the commitment to include disabled children, but we did not really believe that they could be in school. Now we have seen for ourselves, and we have moved from commitment to conviction.'

EDUCATION FOR ALL THROUGH INCLUSIVE EDUCATION

The Education for All (EFA) movement was launched at the World Conference on Education for All in Jomtien, Thailand in 1990 and it aims to give all children, young people and adults the right to education. The Jomtien World Education Declaration (article 2.2) sets out the main components of an 'expanded vision' of basic education.

- Give all children, young people and adults' universal access to education, and promoting equality – by, for instance, ensuring that girls and women and other under-served groups have access to basic education
- Focus on learning acquisition and outcome – rather than simply on enrolment
- Broaden the means and scope of basic education – partly by ensuring the availability of universal primary education, but also by calling upon families, communities, early childhood care, literacy programmes, non-formal education programmes, libraries, the media and a wide range of other 'delivery systems.'
- Enhance the environment for learning – by ensuring that learners receive the nutrition, health care and general physical and emotional support they need to benefit from education
- Strengthen partnerships – between all sub-sectors and forms of education, government departments, non-governmental organizations, the private sector, religious groups, local communities and, above all, families and teachers.

A decade after the Jomtien Declaration, its vision was reaffirmed at the World Education Forum meeting in Dakar, held to review progress in achieving Education for All (World Education Forum, 2000). The Forum highlighted the continuing barriers to education experienced by disadvantaged groups and called for positive action to overcome them.

SUPPORTS OF INCLUSIVE EDUCATION

The major impetus for inclusive education came from the 1994 World Conference on Special Needs Education in Salamanca. The conference recommendations were based on the principle of inclusion:

'... Schools should accommodate all children regardless of their physical, intellectual, social, emotional, linguistic or other conditions. This should include disabled and gifted children, street and working children, children from remote or nomadic populations, children from linguistic, ethnic, or cultural minorities and children from other disadvantaged or marginalized areas or groups.'

(UNESCO, 1994, Framework for Action on Special Needs Education)

JUSTIFICATION OF INCLUSIVE EDUCATION

- ***There is an educational justification**:* The requirement for inclusive schools to educate all children together means that they have to develop ways of teaching which respond to individual differences and therefore benefit all children.
- ***There is a social justification:*** Inclusive schools are able to change attitudes to difference by educating all children together, thereby forming the basis for a just and non-discriminatory society which encourages people to live together in peace.
- ***There is an economic justification**:* It is likely to be less costly to establish and maintain schools which educate all children together than to set up a complex system of different types of schools specializing in the education of specific groups of children. Inclusive schools offering an effective education to all of their students are a more cost-effective means of delivering Education for All.

DEVELOPMENT OF INCLUSIVE POLICIES AND PRACTICES

The move to more inclusive education does not happen overnight. The change, however gradual, should be based on clearly articulated principles, which address system-wide development. If the barriers to inclusive education are to be reduced, policy-makers and managers need to:

- Mobilize opinion
- Build consensus
- Carry out a situation analysis
- Reform legislation
- Support local projects.

Education administration systems often need to change to enable inclusive education to develop. For example, uniting the management of special and mainstream education helps to promote inclusive education. The process of change itself requires financial, human and intellectual resources. A good first step is to identify a pool of resources to support the implementation of legislative change or to pump-prime experimental developments. Building partnerships with stakeholders, international organisations, and non-governmental organisations (NGOs) is also crucial.

NEED OF PROFESSIONAL DEVELOPMENT FOR INCLUSIVE EDUCATION

The development of a teaching force skilled in inclusive practices is vital to the campaign for inclusive education. The most urgent need for teacher development is in mainstream schools. Where training resources are scarce and not all teachers can attend training sessions, a 'cascade' model3 enables training to be disseminated throughout the system. Distance learning is an effective mechanism for giving teachers in remote areas access to training. If inclusive education is to be sustainable, training must be planned, systematic and long term.

ROLE OF EDUCATIONAL ASSESSMENT IN QUALITY EDUCATION

In an effective education system, all students are continuously assessed on their educational progress in relation to the curriculum. In inclusive education, teachers have to respond to a wide diversity of students, using a range of techniques. Assessment should focus on the characteristics and attainments of the students, as well as on how each student can learn within the curriculum. Assessment techniques should enable students to demonstrate their strengths and their potential and should not unfairly discriminate between groups of students.

Parents and students are key contributors to the assessment process. Parents can provide information on how a student behaves outside the school, describe the student's early childhood development and give teachers feedback on the effectiveness of their work with the student.

If a student's difficulties are more complex, the teacher needs to work with professionals who have specialist skills. This is best achieved when teachers have access to specialists in the school and to multi-disciplinary teams working locally. Early assessment of a child's difficulties is an important part of the assessment process. Early assessment and intervention minimises the impact of any difficulties, reduces the need for costly programmes of rehabilitation and remediation and makes it more likely that the students can be met in a mainstream environment.

EFFECTIVE SUPPORT FOR INCLUSIVE SYSTEMS

An effective support system is essential if schools are to give every learner the opportunity to become a successful student. 'Support' includes everything that enables learners to learn. The most important forms of support are available to every school: children supporting children, teachers supporting teachers, parents becoming partners in the education of their children and communities supporting their local schools.

There are also more formal types of support; for example, from teachers with specialist knowledge, resource centres and professionals from other sectors. A coordinated approach to the provision of formal support is critical, with services and agencies working together. This may require changing local management structures to facilitate a 'joined-up' approach to delivering support to schools.

COMMUNITY PARTICIPATION IN INCLUSIVE EDUCATION

The involvement of families and local communities is essential in achieving a quality education for all. Families and community groups can take an active role in promoting inclusive education, advancing changes in policy and legislation. Successful partnerships with families can be developed if both the professionals and families understand and respect each other's roles in those partnerships. Although it can take time to develop, trust between the partners is vital. Encouraging marginalised groups to become involved can be particularly difficult. The importance of family involvement in education can be reinforced by embedding it in the way schools are run and by appropriate legislation. Partnership with the wider community is a significant opportunity for schools and mutually beneficial; both have resources to share.

INCLUSIVE EDUCATION-CURRICULUM DEVELOPMENT

Developing a curriculum, which is inclusive of all learners, may involve broadening current definitions of learning. Inclusive curricula are based on a view of learning as something, which takes place when students are actively involved in making sense of their experiences. This emphasizes the role of the teacher as facilitator rather than instructor.

The curriculum should be flexible enough to respond to the needs of all students. It should not therefore be *rigidly* prescribed at a national or central level. Inclusive curricula are constructed flexibly to allow not only for *school-level* adaptations and developments, but also for adaptations and modifications to meet the *individual* student's needs and to suit each teacher's style of working. A key issue for policy-makers is how they enable schools to modify the curriculum to meet the needs of individual students and how they can encourage this approach.

More inclusive curricula make considerable demands on teachers. They have to become involved in curriculum development at a local level and to be skilled in curriculum adaptation in their own classrooms.

In addition they have to manage a complex range of classroom activities, be skilled in planning the participation of all students and know how to support their students' learning without giving them predetermined answers. They also have to understand how to work outside traditional subject boundaries and in culturally sensitive ways.

Inflexible and content-heavy curricula are usually the major cause of segregation and exclusion. The development of an inclusive curriculum is arguably the most important factor in achieving inclusive education.

FINANCIAL MANAGEMENT ASSISTS IN SUPPORTING INCLUSIVE SYSTEMS

Funding provision for learners who experience difficulties is always problematic. However well resourced a system may be overall, there is almost always a feeling that resources are inadequate to meet learners' needs.

A number of countries have broadened their approach to funding and resourcing education. They have developed responses to learning difficulties, which are not dependent on additional funding. These responses include: collaborative work by students; parental involvement in the classroom; and teacher problem-solving and mutual support.

Few education systems can provide all the resources they would wish to from state funds alone. It is therefore essential for national and local governments to establish partnerships with potential funding partners. International donors and NGOs are obvious sources of additional resourcing, but so are the business and industry sectors, which have a vested interest in establishing goodwill and helping to produce a well-educated workforce.

In many countries, there are separate funding streams for mainstream and special education. Where this occurs, there are often administrative barriers preventing mainstream schools from accessing the funds they need to support inclusive approaches. Inclusive systems therefore need a mechanism for channelling additional funds into mainstream schools.

Further strategies are needed if the aim is to go beyond accommodating a diverse range of students to redressing some of the specific disadvantages experienced by certain groups. Many countries have developed programmes, which promote equality of opportunity by allocating specific funds to areas of social and economic need.

TRANSITIONS FROM ONE PHASE OF EDUCATION TO ANOTHER

A good education system ensures a smooth transition between different phases of education. Ideally, all students, regardless of their difficulties or disabilities, should be able to enter the education system as young children, progress through each phase and emerge into a meaningful and useful adult life. This can only happen if barriers at key transition points are identified and removed. Key transition points include: the transition from home to school; the transition between phases or cycles of schooling; and the transition between schooling, lifelong learning and the world of work.

There are clear structural barriers, which make transition within and between different phases of schooling, further, and higher education and employment difficult. These include:

- Separate funding, administrative and legislative systems in primary, secondary and tertiary education
- The impact of selection in further and higher education
- The transfer from children's to adult's services
- The impact of selection in the labour market. If education systems are to become more inclusive, transition has to be managed so that all learners progress smoothly from one stage to another, maximizing the opportunities available to them.

IMPLEMENTATION OF INCLUSIVE EDUCATION

The implementation of more inclusive systems of education is possible only if schools themselves are committed to becoming more inclusive. The development of enabling mechanisms such as national policies on inclusion, local support systems and appropriate forms of curriculum and assessment are important in creating the right context for developing inclusive education. However, the involvement of schools in inclusion projects is essential if national policy is to be translated into the realities of practice.

The most common strategy in promoting inclusive education is to initiate an inclusion 'project' in which one or more schools are supported in developing more inclusive practices. Projects can build on schools' own initiatives or can be centrally-run. Special projects alone are unlikely to create a more inclusive education system, but they have an important role to play. All projects work differently, but there are some common success criteria:

- Clarity over roles and responsibilities

- Effective support for schools
- Clear mechanisms for developing practice
- A good dissemination process.

Projects need to help schools change their culture and practice. If the school culture currently takes little account of the principles of participation, collaboration and inclusion, developing more inclusive practices will inevitably challenge existing values, assumptions and practices. This can disrupt the status quo and requires careful management and sensitive support. Frequently, schools work in isolation or at best with a central project team. Whilst much good work can be done in this way, schools can offer valuable support to each other. Through networking, schools can:

- Share experiences and expertise
- Develop joint policy and practices
- Replace competition and self-interest with a sense of shared investment in the network
- Develop shared resources such as specialist expertise and innovative delivery mechanisms
- Create economies of scale which enable them to respond more easily to a greater diversity of student need.

Not about money

It is not simply a question of funding. It is a common assertion that 'full' inclusion - all children and young people learning together, including all disabled children - would be too expensive. Yet the example from Mali demonstrates that inclusion can happen whatever resources are available.

International work by both the World Bank and OECD has shown that it is far more expensive to operate dual systems of ordinary and 'special' education than it is to operate a single inclusive system. In Reykjavik, Iceland, local authority staff calculated that the cost of educating a child requiring the most intensive support in a mainstream school was no greater than the average cost of sending students to 'special' schools.

The real problem lies with the historical investment in separate, segregated systems of 'special' schools, the lack of political will to make inclusive education available to all, and the uncertainties of some parents that inclusion will benefit their children. But throughout the world, people are seeing the benefits of inclusion for themselves. Everywhere, those who have experienced inclusive education - including providers and disabled and non-disabled students - are convinced that inclusion is the way forward.

From strength to strength

These experiences must be built on. The urgent task is to change hearts and minds, encouraging openness to the values and aims of inclusive education and a commitment to the human rights of all children and young people. Non-government organisations and individuals must also continue to lobby Governments, and raise awareness among teachers and parents of the advantages of inclusion. People directly involved in inclusive education need to share their knowledge and experiences with those just starting out.

Progress needs to happen on all fronts, from Governments passing legislation and formulating policy to people in schools working inclusively with real students. As one school director in Swaziland said: 'I had thought the problem of integration of children with difficulties was difficult to solve, and a problem of the state. But all my conversations have now confirmed my opinion that someone had to start, to break the mould, and fight against the isolation of children with special needs.'

Exchanging information about examples of good practice in the restructuring of mainstream schools in the UK and overseas is an essential step towards ending discrimination in education. In persisting with these efforts to secure a worldwide move from ordinary and 'special' education to inclusive education, we can press on towards the goal of making inclusion an everyday

BENEFITS OF INCLUSIVE EDUCATION

The benefits of inclusive education are numerous for both students with and without disabilities.

Benefits of Inclusion for Students with Disabilities

- Friendships
- Increased social initiations, relationships and networks
- Peer role models for academic, social and behavior skills
- Increased achievement of IEP goals
- Greater access to general curriculum
- Enhanced skill acquisition and generalization
- Increased inclusion in future environments
- Greater opportunities for interactions
- Higher expectations
- Increased school staff collaboration
- Increased parent participation
- Families are more integrated into community

Benefits of Inclusion for Students without Disabilities

- Meaningful friendships
- Increased appreciation and acceptance of individual differences
- Increased understanding and acceptance of diversity
- Respect for all people
- Prepares all students for adult life in an inclusive society
- Opportunities to master activities by practicing and teaching others
- Greater academic outcomes
- All students' needs are better met, greater resources for everyone

There is not any research that shows any negative effects from inclusion done appropriately with the necessary supports and services for students to actively participate and achieve IEP goals.

CONCLUSION

Inclusive schools no longer distinguish between "general education" and "special education" programs; instead, the school is restructured so that all students learn together. Proponents want to maximize the participation of all learners in the community schools of their choice, make learning more meaningful and relevant for all, particularly those learners most vulnerable to exclusionary pressures, and to rethink and restructure policies, curricula, cultures and practices in schools and learning environments so that diverse learning needs can be met, whatever the origin or nature of those needs

- All students can learn and benefit from education.
- Schools adapt to the needs of students, rather than students adapting to the needs of the school.
- Individual differences between students are a source of richness and diversity, and not a problem.
- The diversity of needs and pace of development of students are addressed through a wide and flexible range of responses (so long as those responses do not include removing a student with a disability from a general education classroom).

Inclusive education is a process of removing barriers and enabling all students, including previously excluded groups, to learn and participate effectively within general school systems. It is possible to provide education for all with mutual co-operation among teacher, students, parents and governments. Without education the development of any society can't take place. It is the primary duty of government to provide education in general and inclusive education in particular for all children in the society. Today's children are tomorrows' citizens. If we take care about present generation, the future will become good.

REFERENCES

1. Ainscow M., Booth T. (2003). "*The Index for Inclusion: Developing Learning & Participation in Schools*". Bristol: Center for Studies in Inclusive Education.
2. Mary Beth Doyle. "*The Paraprofessional's Guide to the Inclusive Classroom*".
3. "*National Policy on Education*" (1986). Government of India, New Delhi.
4. "*Persons with Disability Act*" (1995). Government of India, New Delhi.
5. "*Programme of Action*" (1992). Government of India, New Delhi.
6. "*The National Trust Act*" (1999). Government of India, New Delhi.
7. "*The Rehabilitation Council of India Act*" (1992), Government of India, New Delhi.
8. Villa, R., & Thousand, J. (Eds.). (2000a). "*Restructuring for caring and effective education*". Baltimore: Brookes.
9. "*UN Convention on the Rights of the Child*" (1989).
10. "*UNESCO Salamanca Statement*" (1994).

23

Upliftment of the Disadvantaged Through Education

INTRODUCTION

Education means an all round drawing out of the best in child and man-body, mind and spirit. The imperative character of education for individual growth and social development is now accepted by everyone. Investment in the education of its youth considered as most vital by all modern nations. Such an investment understandably acquires top priority in developing countries. The end of all education, all training should be man making. The end and aim of all training is to make the man grow. The training by which the current and expression are brought under control and become fruitful is called education. Education plays a vital role in giving human beings proper equipment to lead a gracious and harmonious life. Education is a fundamental means to bring any desired change in society, which is an accepted fact throughout the world. This can be attained only if schools become real centres of learning. Education not only helps in the development of personality of the child but also determines his future. Recent psychological research has shown that favourable attitudes towards life develop in the earliest stages of child growth. Value oriented education is necessary. All men and women are equal. Caste, colour, religion and region are only labels. Education helps to change the attitude of all human beings. Education is a good weapon to change the lives of disadvantaged in the society.

SOCIAL PROBLEMS IN INDIA

Historical Phases

The Indian society, being part of an ancient civilization, has passed through different historical phases. The *Vedic* period in India sowed the seeds of a civilization - characterized by the emergence of sophisticated philosophy, religion, astrology, science and medicine. Its institutional base centered on *Varnashram* and caste, emphasis on rituals, higher position of ritual performers over others and the sacrifice of animals.

In the medieval period, the Bhakti movement, reassert the humanist elements of the Indian civilisation by preaching equality, speaking against rituals, the caste rigidity and untouchability. The practices of untouchability, child marriage, sati, infanticide, organised thagi (cheating) increased in the Indian Society particularly during the declining phase of the Mughal Empire. Even the religious beliefs encouraged the addiction of tobacco, hashish and opium.

By the early part of the 19th Century, the colonial administration in India was fully established. After 1820, it adopted reformist zeal. There were several social reform programmes to eradicate the practices of Sati and the Thagi -widely prevalent during this period.

In the early 19th Century, the questions related to the social problems of *sati*, remarriage of widows, spread of modern education, evils of child marriage and of untouchability were raised by social reformers.

In the 19th century, there were four major reform movements:

- Brahmosamaj–led by Raja Rammohan Roy,
- Aryasamaj–led by Swami Dayanand Sarawati,
- Prarthana Samaj–led by Mahadeva Govind Ranade,
- Ramakrishna Mission–inspired by Ramkrishna Paramhansa and led by Swami Vivekanand.

These reform movements opposed the practice of untouchability, *Sati*, infanticide and propagated in favour of the remarriage of widows and the modern education. Due to the tireless efforts of Raja Rammohan Roy, the practice of *Sati* was legally abolished in 1829. The *Arya Samaj* contributed significantly in weakening the caste-rigidity and reducing the practice of untouchability in the Punjab, Haryana and the Western Uttar Pradesh. The activities of the *Prarthana Samaj* were mainly confined to the Bombay Presidency. The Ram Krishna Mission contributed significantly in the field of educations and health services.

Contemporary Phase

In contemporary India, there are several social problems. Though, they are called as social problems, yet, in some problems socio-cultural overtones are more prominent, whereas, in some others, the economic and legal overtones are conspicuous. Thus, the contemporary social problems may be classified in the following categories:

i) Socio-cultural problems: communalism, untouchability, population explosion, child-abuse, problems of the scheduled castes, the scheduled tribes, the backward classes, women, alcoholism and drug addiction,
ii) Economic problems: poverty, unemployment, black money;
iii) Legal problems: crime, delinquency, violence, terrorism.

Social and political movements were launched in the contemporary period against communalism, untouchability, illiteracy, alcoholism and drug addiction. Gandhi–as the leader of the national movement after 1919, devoted a considerable part of his action-programme for the uplift of *Harijans*, *Adivasis* and Women. He tried to reorganise education and village industries. He fought relentlessly against communalism, untouchability and alcoholism. In the contemporary period, there are organised movements of women, Scheduled Castes, Scheduled Tribes, backwards castes and labour to protect their interests.

DISADVANTAGED IN INDIA

The term **'disadvantaged'** can be defined as a general condition of being denied certain basic facilities that are otherwise available to most other members. The denial of these facilities can cause problems and create barriers/difficulties for those men/women in achieving success in their life. There are different kinds of disadvantages such as physical, social, familial, emotional, cognitive, linguistic, environmental, economic and sex.

As Oliver Wendell Holmes said, "There is no greater inequality than the equal treatment of unequals." Here, arises the need for such positive discrimination which would make humanity more humane and progressive.

Aristotle in his *Nichomchean Ethics* wrote, justice is equality, as all men believe it to be quite apart from any argument. Indeed, in Greek, the word equality means justice. To be just is to be equal and to be unjust is to be unequal.

According to Aristotle, equality means that things that are alike should be treated alike and things that are unalike should be treated unalike. Injustice arises when equals are treated unequally and also when unequals are treated equally.

There is a need to look inward, within the country to identify groups that fare poorly in human development as against spatially in terms of how districts fare or sector fare. Deprivation in India has an obvious face of exclusion, the Schedule Castes due to social exclusion, and the Schedule Tribes due to geographical and cultural exclusion. The Schedule Castes suffer from deprivation on account of the residual power of a discriminatory caste system, which though made illegal, continues to sway as a social force, whereas the Scheduled Tribes see their predicament as victims of the state, which denies them property rights to their habitat. A Scheduled Caste and Scheduled Tribe development index needs to be developed by professionals to capture their deprivations, so as to goad the state policy to address them. A broad attainment index, does not effectively address the roots of these very important deprivations in the Indian context. The process of democracy is at work drawing these people in the mainstream and seeking to address their specific concerns. How well this is being done needs to be assessed through the development of Scheduled Caste-/Schedule Tribe development index.

AMBEDKAR - UPLIFTMENT OF THE DISADVANTAGED

Bhimrao Ramji Ambedkar was born on 14 April, 1891 in Mahar caste. The Mahar caste was one of the 'untouchable' castes. This created many difficulties in Ambedkar's higher education. With the help of a scholarship from Sayajirao Gaekwad, Maharaja of Baroda, he attended Columbia University, USA, and later on with hard work managed to study at the London School of Economics. In England he attained a doctorate and also became a barrister. On returning to India he virtually dedicated himself to the task of upliftment of the untouchable community. Soon he won the confidence of the- untouchables and became their supreme leader. To mobilise his followers he established organisations such as the Bahishkrit Hitkarni Sabha, Independent Labour Party and later All India Scheduled Caste Federation. He led a number of temple-entry Satyagrahas, organized the untouchables, established many educational institutions and propagated his views from newspapers like the 'Mooknayak', 'Bahishkrit Bharat' and 'Janata'. He participated in the Round Table Conference in order to protect the interests of the untouchables. He became the Chairman of the Drafting Committee of the Constituent Assembly and played a very important role in framing The Indian Constitution. He was also the Law Minister of India up to 1951. Right from 1935 Ambedkar was thinking of renouncing Hinduism. Finally, in 1956 he adopted Buddhism and appealed to his followers to do the same. He felt that the removal of untouchability and the spiritual upliftment of the untouchables would not be possible by remaining a Hindu. Hence, he embraced Buddhism.

Ambedkar was not only a political leader and social reformer but also a scholar and thinker. He has written extensively on various social and political matters. 'Annihilation of Castes', 'Who Were the Shudras', 'The Untouchables', 'Buddha and His Dharma' are his more important writings. Besides these, he had also published many other books and booklets propagating his views. His thinking was based on a deep faith in the goals of equity and liberty. Liberalism and the philosophy of John Dewey also influenced his thinking. Jotirao Phule and Buddha have exercised a deep influence on Ambedkar's ideas on society, religion and morality. His political views were also influenced by his legal approach. Ambedkar's personal suffering, his scholarship and his constant attention to the problem of bringing about equality for the downtrodden untouchable community forms the basis of his thinking and writings.

AMBEDKAR'S VIEWS ON EDUCATION

Ambedkar believed that education would greatly contribute to the improvement of the untouchables. He always exhorted his followers to reach excellence in the field of knowledge. Knowledge is a liberating force. Education makes man enlightened, makes him aware of this self-respect and also helps him to lead a better life materially. One of the causes of the degradation of the untouchables was that they were denied the right to education. Ambedkar criticized the British policy on education for not adequately encouraging education among the lower castes. He felt that even under the British rule education continued mainly to be an upper caste monopoly. Therefore, he mobilized the lower castes and the untouchables and funded various centres of learning. While a labour member in the executive council of the Governor-general, he was instrumental in extending scholarships for education abroad to the untouchable students. Ambedkar wanted the untouchables to undergo both liberal education and technical education. He was particularly opposed to education under religious auspices. He warned that only secular education could instill the values of liberty and equality among the students.

EDUCATION FOR ALL

All over the world educationists are grappled with one central and all-encompassing question; what kind of education is needed for what kind of society of tomorrow? They are conscious of the new role of education and the new demands made on educational systems in a world of accelerating economic, environmental and social change and tension (Kireet Joshi, 2000a; Marmar Mukhopadhyay, 2005; Arun Kapur, 2007). They have come up with some of the underlying principles which are universal and common to the aims of educators, citizens, policy-makers, and other partners and participants in the process of education at all levels.

According to them education, formal and non-formal, must serve society as an instrument for fostering the creation of good citizens. All approaches to redesign the educational processes must take into account the basic and agreed-upon values and concerns of the international community and of the United Nations system such as human rights, tolerance, and understanding, democracy, responsibility, universality, cultural identity, the search for peace, the preservation of the environment and the sharing of knowledge.

It is universally acknowledged fact that an educated and enlightened citizenry is an essential condition for the successful functioning of a democracy. Education, at least up to the elementary level, is considered essential for every individual in a democratic country. Primary education provides the necessary foundation for strengthening human resources because the quality and efficacy of human resources assume special significance for our personal, social and national development. The entire edifice of our national development is based on the availability and quality of primary education.

At the time of independence, India inherited an educated system which was not only quantitatively small but was characterized by striking regional and structural imbalances. Education was not accessible to all and some regions were more developed than the others as far as education was concerned. Some sections of the population were socially and educationally backward due to socio-cultural and economic reasons. Girls, children from weaker section of society, SC/ST, backward minorities and disabled children were educationally disadvantaged. Several measures have been taken after independence to provide educational opportunities to all sections of Indian society and to remove disparities. Our Constitution made special provisions to equalise educational opportunities among these groups. National Policy on Education, 1968 and that of 1986 also recommended equal educational opportunities for all children. NPE 1986 provides several guidelines to achieve this.

ECONOMY, POVERTY, EDUCATION

Economically, India remains predominantly an agricultural society. Naturally, there is an excessive dependence of labour force on agriculture. This overdependence of the labour force on the underdeveloped agriculture is the major cause of many of the social problems in India. It directly leads to poverty which is one of the basic causes of many other social problems in India. The malnutrition, ill-health, beggary, prostitution, etc. are rooted in the large-scale poverty in India.

Indian society is characterised by the unequal distribution of wealth. One observes affluence amidst pervasive poverty in both the rural and urban area of India. On account of this disparity, benefits of development and welfare services also accrue unequally to the different sections of the society. The benefits that the poor gain are comparatively low. Consequently, the lot of the poor and the backward sections of the society have not improved as expected. There is a close linkage between economy, poverty and education.

CRIMES AGAINST SC/ST IN INDIA

The crimes against SC/ST are mentioned below:

Every 18 minutes:

A crime is committed against a SC/ST

Every day:

- 3 SC/ST women are raped
- 2 SC/ST are murdered & 2 SC/ST Houses are burnt in India
- 11 SC/ST are beaten

Every week:

- 13 SC/ST are murdered
- 5 SC/ST home or possessions are burnt
- 6 SC/ST are kidnapped or abducted

Social and Economic condition of SC/ST:

- 37 percent of SC/ST living below poverty in India
- More than half (54%) of their children are undernourished in India
- 83 per 1000 live birth children born in SC/ST community are probability of dying before the first birthday
- 45 percent of SC/ST does not know read and write in India
- SC/ST women burden double discrimination (gender and caste) in India
- Only 27 percent of SC/ST women give institutional deliveries in India
- About one third of SC/ST households do not have basic facilities
- Public health workers refused to visit SC/ST homes in 33% of villages
- SC/ST were prevented from entering police station in 27.6% of villages

- SC/ST children had to sit separately while eating in 37.8% of Govt. schools
- SC/ST didn't get mail delivered to their homes in 23.5% of villages
- SC/ST were denied access to water sources in 48.4% of villages because of segregation & untouchabilty practices
- Half of India's SC/ST children are undernourished, 21% are severely underweight & 12% DIE before their 5th birthday
- Literacy rates for SC/ST women are as low as 37.8% In Rural India

Status of Prevention of Atrocities Act:

The conviction rate under SC/ST Prevention of Atrocities Act is 15.71% and pendency is as high as 85.37%.

Source: National Human Rights Commission Report on the Prevention and Atrocities against SC/ ST.

According to National Crime Records Bureau India Report

- Uttar Pradesh reported 20.5% of total crimes against Scheduled Castes (6,144 out of 30,031) and Madhya Pradesh reported 27.1% of total (1,501 out of 5,532) crimes against Scheduled Tribes in the country.
- Rajasthan reported the highest rate of crimes (6.5) against Scheduled Castes as compared to the National average of 2.6. Arunachal Pradesh reported the highest rate of crime against Scheduled Tribes (2.7) as compared to the National average of 0.5.
- The rate of crime against Scheduled Castes increased from 2.4 in 2006 to 2.6 in 2007 while rate of crime against Scheduled Tribes in 2007 remained 0.5 – the same as in 2006.

Through education/awareness only it is possible to minimize crimes against SC/ST in India. Education gives courage and strength to the individual. It gives authority of questioning. It gives discriminative power. All round development takes place only through education in the individuals.

CONCLUSION

India, the biggest democratic system of the world, with a thousand million plus population and a mind-boggling variety, a system which boasts of more than 5000 years of history and continued civilization and a hoary past, has been experimenting with protective discrimination programmes on an unprecedented variety. Reservations in jobs, educational institutions, legislatures and in local self-governing institutions, better known as *Panchayati Raj* institutions for scheduled castes, scheduled tribes, other backward classes and now women has been a grand experiment by any standard. It may also be noted that scheduled castes, scheduled tribes and other backward classes are a whole cluster of thousands of castes spread over the length and breadth of the country. However, it has succeeded to some extent in achieving the target. By providing education for all, it is possible to succeed the target at 2020. Education has a prominent role in the development of society in general and the disadvantaged in particular.

REFERENCES

1. Bharill, Chandra. (1977): *'Social and Political Ideas of B. R. Ambedkar'*, Jaipur.
2. Keer, Dhananjay. (1961): *'Ambedkar - Life and Mission'*, Bombay.
3. Government of India, *Programme of Action* (1992), New Delhi, Department of Education, Ministry of Human Resource Development.
4. Lokhande, G.S., (1977): *'B. R. Ambedkar: A .Study in Social Democracy'*, New Delhi.
5. National Council of Teacher Education, (2003), *Discrimination Based on Sex, Caste, Religion and Disability:* A Handbook for sensitizing Teachers Educators, under Aegis of Human Rights Commission.

24

Educational Access in Urban India

INTRODUCTION

Education is a key factor not only for social development, but also for economic development of any nation in the world. Education in general and quality education in particular has a prominent role to change the lives of the students. Today's children are tomorrow's citizens. The future of the nation depends on the roles of the youth. Many researchers say that there is a positive correlation between e education and economic development. Urbanization is a symbol for economic development. Some of the rural populace of India is moving to towns and cities for happy and wealthy life and some other to get employment.

According to the latest survey by the National Sample Survey Office (NSSO) in June 2008, the literacy rate among the population with age 7 and above was 72 per cent whereas the adult population (age 15 and above) had a literacy rate of 66 per cent. The level is well below the world average literacy rate of 84 per cent and India currently has the largest illiterate population of any nation on earth. According to 2001 census the urban literacy of India was 79.9 per cent (rural literacy was 58.7 per cent). McKinsey Global Institute estimates that India's population will reach 1.47 billion with around 40% urbanization. That means close to 590 million will be living in cities. There are so many problems for urban people in India. The population of India is increasing day by day. What is the status of provision of primary needs of its citizens including Education?

URBANIZATION

Urbanization is an index of transformation from traditional rural economies to modern industrial one. It is progressive concentration (Davis, 1965) of population in urban unit. Quantification of urbanization is very difficult. It is a long term process. Kingsley Davis has explained urbanization as process (Davis, 1962) of switch from spread out pattern of human settlements to one of concentration in urban centers. It is a finite process—a cycle through which a nation pass as they evolve from agrarian to industrial society (Davis and Golden, 1954). He has mentioned three stages in the process of urbanization. Stage one is the initial stage characterized by rural traditional society with predominance in agriculture and dispersed pattern of settlements. Stage two refers to acceleration stage where basic restructuring of the economy and investments in social overhead capitals including transportation, communication take place. Proportion of urban population gradually increases from 25% to 40%, 50%, 60% and so on. Dependence on primary sector gradually dwindles. Third stage is known as terminal stage where urban population exceeds 70% or more. At this stage level of urbanization (Davis, 1965) remains more or less same or constant. Rate of growth of urban population and total population becomes same at this terminal stage.

The onset of modern and universal process of urbanization is relatively a recent phenomenon and is closely related with industrial revolution and associated economic development. As industrial revolution started in Western Europe, United Kingdom was the initiator of Industrial Revolution. Historical evidence suggests that urbanization process is inevitable and universal. Currently developed countries are characterized by high level of urbanization and some of them are in final stage of urbanization process and experiencing slowing down of urbanization due to host of factors (Brockerhoff, 1999; Brockerhoff and Brennam 1998)). A majority of the developing countries, on the other hand started experiencing urbanization only since the middle of 20th century.

Indian Census Definition of Urban Area

In Census of India, 2001 two types of town were identified:

a) Statutory towns: All places with a municipality, corporation, Cantonment board or notified town area committee, etc. so declared by state law.

b) Census towns: Places which satisfy following criteria:-

i) A minimum population of 5000;

ii) At least 75% of male working population engaged in non agricultural pursuits; and

iii) A density of population of at least 400 persons per sq km

TABLE-1 URBAN POPULATION

YEAR/SECTOR		POPULATION			DECADAL VARIATION
		Male	Female	Persons	Persons
1951					
	RUAL	153,444,642	145,199,739	298,644,381	-
	URBAN	32,083,820	30,359,889	62,443,709	-
	TOTAL	185,528,462	175,559,628	361,088,090	-
1961					
	RUAL	183,504,095	176,794,073	360,298,168	20.64
	URBAN	42,789,106	36,147,497	78,936,603	26.41
	TOTAL	226,293,201	212,941,570	439,234,771	21.64
1971					
	RUAL	225,319,943	213725732	439,045,675	21.86
	URBAN	58,729,333	50,384,644	109,113,977	38.23
	TOTAL	284,049,276	264,110,376	548,159,652	24.80
1981					
	RUAL	270,910,547	252,956,003	523,866,550	19.32
	URBAN	82,463,913	76,998,634	159,462,547	46.14
	TOTAL	353,374,460	329,954,637	683,329,097	24.66
1991					
	RUAL	324,321,614	304,370,062	628,691,676	20.01
	URBAN	114,908,844	102,702,168	217,611,012	36.47
	TOTAL	439,230,458	407,072,230	846,302,688	23.85
2001					
	RUAL	381,602,674	360,887,965	742,490,639	18.10
	URBAN	150,554,098	135,565,591	286,119,689	31.48
	TOTAL	532,156,772	496,453,556	1,028,610,328	21.54

Source: Census of India

The table-1 shows the full information regarding urban population sex wise from 1951 to 2001.

WHY EDUCATIONAL ACCESS IS IMPORTANT IN INDIA

In 1950 India made a Constitutional commitment to provide free and compulsory education to all children up to the age of 14. In 2002 constitutional amendment made free and compulsory education a fundamental right for children aged 6-14. Yet, universal access to elementary education remains elusive and quality of provision erratic. Provision of quality education in India is an enormous quantitative challenge. In 2004-2005, data available from the Ministry of Human Resource Development (MHRD) showed that 182 million students were enrolled in 1.04 million elementary schools (grades 1-8) across the country (GoI, 2007a). This accounted for approximately 82% of children in the 5-14 year age group in that year (GoI, 2007b).

Over the past two decades demand for schooling in India has increased, but provision is unequal. The National Policy on Education (NPE) (1986) and its Programme of Action (POA) (1992) state that all children, irrespective of caste, creed, location or gender, should have access to elementary education of a comparable quality. But in reality, schooling provision favours those better off, and disadvantaged groups (including poor children, girls, children from Scheduled Caste (SC), Scheduled Tribe (ST), Other Backward Class (OBC) groups) have less access and access to poorer quality education. Large variations in access exist across different states, geographical areas, and social categories such as gender, caste and ethnicity. Policy makers whilst making great strides to improve physical access to schools, have ongoing challenges to provide meaningful access for all children in India.

Indian Policy Context

Education in India is the joint responsibility of the central and state governments, and educational rights to education are provided for within the Constitution. Further commitments to the universalisation of education as well as the legal, administrative and financial frameworks for the government-funded education system are found in two main sources. These are the on-going series of Five Year Plans for National Development and the National Policy on Education (NPE) (1986), with its Programme of Action (1992). Additionally, Sarva Siksha Abhiyan (SSA) is a programme which aims to achieve universal elementary education of satisfactory quality by 2010.

The general pattern of education adopted at the national level, commonly known as the 10+2+3 pattern, envisages a broad-based general education for all pupils during the first ten years of schooling. The elementary education which has now been made free and compulsory for the children of 6-14 years age group includes primary (I-V) and upper-primary/middle (VI-VIII) stages. Most states conduct examinations after class VIII for entry to secondary school. A policy of automatic promotion has been introduced at the elementary stages to encourage children to continue their education to at least Grade 8, whilst minimizing repetition and dropout.

As a result of the NPE policy initiatives changes are being made on the ground. A massive infrastructure development and teacher recruitment drive was initiated nationally. NPE (1986) focused on the need for improvements to school environments (including building conditions, availability of tap water and toilet facilities), instructional material and teacher training. The District Primary Education Programme (1994) brought additional resources to the sector through the involvement of bilateral and multilateral donors. Village education committees, parent-teacher and mother-teacher associations have become active across the country. Legislative moves to bring elementary education under Panchayati Raj Institutions (local self-governments) have given further impetus to community mobilization at the grassroots level. Despite these changes, quality of provision continues to be a concern and is highlighted in the Tenth (2002-2007) and Eleventh (2007-2012) Five Year Plans, as well as SSA.

Various government schemes target disadvantaged children. The Alternative, Innovative and Education Guarantee Scheme (EGS/AIE) provides education in smaller, isolated habitations in rural areas and / or urban slums that do not qualify as regular formal schools; and schooling to difficult-to-reach groups such as working and migrating children. The National Programme for Education of Girls at Elementary Level (NPEGEL) and Kasturba Gandhi Balika Vidyalaya (KGBV) target girls often from scheduled castes, scheduled tribes and minorities in difficult areas. Through these programmes scholarships, free uniforms and textbooks are being given to recipients. The Midday-meal Scheme offers free lunch to all children attending primary schools and EGS/AS throughout India. Anganwaris provides nutritional support and pre-school education to children aged 0-6 years and early childhood care and education (ECCE) centres are operational in some selected areas. These initiatives have had considerable impact on children's access to education.

Patterns of educational access in India

Access to basic education in India is improving, but areas of concern remain:

School supply: The number of primary schools has grown rapidly from 529,000 in 1986 to

767,000 in 2005 and at upper primary from 134,000 to 275,000.

In 2003 around 87% of habitations had a primary school within a distance of 1 km and 78% of habitations had an upper primary school within 3 km (NCERT, 2005).

In addition, the number of private pre-primary, primary and upper primary schools has also increased considerably. However, government and local bodies continue to be the main providers managing around 91% of primary and 73% of upper primary schools. Many new schools particularly those opened under the EGS/AIE scheme are small in size. Most are located in rural areas. Around 28% of children are educated in primary schools with 50 students or fewer (DISE 2005-6). Questions of quality of provision persist with many schools having weak infrastructure and poor teaching and learning conditions.

EDUCATIONAL ACCESS IN URBAN INDIA

The essence of human resource development is that education must play a significant and interventionist role in remedying imbalances in the socio-economic fabric of the country. Basic education has also greatly contributed to the quality of human life, particularly with regard to life expectancy, infant mortality, learning levels and nutritional status of children, etc. Several new initiatives have been taken by the Government placing emphasis on decentralization with the participation of people at the grass root level. Consequently, universal basic education has vastly contributed to social justice and equity, and participative economic growth. Education for all programme, makes an effort to universalize elementary education by community ownership of the school system. It is a response to the demand for quality basic education all over the country and seeks to ensure access, retention and quality improvement. It reiterates the need to focus on girls' education to equalize educational opportunities and eliminate gender disparities.

The international movement towards Education for All (EFA) encompasses six goals of early childhood care and education, universal elementary education, adult literacy, adolescent and life skill education, gender equality and all aspects of quality education. These goals are designed to enable children and young adults to realize their right to learn. The Government of India is committed to the Education for All (EFA) goals, which encompass early childhood care and education, primary education, girls' education, as also adult education. Government of India implements a number of programmes for the achievement of the EFA goals, including, inter alia, Sarva Shiksha Abhiyan (SSA), Mid Day Meal Scheme (MDM) and National Literacy Mission (NLM). Sarva Shiksha Abhiyan (SSA), which is a major flagship programme of the Government, addresses the national resolve of universalizing elementary education. Under SSA, special focus is on girls, children belonging to SC/ST communities, other weaker sections, minorities and urban deprived children.

TABLE-2 URBAN LITERACY RATE

YEAR	MALE	FEMALE	PERSONS
1991 (7 YEARS AND ABOVE)			
RURAL	57.87	30.62	44.69
URBAN	81.09	64.05	73.08
TOTAL	64.13	39.29	52.21
2001 (7 YEARS AND ABOVE)			
RURAL	70.70	46.13	58.74
URBAN	86.27	72.86	79.92
TOTAL	75.26	53.67	64.84

Source: Census of India

From the table-2 we conclude that the literacy rate of urban India is better than rural India. Urban literacy rate of India is low when compared to other developed countries in the world. It is the duty of government and NGOs to take good steps to increase urban literacy rate of India.

Urban Poverty and Education

India Urban Poverty Report-2009 using human development framework provides a good insight on various issues of urban poverty such as basic services to urban poor, migration, urban economy and livelihoods, micro finance for urban poor, education and health, unorganized sector and livelihoods.

- Quality of employment, productivity and returns on education are likely to be better in large cities than small towns.
- Education infrastructure is poorer in cities with larger population base and higher urbanization, thus increasing the possibility of marginalizing children of urban poor from education.
- There is a big difference between the proportion of children accessing education in million plus cities compared to smaller cities. The two critical problems pointing out by the author in this field are access and the quality of education. Quality defines in terms of poor

teaching standard and facilities, teacher absenteeism, insensitive curriculum and content, poor motivation of teachers. This is compounded with lack of physical access and infrastructure.

- The analysis also shows that smaller million-plus cities have more schools per capita population when compared to four mega polis. Contrary to health services, education infrastructure is poorer in cities with larger population and there is a huge gap in achieving universal access to education in all cities, impacting the disadvantaged children the most and million plus cities, which are hub of economic activities, need to improve access of girl children to education. The proportion of children from marginalised communities in mega cities is very low compared to smaller towns.
- There is still a huge gap in achieving universal access to education in all cities, impacting the disadvantaged children the most.
- Million plus cities, which are hub of economic activities, need to improve access of girl children to education.
- Effective monitoring and surveillance system for improving the student-to-classroom and student-to-teacher ratio in the cities.
- Vigorous community mobilization campaigns need to be initiated in urban slums urging the poor households to send their children to schools.
- Innovative approaches to increase school enrollment at primary level and retention rate in schools, particularly for girls
- Convergence of health and education with other basic services for achieving synergy.

Main Features of Right to Education 2010 Act

- The salient features of the Right of Children for Free and Compulsory Education act are -
- Free and compulsory education to all children of India in the six to 14 age group;
- No child shall be held back, expelled, or required to pass a board examination until completion of elementary education;
- A child above six years of age has not been admitted in any school or though admitted, could not complete his or her elementary education, then, he or she shall be admitted in a class appropriate to his or her age; Provided that where a child is directly admitted in a class appropriate to his or her age, then, he or she shall, in order to be at par with others, have a right to receive special training, in such manner, and within such time limits, as may be prescribed: Provided further that a child so admitted to elementary education

shall be entitled to free education till completion of elementary education even after fourteen years.

- Proof of age for admission: For the purposes of admission to elementary education. The age of a child shall be determined on the basis of the birth certificate issued in accordance with the provisions of the Births. Deaths and Marriages Registration Act, 1856 or on the basis of such other document, as may be prescribed. No child shall be denied admission in a school for lack of age proof
- A child who completes elementary education shall be awarded a certificate;
- Calls for a fixed student-teacher ratio;
- Will apply to all of India except Jammu and Kashmir;
- Provides for 25 percent reservation for economically disadvantaged communities in admission to Class One in all private schools;
- Mandates improvement in quality of education;
- School teachers will need adequate professional degree within five years or else will lose job;
- School infrastructure (where there is problem) to be improved in three years, else recognition cancelled;
- Financial burden will be shared between state and central government

CONCLUSIONS

Educational access in urban India is better than rural India. At the same time it is not so better than neighboring countries like China and Sri Lanka and other developed countries in the world. The poverty rate of urban India is increasing gradually when compared to rural India. Poverty is the main cause for low access of Education. It is the fore most duty of governments (State and Central) to take necessary actions towards quality and quantity education. Without education the development of any nation can't take place. Education is the base for all types of development in the world.

REFERENCES

1. Geetha Gandhi Kingdom, 2007; "*The Progress of School Education in India*", Report of Global Poverty Research Group, Oxford.
2. Government of India, 2001; "*Census of India-2001*", New Delhi.
3. Government of India, 2007; "*Time Series Data*", New Delhi.
4. Government of India, 2009; "*Urban Poverty Report-2009*", New Delhi.
5. Report of Crete, 2009; "*Educational Access in India*".
6. Reports of Ministry of Human Resource Development, Government of India, New Delhi.
7. Reports of NCERT, New Delhi.

25

Economics of Education at School Level

INTRODUCTION

We are living in the highly modernized society. With the help of science and technology we are enjoying each and every moment with great pleasure. We are seeing day and night one after another. In the same manner problems and solutions are always move towards side by side. But to find a solution we want some exercise. Nothing will happen if any one sits like a stone. The development of any nation depends mainly on its human resources and education including technology. The standards of any nation depends mainly on its' educational institutions. It is more important to give priority for economics of education at school level. Economic stability is important for national development.

The word "economics" is derived from 'oikonomikos', which means skilled in household management. Although the word is very old, the discipline of economics as we understand it today is a relatively recent development. Modern economic thought emerged in the 17th and 18th centuries as the western world began its transformation from an agrarian to an industrial society.

Another, slightly different, definition of economics, favored by many economists, is this: Economics is the study of how our scarce productive resources are used to satisfy human wants. This definition emphasizes two central points. First, productive resources are scarce, in the sense that we are not able to produce all of everything that everyone wants free; thus, we must "economize" our resources, or use them as efficiently as possible.

Second, human wants, if not infinite, go so far beyond the ability of our productive resources to satisfy them all that we face a major problem in "economizing" those productive resources so as to satisfy the largest possible number of our wants. Indeed, most major economic problems arise from this fact of scarcity, and the need to make effective use of our resources to satisfy our wants. If there were plenty of everything for everyone to have without working or paying for it, there would be no economic problem. In the recent years we are facing problem of economic crisis by some of the unethical officials.

NEED OF THE STUDY

Understanding economics is essential to becoming an involved and productive citizen that makes wise financial choices. Getting informed about supply, demand and real cost makes us all better consumers.

Economics is the social science that studies the methods by which individuals and societies organize production activities and allocate scarce resources to meet material wants and needs. Economics is a logical way of thinking about economic matters rather than a set of answers. An important part of economics is the analysis of the interaction of economic policy and economic activity with the objective of selecting policies which will encourage the desired outcome.

The study of Economics helps to prepare students to make rational economic choices both in their own lives and in their participation in policy decisions as citizens of a city, state, nation, and the world. The study of Economics provides students with analytical tools for interpreting economic events and making personal economic choices, even under changed conditions.

Economics is the study of how the goods and services we want get produced, and how they are distributed among us. This part we call economic analysis. Economics is also the study of how we can make the system of production and distribution work better. This part we call economic policy. Economic analysis is the necessary foundation for sound economic policy.

OBJECTIVES

The study is designed with the following specific objectives:

- To study the attitude of IX class students towards economics.
- To know the methods of teaching in economics.
- To know the status of learning through activities.
- To know the importance of field work in economics.

- To study the status of usage of economics in daily life.
- To find how many students are encouraged by their parents to study economics.
- To find the rate of students to study economics at higher level.

METHODOLOGY

Tools for the data collection:

The investigator searched for the tools for economics of education. The investigator has not found suitable tool for economics of education. Hence, the investigator planned to develop a tool for economics of education.

On the basis of review of literature, a list of 33 items on economics of education was prepared. These items were given to some experts. The experts had checked the suitability and vocabulary used in the items. 8 items were deleted on the advice of the experts and 25 items retained were suitable to measure the attitude of IX class students towards economics of education. Each item of the inventory was arranged on a 5 point scale with responses: Strongly Agree (SA), Agree (A), Doubtful (D), Disagree (DA) and Strongly Disagree (SDA). A personal data sheet was prepared to collect personal information of the IX class students.

Locale, Sample, Data Collection and Analysis

The data was collected from IX class students in both rural and urban areas of Chittoor District (Z.P.H.School, 49. Kothepalle Mitta-Rural and S.V.Campus School, Tirupati-Urban). The total number of sample was 120. The data thus collected was pooled and analyzed keeping in view of the objectives of the study.

FINDINGS OF THE STUDY

1. Characteristics of the sample

To understand the characteristics of the sample, the sample were classified into different groups based on their characteristics and percentage were calculated for each group. The classified information is presented in the table-1.

The characteristics of the sample reveal that the data were collected from 50 per cent of boys and girls in both rural and urban areas of Chittoor District. The total number of the sample was 120. 82.5 per cent of students are belongs to the age 14 years; 12.5 and 3.33 per cent of students are belongs to < 13 years and > 15 years age group respectively. Among the sample 20 per cent are belongs to OC community; 52.41 per cent are BC community students and remaining 25.83 per cent are SC/ST students. In the case of religion 80.00 per cent students belongs to Hindu; 5.83 per cent are belongs to Muslim and 14.16 per cent are belongs to Christian. The occupation of father and mother; educational qualifications of father, mother and teacher and annual income of the family were given in the table-1.

Table-1 Characteristics of the Sample

S. No.	Variable	Group	N	%
1	Sex	Boys	60	50.00
		Girls	60	50.00
2	Age	<13 years	17	12.50
		14 years	99	82.50
		> 15 years	4	03.33
3	Locality	Rural	60	50.00
		Urban	60	50.00
4	Caste	OC	24	20.00
		BC	65	52.41
		SC/ST	31	25.83
5	Religion	Hindu	96	80.00
		Muslim	7	05.83
		Christian	17	14.16
6	Occupation of father	Govt. employee	21	17.5
		Private employee	32	26.66
		Agriculture	50	41.66
		Business	10	08.33
		Part time/Others	7	05.83
7	Occupation of mother	Govt. employee	12	10.00
		Private employee	23	19.16
		Agriculture	37	30.83
		Business	14	11.66
		Part time/Others	10	08.33
		House wife	24	20.00
8	Educational Qualification of father	Illiterate	9	07.50
		I-X	38	31.66
		XI- Degree	40	33.33
		P.G. and above	33	27.50
9	Educational Qualification of mother	Illiterate	15	12.50

		I-X	69	57.50
		XI- Degree	23	19.16
		P.G. and above	13	10.83
10	Educational Qualification of economics teacher	B.A. with B.Ed.	71	59.16
		M.A.	37	30.83
		M. Phil. /Ph.D.	12	10.00
11	Annual Income of the family	Up to Rs. 50,000/-	4	03.33
		Rs. 50,001/- to 1,00,000/-	32	26.66
		Rs. 1,00,001/-to 2,00,000/-	69	57.50
		Above Rs. 2,00,000/-	15	12.50

2. Attitude of IX Class Students towards Economics of Education.

Table-2 Attitude of IX Class Students towards Economics of Education

S.No.	Statement	Strongly Agree (SA) % (N)	Agree (A) % (N)	Doubtful (D) % (N)	Disagree (DA) % (N)	Strongly Disagree (SDA) % (N)
1	I like economics very much.	3.33 **(4)**	56.66 **(68)**		38.33 **(46)**	1.66 **(2)**
2	The way of economics teaching of my teacher is excellent.	3.33 **(4)**	55.83 **(67)**		35.00 **(42)**	05.83 **(7)**
3	Activity based learning of economics is available in our school.	10.00 **(12)**	23.33 **(28)**		58.33 **(70)**	08.33 **(10)**
4	I am learning Economics through society.	20.83 **(25)**	31.66 **(38)**		37.50 **(45)**	10.00 **(12)**
5	I like to read economic matters in the news paper.	18.33 **(22)**	05.83 **(7)**		55.83 **(67)**	20.00 **(24)**

6	It is important to know about Indian economy and economists.	20.83 **(25)**	60.00 **(72)**	09.16 **(11)**	10.00 **(12)**
7	Economics is important for everybody in the society.	90.83 **(109)**	01.66 **(2)**	01.66 **(2)**	05.83 **(7)**
8	Economics is useless subject.				100 **(120)**
9	I learned saving method through economics.	46.66 **(56)**	07.50 **(9)**	26.66 **(32)**	19.16 **(23)**
10	It is important to give more value for economics than any other subjects.	03.33 **(4)**	01.66 **(2)**	85.00 **(102)**	10.00 **(12)**
11	I feel some times economics is difficult.	19.16 **(23)**	05.83 **(7)**	56.66 **(68)**	18.33 **(22)**
12	I like to study economics at higher level.	03.33 **(4)**	05.00 **(6)**	35.00 **(42)**	56.66 **(68)**
13	I don't watch TV programmes related to economics.	35.00 **(42)**	30.00 **(36)**	13.33 **(16)**	21.66 **(26)**
14	The impact of economics is much on national development.	68.33 **(82)**	24.16 **(29)**	01.66 **(2)**	05.83 **(7)**
15	Our parent encourages studying economics well.	30.83 **(37)**	35 **(42)**	11.66 **(14)**	22.50 **(27)**
16	I don't like field works in economics.	01.66 **(2)**	05.83 **(7)**	23.33 **(28)**	69.16 **(83)**
17	I like lecture cum demonstration method in economics teaching.	85.00 **(102)**	11.66 **(14)**	0.83 **(1)**	02.5 **(3)**

18	I read economics well.	60.00 **(72)**	06.66 **(8)**	10.83 **(13)**	22.50 **(27)**
19	Economics is an important subject for all students.	60.00 **(72)**	10.83 **(13)**	10.00 **(12)**	19.16 **(23)**
20	I am frequently discussing economics with my friends.	18.33 **(22**	25.83 **(31)**	25.00 **(30)**	30.83 **(37)**
21	I have much interest to learn economics effectively.	05.00 **(6)**	01.66 **(2)**	45.00 **(54)**	48.33 **(58)**
22	The economics syllabus was not good.	17.50 **(21)**	05.00 **(7)**	37.50 **(45)**	39.16 **(47)**
23	I use economics in my daily life.	89.16 **107)**	04.16 **(5)**	04.16 **(5)**	02.50 **(3)**
24	I give priority for marks than subject knowledge of economics.	44.16 **(53)**	14.16 **(17)**	12.50 **(15)**	29.16 **(35)**
25	The encouragement of teacher is not good in the process of learning economics.	27.50 **(33)**	10.00 **(12)**	32.50 **(39)**	30.00 **(36)**

MAJOR FINDINGS OF THE STUDY

The following results were found in the present study:

1. Attitude of IX class students towards economics of education.

Overall 60 per cent of IX class students were liked economics very much. Among the 60 per cent, 3.33 per cent of students were strongly agreed and 56.66 per cent of students were agreed the statement-1. 40 per cent of students were disliked economics. Among the 40 per cent 1.66 per cent were strongly disagreed the statement-1 and 38.33 per cent were disagreed the statement-1.

2. Method of Teaching in economics

59.16 per cent of IX class students were liked their teachers' way of economics teaching. Among 59.16 per cent only 3.33 per cent of students were strongly agreed the statement-2 and remaining 55.83 per cent were agreed the statement-2. 40.83 (35.00 per cent- DA, 5.83 per cent-SDA) per cent of students were not liked their teachers' way of economics teaching.

96.66 per cent of students were liked 'Lecturer cum demonstration method' (85.00 per cent and 11.66 per cent of IX class students are strongly agree and agree the statement-17).

3. Learning economics effectively.

Only 6.66 per cent of IX class students were ready to learn economics effectively. Among this 5.00 per cent students were strongly agreed and 1.66 per cent students were agreed the statement-21. 93.33 (45.00 per cent of students –DA, 48.33 per cent of students-SDA) per cent of students were just learning the economics.

76.66 per cent of IX class students were believed that the economics syllabus was good and only 23.33 per cent of students were didn't liked the economics syllabus.

4. Importance of field work in economics.

92.49 per cent of IX class students were liked the field work in economics and only 7.51 per cent of students were disliked the field work in economics.

5. Practice of economics in daily life.

93.32 per cent of students are practicing economics in their daily life. 89.16 per cent and 4.16 per cent of IX class students are strongly agree and agree the statement-23 respectively. 92.49 per cent of students are feeling that economics is important for everybody in the society and only 7.51 are not agreeing the statement-7 (1.66 per cent of students-DA, 5.83 per cent of students-SDA).

6. Encouragement of students to study economics.

65.83 per cent of students are getting encouragement of parents to study economics. Among 65.83 per cent of students 30.83 per cent and 35 per cent of students are strongly agree and agree the statement-15. 34.16 per cent of IX class students were not agreed the statement-15 (11.66 per cent of students were disagreed and 22.50 per cent of students were strongly disagreed the statement-15).

37.50 per cent of IX class students were believed that the teacher encouragement was not good in the process of learning economics. 62.50 per cent of students were believed that the teacher encouragement was good in the process of learning economics.

7. Willing of study of economics at higher level.

Only 8.33 (3.33 per cent-SA, 5.00 per cent A) per cent of IX class students were willing to study economics at higher level and remaining 91.66 (35.00 per cent DS, 56.66 per cent-SDA) per cent were not willing to studying economics at higher level. But 70.83 per cent of student were feeling that economics is important for all students and only 29.17 per cent of students were not agreed the statement-19.

8. Learning of economics through society

52.49 per cent of IX class students are learning economics through society and the remaining 47.51 per cent of IX students are not agreed the statement-4. It shows that 47.51 per cent of IX class students are unable to learn economics through society.

9. Watching and reading of economic matters

24.36 per cent of IX class student are reading economics matters in the news paper and the remaining 75.64 per cent of IX class students are not concentrating economics matters in the news papers.

65.00 per cent of IX class students are watching economics programmes on TV. Only 35.00 per of students are unable to view economics programmes on TV.

10. Useful subject

All the students of IX class believe that the economics is useful subject. 66.66 per cent of IX class students are reading economics well. 80.83 per cent of students are like to know about Indian economists. 92.49 per cent of students are feeling that the impact of economics is much on national development.

SUGGESTIONS

With the help of the study some suggestions were given below:

- It is necessary to arrange lectures of eminent personnel of economics to motivate the students towards economics reading and loving.
- Celebrations of birthdays of great economists are important.
- Encourage the students to participate in the field works of economics regularly and also it is the duty of teacher to conduct the field work at least once in a month.
- Encourage the students to read news papers daily and focus on economic issues. Encourage the students to watch budget live programmes of Assembly and Parliament.

- Explain the students about the job opportunities by studying economics.
- Explain the students about the importance of economics in daily life.
- Explain the students about the sources of economics at higher level.
- It is the duty of parents to encourage the students to study higher studies in economics.

Effective curriculum is important to reach our goal in economics. The below given frame work for teaching the basic concepts of economics is very useful for students. Keep these concepts in mind while preparation of text books for school students.

Framework for Teaching the Basic Concepts of Economics:

Fundamental Economic Concepts

1. Scarcity
2. Opportunity Cost and Trade-offs
3. Productivity
4. Economic Systems
5. Economic Institutions and Incentives
6. Exchange, Money, and Interdependence

Microeconomic Concepts

7. Markets and Prices
8. Supply and Demand
9. Competition and Market structure
10. Income Distribution
11. Market Failures
12. The Role of Government

Macroeconomic Concepts

13. Gross National Product
14. Aggregate Supply
15. Aggregate Demand
16. Unemployment
17. Inflation and Deflation
18. Monetary Policy
19. Fiscal Policy

International Economic Concepts

20. Absolute and Comparative Advantage to Barriers to Trade

21. Exchange and Rates and the Balance of Payments
22. International Aspects of Growth and Stability

Measurements Concepts and Methods Students Should Know

Tables
Charts and Graphs
Ratios and Percentages
Percentage Changes
Index Numbers
Real vs. Nominal Values
Averages and Distributions around the Average

CONCLUSION

The development of any nation depends mainly on its' standards of educational institutions. The present study has given a lot of information about IX class students towards economics of education. The students like economics much. At the same time they are not willing to study economics at higher level. The attitude of parents of students is also different. They are encouraging their students to study engineering and medicine. Majority of schools are giving coaching for EAMCET, IIT and other competitive exams from VIII class onwards. They are giving much priority for science and mathematics. The students are also attracted towards science subject compared to arts, especially economics. The students are studying economics to get marks only. They don't know about the job opportunities for economics students. It is the duty of parents and teachers to motivate the students towards economics. It is important to remember that our honorable Prime Minister, Sri Manmohan Sing, Sri Pranam Mukharjee, Sri Chidambaram, Sri MS Ahluvalia, Sri YV Reddy and C. Rangarajan are best economists of India. They are role models for students who like and love economics. It is important to change the attitude of students and parents towards economics.

26

Environmental Awareness Through Education

INTRODUCTION

Man is living in the highly modernized and technological world. Environment does not belong to man, man belongs to environment. Environment means surroundings. It is a system in which various living beings like man, animals, birds, insects, microorganisms like algae, fungi, protozoa and nonliving beings like the soil, the water, the air are interrelated, interconnected and interdependent in a life sustaining system. Man is one among the many species competing with all others for survival. In the name of progress, the human race has changed from being hunter-gatherer to a self-centered modern man, a destroyer of nature, has become synonymous with environmental degradation and progress with pollution.

Environmental Pollution and the resulting global warming is one of the most challenging problems posing a threat to the very survival of mankind. Despite global and national policies and efforts of governmental and non-governmental organizations striving to mitigate or overcome this problem, pollution free environment is an unrealized dream.

The Rio Declaration on Environment and Development states; "Human beings are at the centre of concerns for sustainable development and that they are entitled to a healthy and productive life, in harmony with nature. There is an urgent need to address the cause of ill health, including environmental causes and their impact on development".

HEALTH EFFECTS OF POLLUTION

By observing the above figure we conclude that each and every part of man would affect the impact of pollution. In the words of Dalia Lama "*If we care Nature, it can be rich, bountiful, inexhaustible and sustainable*". Nature is a wonderful book authored by God. She is full of profound meaning which is open to all of us, and which all of us can read, but she is also a dark mine that conceals immense treasures in her depths which we need to explore.

POLICIES TOWARDS ENVIRONMENTAL PROTECTION IN INDIA

Plan and creativity is necessary to do any work. Along with good plan proper implementation is also important. Proper plan and implementation are two faces of a single coin. If both co-exist then only we will reach the goal. The Constitution of India provides in Article 48 A, the provision of Environmental protection and improvement as of a state policy; it declares "*The state shall endeavour to protect and improve the environment and to safeguard the forest and wild life of the country*". Article 51 (A) (G) says that "*every citizen shall have the duty to protect and improve the natural environment including forest, lakes, rivers and wild life and to have compassion for living creatures*".

Important Legislations dealing with Water and Air Pollution Control and Environment Protection:

- National Environment Policy, 2006.
- National Water Policy, 2002.
- National Population Policy, 2000.
- National Agricultural Policy, 2000.
- National Forest Policy, 1998.
- Policy Statement on Abatement of Pollution, 1992.
- National Conservation Strategy and Policy Statement on Environment and Development, 1992.

Environmental Enactments, Rules & Legislative Changes:

- The Air (Prevention and Control of Pollution) Act, 1981.
- The Environment (Protection) Act, 1986.
- The National Environment Appellate Authority Act, 1997.
- The National Environment Tribunal Act, 1995.
- The Public Liability Insurance Act, 1995.
- The Water (Prevention and Control of Pollution) Act, 1974.
- The Water (Prevention and Control of Pollution) Cess Act, 1977.

Rules under the Environmental Protection Act, 1986:

- The Batteries (Management and Handling) Rules, 2001.
- The Bio-Medical Waste (Management and Handling) Rules, 1998.
- The Chemical Accidents (Emergency Planning, Preparedness and Response) Rules, 1996.
- The Hazardous Wastes (Management and Handling) Rules, 1989.
- The Municipal Solid Wastes (Management and Handling) Rules, 2000.
- The Noise Pollution (Regulation and Control) Rules, 2000.
- The Ozone Depleting Substances (Regulation) Rules, 2000.
- The Recycled Plastics Manufacture and Usage Rules, 1999.

Environmental Protection - International Level:

- Kyoto Protocol, 1997.
- Montreal Protocol, 1989.
- United Nations Frame Work Convention on Climate Change (UNFCCC), 1992.

ENVIRONMENTAL AWARENESS

In recent times, industrialization and urbanization have had a strong impact on the environment. Development and pollution have a positive relationship, and may affect the life of human beings, livestock, property, historical buildings, etc. The importance of ancient structures also should be included in environmental awareness program. The architectures, art and crafts, sculpture are also environmental assets. These are left to us by our ancestors, and while using them we have the responsibility to keep them safe for the generations to come. We all know that day by day our environment is getting destructed and we are responsible for this. Environmental awareness has to be created within all people of every level by educating them about how important our environment is and how can we make a good environment to stay in.

The protection and preservation of environment is a pressing issue. Every person, organization and institution has an obligation and duty to protect it. Environmental Education is a process of recognizing values and clarifying concepts in order to develop skills and added tools necessary to understand and appreciate the inter-relationship among man, his culture and his bio-physical surrounding. It creates an overall perspective, which acknowledges the fact that natural environment and man-made environment are interdependent. It should consider the environment in its totality and should be a continuous lifelong process beginning at the pre-school level and continuing through all stages. It should be inter-disciplinary and examine major environmental issues from local, national and international points of view. It should utilize various educational approaches to teach and learn about and from the environment with stress on practical activities and first-hand experience. It is through this process of education that people can be sensitized about the environmental issues.

People should know that 'Man' is one amongst billions of other species in nature rather than thinking that *'nature is only for man and man is the master of nature.'* Man belongs to a global community that includes 1.8 million known living forms and a lot of unknown ones. We must live on earth as a part of it. So we have a great responsibility in protecting other living beings also, as they help in keeping our environment in its glorious form.

Indian thought have always respected and supported different forms of nature in the form of poetry, stories, sayings etc. Tribal people have a deep respect for the nature, they understand about the importance of nature.

India need economic development, but people don't want it at the cost of environment. We don't want progress at the cost of disasters, destruction of natural resources and nature's beauty, loss of mental peace, health hazards. We can get a healthy environment to live in by creating awareness about environment within ourselves and among others.

Take care about the following:

A) AIR & WATER

"Don't breaths air in the developed countries"
"Don't drink water in the underdeveloped countries"

Water is a natural resource which is an essential content in every part of life on the earth. Everything is originated from water and everything is sustained by it. "*Water*" said the eminent Greek Philosopher Pindar "*is the best of all things*". Water is the most precious natural resource for the existence of life on the earth. A United Nations report has ranked India a poor 120th country for water quality among 122 countries, making it the third worst after Belgium. So take care about ponds, rivers and seas.

The major causes of air pollution are deforestation, industrialization and automobiles. Plato wrote about the Greek peninsula 2400 years before, which was once blessed with fertile soil and thick forests of fine trees. "*After the trees were cut to build houses and ships, a heavy rain washes the soil into the sea, leaving only a rocky skeleton of a body washed by disease. Springs and rivers dried up while farming became a farce*".

B) PLANTS:

It is possible for anyone to live without using a single part of living or dead plant directly or indirectly? No, impossible. Charaka is considered to be the father of Ayurvedic medicine. Once his teacher asked to his disciples to bring plants that are of no use in medicine. Some of the students returned with ten some with twenty but Charaka returned bare handed after several weeks. He said "*I could not find a single plant that has no medicinal value. Indeed, every plant is a hidden treasure*".

Everyone should be aware about the need of keeping their surroundings clean. We can prevent our environment from degrading following these steps.

1. Understanding the benefits of plants, growing more plants and creating a green surrounding.
2. Saving water by minimizing unnecessary use of water.
3. Keeping water resources clean. Ponds, river, sea are natural water resources, we should not pollute them.
4. Using less fertilizers and pesticides in crops, so that we can prevent our soil from getting polluted and also we will get healthy food to eat.
5. Separating garbage to degradable and non-degradable before disposal, so that the degradable waste can be used as fertilizers and the non-degradable can be recycled or safely disposed so that they will not pollute water and our surrounding.
6. The harmful chemical gases from industries should be filtered properly before disposing to atmosphere and also the chimney exit should be high.

Some Facts

According to recent survey on environmental pollution some facts are given below.

1. 40 per cent of deaths worldwide are caused by Water, Air and Soil Pollution.
2. Of the world population of about 6.5 billion, 57 per cent is malnourished of pollution.
3. Air pollution kills 3 million people a year.
4. Unsanitary living conditions account for more than 5 million deaths each year, of which more than half are children.
5. Environment pollution is causing a lot of distress not only to humans but also animals, driving many animal species to endangerment and even extinction.

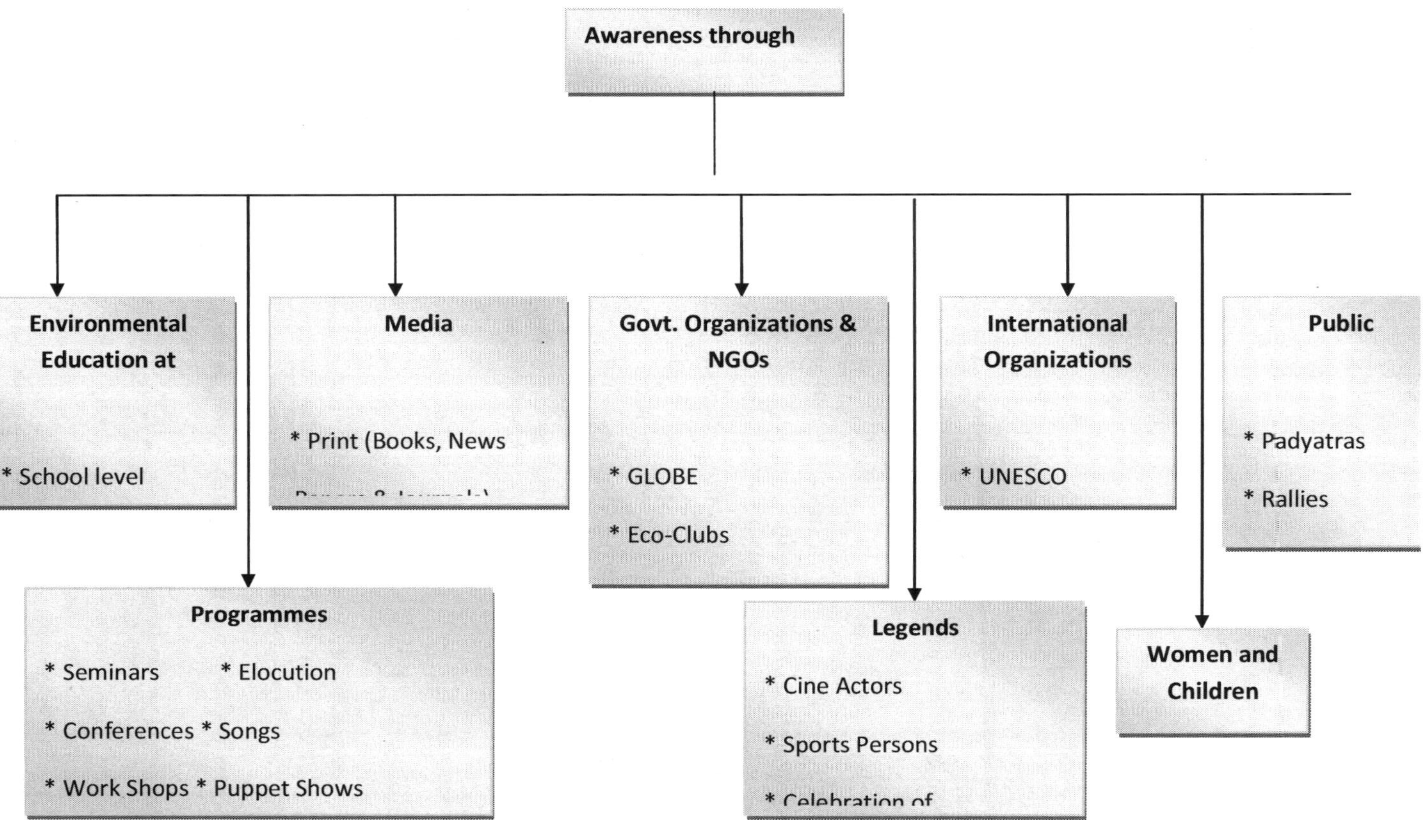
Awareness through
Environmental Education at
* School level
Media
* Print (Books, News
Govt. Organizations & NGOs
* GLOBE
* Eco-Clubs
International Organizations
* UNESCO
Public
* Padyatras
* Rallies
Programmes
* Seminars * Elocution
* Conferences * Songs
* Work Shops * Puppet Shows
Legends
* Cine Actors
* Sports Persons
Women and Children

CONCLUSION:

Earthquakes, Landslides, Floods, Cyclones, Fires, Explosions, War, Riots Epidemics, Accidents, Technological failure etc., that cause sudden damage on a very large scale. The absence of well conceived disaster planning can ruin not only public health but also environmental resources. So proper planning should be done to meet any emergency. It is the moral responsibility of every human being to bequeath a safer heaven to future generations. All nations need to shoulder responsibility on an equal footing to protect the planet earth as it is a global concern.

Awareness and involvement of the civil society is a precondition of checking environmental degradation. This would put pressure on the policy to have fully fledged environmental policy for long run. Although there is no dearth of policies the crux of the problem lies with implementation. Compliance to rules and regulations can be achieved only through strengthening the hands of the implementing agencies and tightening the environmental legislation.

Finally it can be concluded that the environment and national development are the two sides of the same coin and we must achieve economic development without destroying the environment and economic development ultimately culminate the concept of sustainable development. The G-8 Summit that concluded in L'Aquila, Italy, on Thursday, 9th July 2009, issued a declaration in which members described how they intend to address desertification, land degradation and drought. The 134-paragraph declaration, titled, **"Responsible Leadership for a Sustainable Future"**, addresses several issues concerning the world economy, sustainable use of natural resources and development.

References:

1. Chhokar, K.B. (2000). Sharing Concerns in Environmental Education. *University News*, 38 (26): 1-3.
2. *"Comparative Analysis of Environmental Activism through Constitutional Rights, Two Case Studies: India and Hong Kong"* by Sukanya Pani, National Academy of Legal Studies and Research (NALSAR), University of Law, Hyderabad, India, December 2002.
3. Krishnamacharyulu, V. *Environmental Education*, New Delhi, Neelkamal Publishers.
4. Selvam, S.K.P. (2004). Role of Universities in Environmental Protection, *University News*, 42 (46): 184-189.
5. *The Time of India*, Just 8 years to fight global warming, 5th May, 2007.
6. United Nations Convention to Combat Desertification, 12th July, 2009.
7. *University News*, Special Issue on "Environmental Issues & Global Warming", Vol. 45, No.44, Oct 29-Nov 04, 2007.

27

Pioneering Institutions In Adult Education

INTRODUCTION

The contribution of the human factor towards progress both in the urban and rural areas, can't be over emphasized, more so in a world of ever-changing social systems and values. Such an endless task – like the development of educational activities for innumerable farmers and workers, illiterate and semi-illiterate adults, men and women, boys and girls – needs a deep involvement of all national forces, government and non-governmental. From even before 1947, voluntary organisations have been playing a significant role in the reconstruction of education and their success has been in no small measure owing to the dedication of social workers and the larger academic and administrative freedom they enjoy to conduct new experiments.

Voluntary organisations are initiating and developing activities and programmes which can be considered to be of relevance to adult education directly or indirectly. This trend needs to be encouraged and supported. Many of them are closely linking their out-of school activities or programmes of social education with other socio-economic or socio-cultural goals which are part of their objectives.

The contribution of voluntary organisations in general has been encouraging, promising and stimulating. It is fervently hoped, that voluntary organisations, both from their headquarters and in the field will expand their interest for adult and youth education, as well as channelise their efforts to common national goals.

The contribution of the following six voluntary agencies to the development of adult education, non-formal education is briefly described.

1. ALL INDIA COUNCIL FOR MASS EDUCATION AND DEVELOPMENT (AICMED), WEST BENGAL.
2. ANDHRA MAHILA SABHA (AMS), HYDERABAD.
3. INDIAN ADULT EDUCATION ASSOCIATION (IAEA), NEW DELHI.
4. LITERACY HOUSE, LUCKNOW
5. RDT, ANATAPUR.
6. SEVAMANDIR, UDAIPUR.

ALL INDIA COUNCIL FOR MASS EDUCATION AND DEVELOPMENT (AICMED), WEST BENGAL

Introduction

All India Council for Mass Education and Development (AICMED), established in 1987 (Regn. No. S/56626 1987-88) is a voluntary non - profiteering registered organisation. It is also covered by Foreign Contribution Regulation Act (FCRA) of the Government of India (Regn. No. 147120474).

It had its genesis in the formation, in 1965, of the West Bengal Students' Council to Eradicate Illiteracy, which was the culmination of large-scale mobilisation of students and youth from the colleges and universities of Calcutta to the villages of West Bengal to launch a mass literacy campaign. The vision of the organisation is to develop an enlightened, empowered and self-sustained rural community - both materially and morally. The mission of AICMED is 'enlightenment' and 'empowerment', particularly of the poor and the underprivileged, with special emphasis on women and the tribal people.

Aims and Objectives

- To encourage and develop adult education programme as a part of the development programme.
- To encourage and promote voluntary actions in the rural areas in favour of rural development and introduction of advanced technology.
- To organise workshop and prepare teaching and learning materials for various programmes.

- To orient adult education functionaries and development activists of different levels so that they can undertake adult education and developmental programmes independently.
- To undertake research and promotional work to develop and sharpen existing technologies and methodologies of rural development. The structure of the organisation provides opportunities to involve people of different kinds drawn from a wide spectrum of the society.

Activities

In the course of implementing National Adult Education Programme, AICMED has developed people's organisation in 13 of the 17 districts of West Bengal and elsewhere. However, presently it has concentrated activities in several districts of West Bengal, Andhra Pradesh, Jharkhand, Orissa and Tripura in other rural development programmes.

AICMED conducts projects, holds seminars & camps, organises exhibitions, runs awareness and training programmes, and such other activities lead to the empowerment of the poor and the underprivileged of our society.

It has successfully completed, and has been continuing, the projects in the following domains in West Bengal and Tripura.

- **Mass Education Programmes:** Adult Education, women's education, early childhood education and non-formal education.
- **Gender & Health Programmes:** Health & Family Welfare especially mother & child health, Family Planning, awareness and different aspects of women's/men's awareness.
- **Livelihood Generation Programmes:** Training in modern fishery activities, poultry farming, piggery, weaving etc. especially among the rural people.
- **Environment Programme:** Safe drinking water, use of eco-friendly organic fertilizers, smoke-less chulhas etc. among villagers.
- **Herbal Programmes:** Capacity building workshops on Herbotherapy, kitchen-gardening of relevant herbs, cottage-scale preparation of herbal products (like spices, pickles, jam), preservation, containerisation and micro-marketing of the products.
- **Arsenic Programmes:** Mass awareness generation and mitigation of arsenic pollution through community participation in forty villages of two districts of West Bengal. The mitigation devices include Arsenic Removal Plants, Rainwater Harvesting Units and Domestic Filters.
- **Other Programmes:** AICMED, through its central resource centre in Calcutta (which houses a modest library of relevant books,

documents, pamphlets, handbills etc.) continually disseminates useful information among potential users.

ANDHRA MAHILA SABHA (AMS), HYDERABAD

Introduction

Andhra Mahila Sabha, a unique institution dedicated to the upliftment of women, was established by Padma Vibhushan Dr. (Smt) Durgabai Deshmukh in 1948 as a registered society under Indian Societies Act (XXI) of 1860 and a Trust in the same year. With its Central Office located in Hyderabad, Andhra Mahila Sabha has 30 units working under its flag – 9 of them in Chennai and rest in the State of Andhra Pradesh. The institutions run by Andhra Mahila Sabha cater to care of Women, Children, Senior Citizens, Disabled, Health and Education.

Aims and Objectives

Andhra Mahila Sabha is a non-profitable voluntary organisation with the specific objective of promoting education and training of women to overcome their socio-economic and political backwardness and empower them to participate in all aspects of national development. It has also established a regional handicraft training institute for the women. AMS runs a hospital and research centre providing various services including outpatient services in eye care, general surgery, orthopaedics and in patient services including neo-natal unit and well equipped air conditioned operation theatres. It also runs a vocational training and rehabilitation centre, girl's high school and colleges and legal aid centre for women.

Activities

Andhra Mahila Sabha is the premier Women's organization in the country, with around 40 units functioning under its logo. These units focus on education, health care, up-liftment, empowerment, old age care of the downtrodden of the society, in particular women, causes dear to Dr Durgabai Deshmukh's legendary figure of 20th Century. The major services provided by the various institutions established under this organization are:

- Education
- Health
- Rehabilitation
- Training
- Women's issues
- Education Provides training and education to women and children and enable them to harness their services for building the nation.

Dr Durgabai Deshmukh was inspired by the work done by Welthy H Fisher, a Canadian literacy worker at Lucknow, Uttar Pradesh. This led to the establishment of Literacy house at Andhra Mahila Sabha during 1967.

The Programmes/ Courses under Andhra Mahila Sabha Literacy House

- Computer Courses
- Fabric Painting
- Glass Painting
- Embroidery
- Tailoring and Maggam work
- Basic Art designers Drawing Grade I & II
- Pre Primary Teacher Training
- Hand Writing
- Speed Mathematics
- Concentration & Memory
- Personality Development

Andhra Mahila Sabha has publications to its credit. AMS, Chennai releases a bi-monthly newsletter. AMS, Hyderabad releases a quarterly newsletter.

- Health Care Outreaches giving free treatment to the needy and dedicated to the rehabilitation and integration of disabled children.
- Upliftment & Empowerment Spreads literacy among women, counsels them on matrimonial and property matters, conducts training for trainers of teachers and teachers and also in various mass media of communication.
- Old Age Care Provides shelter and food at affordable price to the needy senior citizens who desired to live the remaining years of respectably.

INDIAN ADULT EDUCATION ASSOCIATION, NEW DELHI

Introduction

Indian Adult Education Association was established on 2nd Dec. 1939, Under the Indian Societies Registration Act. 1860. With unflinching faith in the effective participation of every citizen in social, economic, religious and political life of the country and consequent there to the imperative need for every citizen to have access to the expanding realms of knowledge through adult and life-long education, IAEA is specially committed to ceaselessly work towards raising the literacy level in its overall bid to safeguard the interests of the illiterates, down-trodden and deprived sections of population so as to enable them to take their rightful place in society.

In the beginning, IAEA's major emphasis was on creation of public opinion for a public policy on adult education, besides mobilising support from government and other public institutions for literacy movement. Today, when adult education has been duly recognised as an essential component of national reconstruction, IAEA functions as a federation of some 500 affiliated organisations spread throughout the length and breadth of the country, supporting their activities by bringing them together in its conferences, seminars, workshops and discussion groups. Through its publications, both periodic and otherwise, IAEA disseminates research findings and field experience on adult/non-formal and life-long continuing education to its more than 2500 'life' and yearly individual members coming from its 16 state branches, and others.

Aims and Objectives

1. Spread knowledge among the people of India on all subjects related to their all-round development, welfare and culture in a popular and attractive manner through suitable agencies.
2. Initiate, wherever necessary, adult education activities in cooperation with various organisations and individuals interested in the work, and to encourage and coordinate local efforts and organisations engaged in promoting the cause of adult education.
3. Serve as a 'Clearing House' for exchange of ideas, information and advice concerning adult education in different States of India.
4. Cooperate with movements aiming at removal of illiteracy and ignorance, and promotion of civic, economic and cultural interests of the people.
5. Serve as a connecting link for inter-State cooperation and coordination among the State Governments and NGOs.
6. Prepare and supply, if necessary, slides, charts, films, booklets, suitable literature, etc., and to undertake publication of bulletins, newsletters and journals. Arrange public lectures, demonstrations, seminars, etc., in furtherance of the objectives of the Association.
7. Organise All India Adult Education Conferences, Zonal, Regional and State level Conferences in furtherance of its objective.
8. Persuade universities, Govt. Depts.; NGOs; colleges and other educational bodies in the country to take up adult education work

and to do all other acts that are incidental to fulfillment of the above mentioned aims and objectives of the Association.

Activities

Functions of IAEA are as varied and wide-ranging as its aims and objectives. The following is a brief account of its activities over the years.

As Catalytic Agent

Being a pioneer, promoter, catalyst and leader, IAEA advises Central/ State Governments, Universities, State Resource Centres, Jan Shikshan Sansthans, Zilla Saksharta Samitis (ZSSs), its member-institutions and other organisations on adult, non formal and population education programmes.

As 'Clearing House'

IAEA has been functioning as a 'Clearing House' to disseminate information on growth and development of adult education through its periodicals, books, correspondence, etc., for the benefit of individuals and organisations.

Training

IAEA accords high priority to training of adult education functionaries. Since 1948, it has been organising training for adult education functionaries and public opinion leaders. It organises intra-state and inter-state training for key-level functionaries of Government Departments, NGOs, Universities, Colleges and trade union workers in different parts of the country, including the far flung areas.

IAEA also provides hands-on training in computer and information technology to women. The Association is recognised as a Study Centre of Makhanlal Chaturvedi University, Bhopal for DCA and PGDCA courses and Accredited Vocational Institute of National Institute of Open Schooling (Previously National Open School). The Association has started Library Science and CCA courses.

Research

IAEA accords high priority to research in adult education to strengthen the programme of adult education. It undertakes surveys and research projects on its own as well as in collaboration with other institutions.

Research Methodology Courses

IAEA also organises Research Methodology Courses for budding researchers in collaboration with Jawaharlal Nehru University, Directorate of Adult Education, Government of India and other agencies. So far 10 courses have been organised by the Association.

Research Fellowship

IAEA instituted Mohan Sinha Mehta Research Fellowship in 1986 in honour of its late President Dr. Mohan Sinha Mehta. This fellowship is awarded every year to individuals to carry out research in the field of Adult Education.

Monitoring and Evaluation

IAEA has, over the years, been engaged in monitoring and evaluation of literacy programmes. Empanelled by the National Literacy Mission for this purpose, IAEA has undertaken external evaluation work of the Total Literacy Campaigns/Post Literacy Programmes in about 22 districts in the country.

Other Activities

Under UNFPA-assisted project on Population Education in Adult Literacy Programme, IAEA houses the National Documentation Centre on Literacy and Population Education (DCLPE). Its activities were given below:

- Publication of quarterly Indian Journal of Population Education containing information on health education, adolescent education and gender issues, family welfare and population education in India
- Bringing out quarterly bibliography/accession list of latest acquisitions on population and population education
- Publication of bi-monthly Newsletter on Population Education
- Repackaging and dissemination of information through networking arrangements with various agencies, institutions and persons.
- Acquiring books and periodicals on the subject from national/ international organisations.

IAEA has established an International Institute of Adult and Life Long Education. The mission of the Institute is to professionalize adult education by strengthening and promoting it as a distinct but distinguished field of practice and discipline of study.

LITERACY HOUSE, LUCKNOW

'Literacy is an idea whose time has come. Local, national and international programmes – public and private-are hard at work on one of the most stubborn problems facing mankind-the development of an articulate and informed citizenry in a free society'.—***Welthy Honsinger Fisher***

Introduction

Literacy House was founded in 1953 by Dr. Welthy H. Fisher. Mahatma Gandhi, Six weeks before his assassination said, "Cities have everything. Our villages have nothing. Go and help the villages". This was the first step shown to Mr. W.H. Fisher. She took the first step in 1953 when she started her literacy work for the villages near Alhabad. At the request of the Governor, the literacy House was moved to Lucknow in 1956 and literacy work began on the present campus. Literacy house is the creation of the Ford Foundation. It is situated six miles from the City on the Lucknow-Kanpur Road.

Aims and Objectives

- To develop through its programmes of education and training, the techniques of communication with the masses.
- To produce educational materials-books, pamphlets, periodicals and simple audio-visual aids such as flash cards, khaddargraphs, puppets and puppet stages etc. for illiterate and literate adults.
- To produce professional literature for adult education and literacy workers.
- To publish books in Hindi, English and other languages dealing with problems such as those of citizenship, cottage industries, folk literature, health and agriculture.

Activities

Illiteracy is strongly linked to poverty, poor health, disadvantage and exclusion, and education is not an issue that stands in isolation from the many challenges that face the poor. As a result, Literacy House has developed a highly integrated approach to literacy that includes community programs that focus on women's rights, social justice, and health care, access to public services, advocacy, and community building.

Adult Literacy Programme

In UP, according to census 2001 survey, the literacy rate in Male are 68.8% and among adult women literacy rates are 42.98% only. In India the overall literacy rate is 64.8 % (Male: 75.3%; Female: 53.7%). Historically, a variety of factors have been found to be responsible for poor female literate rate viz., gender based inequality, social discrimination and economic exploitation, occupation of girl child in domestic chores, low enrolment of girls in schools and low retention rate and high dropout rate.

Children's Education Programme

In India, only 62% of children reach grade 5 and one-third of all children aged 6 to 14 do not attend school. Presently 62 Balwadi Kendras are running either through literacy house directly or rural NGO partners in 9 districts of eastern UP where over 1600 kids are receiving informal education.

Health Awareness Programme

Major Activities of Health Program are: Clinical Support, House Visit, Immunization, Health Awareness Meeting, Pregnant women check up and distribution of Iron / Folic acid tab, Health awareness Camp, Sterilization and distribution of family planning material, networking for health facilities, Special Cases, Health Staff Training etc.

Health Awareness Meetings

A combined total of 300 Health awareness meeting were held in the period April 2005 to March 2006.

Social Enterprise Programme

The term 'Social Enterprise' implies a linking of business ventures to achieving social good. 'Social enterprise' program consists of assisting poor women in developing new methods of income generation, especially through small business ventures, in order to improve the income and quality of life of their families.

Advocacy Programme

The advocacy program works to actively engage targeted communities on issues of human rights, women's empowerment, literacy, democratization and good governance. Our goal is to help these people understand the larger issues that affect the quality of their lives, and to enable them to make their voices heard for change.

RDT, ANATAPUR

Introduction

The Rural Development Trust (RDT) is a voluntary organisation working in Anantapur District of Andhra Pradesh, India. Fr. Vincent Ferror was established RDT in the year 1969. Anantapur district is the second most drought prone district in India due to failure of monsoons coupled with untimely and erratic rains and also high wind velocity and extreme heat. The average rainfall in the district is around 520 millimeter per annum, ranging from 120 millimeters in some parts to 650 millimeters in some other parts of the district. Temperatures normally up to 45 degrees centigrade in summer and wind velocity reaches 50 to 60 kilometers per hour during the wind season. The district lies between 13'-40' and 15'-15' northern latitude and 76'-50' and 78'-30' eastern longitude.

Aim and Objective

The main aim and objective of RDT is overall rural development in Anatapur District.

Activities

- Rural Development
- Women empowerment
- Child Education
- Health Facility
- Cultural Development
- Old age Homes

SEVA MANDIR

Introduction

Dr Mohan Singh Mehta a social worker and an educationalist, founded Seva Mandir. Udaipur, in the pre-independence period 1900-1947, was witness to an increasing awareness among educationalists and liberal thinkers of the particular backwardness and political stagnation of Rajasthan. This realisation provoked a move to change, and inspired certain individuals, who had imbibed ideas of voluntarism, to seize the initiative. Dr Mehta, not only played a very important role in founding Seva Mandir in 1966, but also was an inspiration to progressive change throughout Udaipur District. He was a true liberal influenced by the thoughts of Tagore, Gandhi, Dr. Kunzru, and Pandit Madan Mohan Malviya and by tenets of the scout movement. In pre-independence time he served as education minister and Prime Minister of Banswara in the State of Mewar and later as an Ambassador of independent India and as Vice Chancellor of Rajasthan University. He set up Vidya Bhavan at Udaipur in 1931, one of the pioneer co-educational institutions, with the philosophy of treating every child as a unique individual and molding them into citizens with sound moral character and a deep sense of social responsibility.

Aims and Objectives

- To create and strengthen institutions for development (at the village, organization and society levels)

- To enhance people's capabilities for self-development (both at individual and community level); and
- To create sustainable improvements in the livelihoods base;
- These three objectives form the basis for Seva Mandir's three program sectors.
- Activities
- Natural Resources Regeneration
- Non Farm Income Generation
- Education
- Health
- Women's Empowerment
- Child and Youth Development
- Village Institution
- Building
- People's Management School

Each of these programs, in achieving its respective goals, is also designed to build values and social capacities needed to achieve development and democracy for the poor.

Note:

- At present there are 165 Balwadi centres in Seva Mandir's work area, reaching out to a total of 3,806 children.
- Today some 9,307 women have managed to amass a total saving of Rs.6, 172,957 at women's groups.

CONCLUSIONS

India is a democratic country. We have freedom to do any type of good work. The literacy rate of India very less when compared to any other developed country or developing in the world. The roles of NGOs' are very important to increase literacy rate. They have a prominent role to do all the activities like literacy improvement, empowerment etc. Education in general, Adult Education in particular gives strength to human beings. Educate all the human beings.

REFERENCES

- All India Council for Mass Education and Development (AICMED).
- Annual Reports. Lucknow, India: Literacy House, 1958, 1959, 1960, 1961, 1962, and 1963.
- Anuradha Prasad et.al., (2005): "Living in Diversity", External Review.
- Complete Puppet Kit. A leaflet, Ibid. Undated.

- "Eleventh Anniversary of Literacy House," National Herald. New York. February 14, 1964.
- Fisher, Welthy M. To Light A Candle. London: Peter Davies, Ltd. 1963.
- Go to Ramon Magsaysay Award Foundation Online
- Grimes, Paul. "Literacy Village near Lucknow Keeps Promise of Aid to Gandhi," New York Times. April 2, 1961.
- Imprint. Bombay: F & S Distributors Private Ltd. Vol. 3, no. 7, October 1963.
- Koshy, T. A. Five Year Plan - A Summary. Lucknow India: Literacy House. November 22, 1960
- Lederer, William J: and Eugene Burdick. "Some Non-Ugly Americans," Life International. New York. March 14, 1960.
- Lekhak. Lucknow, India: Literacy House, Vol. 2, no. 2, April 1962; Vol. 3, no. 3, 4, January 1964.
- "Light for the Illiterate," Asia Magazine. Hong Kong. December 3, 1961.
- Literacy House, The First Decade. Delhi Publications Division, Indian Cooperative Union. 1963.
- Messages Received on the 10th Anniversary of the Founding of Literacy House, Lucknow, India. February 15, 1963.
- News Circle. Delhi: American Women's Club. Vol. 4, no. 9, May 1959.
- Shah, M. A. Hyder. "The Literacy Village in Lucknow," The Asian Student. San Francisco: Asia Foundation. May 13, 1961.
- Siddiqi, Abdur Rashid. An Approach to Educating Adults for Functional Literacy in India. A thesis presented to the Faculty of the Graduate School of Cornell University for the Degree of Master of Science, September 1963.
- Simple Visual Aids on Development Problems. Lucknow, India: Literacy House. Undated.
- "Teaching People to Teach People to Read and Write," Yojana. India. February 19, 1961.
- Visit to Literacy House and its field work in the villages. Interviews with persons acquainted with Mrs. Fisher and her work.
- www.andhramahilasabha.com
- www.sevamandir.com

28

Access to Higher Education For Disability – A Case Study

INTRODUCTION

India, as one of the oldest civilizations of the world and with its rich cultural heritage, has traversed a long distance during the last 64 years of its independence. The Education system of a country does not function in isolation from the society of which it is a part. Hierarchies of castes, economic status, gender relations and cultural diversities as well as uneven economic development also deeply influence issues relating to access and equity in education. Though India was widely acclaimed as a land of knowledge and wisdom during ancient times yet access to education was limited to select strata of the society. The societal distribution of responsibility and accountability may have been justified in those days but in today's context deeply entrenched social inequalities between various social groups and castes, the century's old social prejudices and inequalities, based on caste at birth, continue to propose challenges for national development. Among these, disability students have also been neglecting. Without inclusive education, it is not possible for overall development of India. Education in general and higher education in particular has a prominent role in the process of national development. It is the time to take care about higher educational access to disability students in India.

IMPORTANCE OF HIGHER EDUCATION

The enrollment of students in higher education in India is only 10-15 per cent where as in developed countries it is above 36 per cent. Prime Minister of India, Dr. Manmohan Singh has recognized the importance of higher education in India. He is planning to establish world class universities in India. The minister for HRD Mr. Kapil Sibal has welcomed the foreign universities to establish their campuses in India.

The President of America, Mr.Obama has emphasized the importance of higher education, urging more Americans to get college degrees. Higher education can lead to prestigious careers and high salaries. It can also broaden one's experience, exposing the student to differing points of view, critical thinking and analytical skills, as well as appreciation of the arts or diverse cultures. These may rival career advancement in importance.

The importance of higher education lies in several areas, including the financial, social, emotional and intellectual realms. University professors Boyce Watkins and Richard Vedder, speaking in a discussion on National Public Radio's Tell Me More (Sept. 1, 2009), emphasized that students should carefully analyze the benefits they wish to gain from higher education.

21st Century Trends for Higher Education

In 2009, the Cisco Internet Business Solutions Group (IBSG) released a series of Points of View regarding key trends for higher education in the 21st century, along with the role of technology in each.

1. Evergreen students
2. Globalization
3. Technical and information literacy
4. Enrollment, retention, and branding
5. Mobility
6. Safety and security
7. Pedagogical centers and innovative campus commons
8. Evolution of teaching and learning
9. Collaboration
10. Strategic plans and technology
11. Edutainment
12. Green

By understanding these trends and technologies, higher-education institutions will be able to prepare students to become the next generation of productive employees and innovative leaders the world needs.

HIGHER EDUCATION – DISABILITY

Education is central to the life of an individual in the community. It provides opportunities for personal, social, and academic growth and development. It sets the stage for later life experiences, most especially in employment. It is also an important venue for integration into the life of the community.

Access and retention in higher education continue to be cornerstones for the democratization of India and achieving a more equitable world. In an increasingly technological world with a globalized economy, a primary role of higher education must continue to be the struggle to create a one-to-one correspondence between access and retention.

Promoting wider and more equitable access to higher education is a key strategic objective of Government and higher education institutions alike. Government called on higher education institutions to widen participation by students who were under represented including mature students, students from socio economically disadvantaged backgrounds and students with disabilities.

India is home to 60 million disabled people. Of them, 48 per cent are visually impaired, 28 per cent are movement impaired, 14 per cent are mentally disabled and 10 per cent have hearing and speech disabilities. Disabled students pose particular challenges to higher education not only in terms of gaining physical access to buildings, but also in relation to much wider access issues concerning the curriculum, teaching, learning and assessment. For these reasons, they may be seen as a litmus test of the ability of higher education to include a diverse range of learners, particularly relevant in light of recent emphasis on initiatives aimed at widening access to higher education to underrepresented groups.

Government of India Announces Plan to Make Education Disabled-Friendly By 2020

"It should, and will be our objective, to make mainstream education not just available but accessible, affordable and appropriate for students with disabilities," promised former Human Resource Development Minister Arjun Singh.

In a comprehensive 'Action Plan for the Inclusive Education of Children and Youth with Disabilities' formulated by the Ministry, the former HRD Minister Arjun Singh has committed that the government will provide education through mainstream schools for children with disabilities, in accordance with the provisions of the Persons with Disabilities Act, 1995. Singh revealed this ambitious plan on 21st March in the Rajya Sabha.

Some of the main objectives of the Action Plan are:

- All universities will have a Disability Coordinator to act as a 'one-stop shop' to assist disabled students in their needs;
- All universities will be assisted by U.G.C. in setting up a separate Department of Disability Studies including modules of inclusion;
- A Chair of Disability Studies will be set up in Central Universities;
- Universities will be encouraged to introduce Special Shuttle Services for disabled students.

To ensure sensitization of teachers to the requirements of disabled students' regular in-service training will be provided. A disability element in the syllabus of B.Ed. and M.Ed. courses will be strengthened. The Minister added that selected schools will be converted into Model Inclusive Schools in order to demonstrate "what is necessary and more importantly, what is possible". As for higher education, all universities will have a Disability Coordinator to act as a 'one-stop shop' for disabled students and assist them in their needs.

In August 2004, N.C.P.E.D.P.'s 'Research Study on Present Education Scenario' revealed that only 0.1% disabled students are in mainstream educational institutions at the university level and 0.51% at the school level.

Status of Mainstream Education of Disabled Students in Universities

National Centre for Promotion of Employment of Disabled people (N.C.P.E.D.P.) has recently conducted a survey on the education scenario for students with disabilities. All the 322 Universities in India were sent the research questionnaire. A total of 119 (36.9%) Universities responded.

- In the total of 119 respondent Universities, only 1,635 students with disabilities are enrolled. Therefore, only about 0.1% of the students were found to be those with disabilities. While 3% seats in educational institutions are to be reserved for disabled students, the figure of 0.1% is nowhere close to this figure!
- About 24 Universities (20%) clearly reported that they did not follow the 3% reservation for disabled students as mandated by the law of the nation! While the Persons with Disabilities (Equal Opportunities, Protection of Rights and Full Participation) Act, 1995 mandates a wide variety of efforts to ensure equal opportunities to disabled students for getting quality education, it also clearly states that 'all Government educational institutions and other educational institutions receiving aid from the Government, shall reserve not less than three per cent seats for persons with disabilities.'

- In all the 119 respondent Universities, only 1,203 students with orthopaedic impairments were enrolled. Furthermore, only 18 Universities (15%) reported that they provided appropriate desks and chairs for students with disabilities, only 11 (9%) provided wheelchairs and only 9 (7.5%) of them provided access to tricycles! It seemed clear that only persons with minor physical impairments, who required minimum physical assistance of any kind, got admission in the Universities.
- In all the 119 Universities, only 311 students with visual impairments were enrolled. While only 16 Universities had special computer software, only 10 (8.4%) Universities provided access to books in Braille!
- In all the 119 Universities, only 38 students with hearing impairments study. Only 9 (7.5%) Universities reported provision of hearing aids for students while 10 (8.4%) of them provided sign language interpreters. Even these figures seem exaggerated as on further investigation one University reported that the sign language interpreters were not provided in classrooms, but arranged for during certain seminars/conferences! Only 11 Universities had students with hearing disability. Most of these had just one such student except Osmania University (Hyderabad) that had 23 of total of 38 students with hearing disability.
- In all the 119 Universities, only 22 students with mental disability were enrolled. Assuming that people with intellectual impairment were unlikely to reach the higher education level, the 1.3 % of students with mental disability in the Universities was likely to be students with mental illness. It was very clear that awareness about the abilities of persons with intellectual impairment and mental illness was lacking.
- Seven Universities (5.8%) categorically mentioned that they do not admit students with disability, conveniently ignoring the law.
- Some of the notable Universities which did not reply to the questionnaire in spite of reminders, were Delhi University, All India Institute of Medical Sciences (New Delhi), Indira Gandhi National Open University (New Delhi), Jamia Millia Islamia University (New Delhi), Bangalore University (Karnataka), University of Calcutta (West Bengal), University of Calicut (Kerala) and Indian Agricultural Research Institute (New Delhi), amongst many others.
- About 76.3% of the disabled students were males, while 23.7% were females. The government focus on educating girls did not seem to have much impact on the education level of girls with disabilities.

- Osmania University (Hyderabad) was the only one that projected a healthier trend in giving opportunities to students with different disabilities - out of its total number of 60 students with disabilities, 13 had orthopaedic disabilities, 3 visual disability, 23 hearing disability and 21 had mental disabilities.
- Banaras Hindu University (U.P.) and Aligarh Muslim University (U.P.) had the number of disabled students in three digits – 208 and 202 respectively. 38 Universities (31%) had no disabled students. These included Tata Institute of Fundamental Research (Mumbai), University of Allahabad, Guru Nanak Dev University (Amritsar), University of Rajasthan, Rabindra Bharati University (Kolkata), and Manipal Academy of Higher Education (Karnataka) among others. 31 Universities projected less than 5 disabled students, which included National Institute of Mental Health and Neuro Sciences (Bangalore), School of Planning and Architecture (Delhi), Indian Institute of Technology (Kanpur), Punjab Agricultural University (Ludhiana), Northeastern Hill University (Shillong), and University of Pune. 23 Universities had more than 5 but less than 20 disabled students. These included Tata Institute of Social Sciences, Mumbai, Punjab University, Chandigarh, Indian Institute of Technology, Chennai, Roorkee, Mumbai, and G.B. Pant University of Agriculture & Technology, Uttaranchal.
- While 112 Universities (94%) mentioned that they gave admission to disabled students, only 24 (20%) of them provided special equipment for the students. Clearly, it was just by chance that the others had a few students with disabilities in their institutions.
- When given a chance to explain reasons for not admitting disabled students, very few Universities were forthcoming. Only 6 admitted to the lack of trained staff and only 5 admitted to lack of infrastructure.
- Out of the 119 respondent Universities, 47 Universities mentioned that they gave scholarships to disabled students and 29 gave financial assistance. It was clear from the minimal number of disabled students in these Universities that these facilities were being provided in general for all students and disabled students could get them by sheer chance. For example, though 73 Universities mentioned that they provided hostel facility for disabled students, it was unlikely that any hostel had even a single toilet/ room/ mess area accessible for a wheelchair user! And it is lack of proper hostels and financial constraints that greatly limit the choices disabled students have for higher education.

- Only 50% of the 119 Universities reported being aware of the UGC schemes and only 11 (9%) Universities had received UGC grant under the schemes including Banaras Hindu University, University of Mumbai, Jawaharlal Nehru University (New Delhi), Tata Institute of Social Sciences (Mumbai), and Aligarh Muslim University. The University Grants Commission initiated two schemes in 1998: one for the preparation of teachers for special education at the B. Ed. and M. Ed. levels and the other for the provision of facilities for promoting higher education for disabled students.
- About 80% of the respondent institutions reported that disabled students were easily able to reach the classrooms, offices, toilets, auditorium, sports area, library, canteen, laboratories and the hostels! The institutions obviously did not understand the issue of access and were under the impression that all the places were accessible for all present and future disabled students.

Top 10 UNIVERSITIES

Name of University	Total Students			Number of Disabled Students		
	Male	Female	**Total**	Male	Female	**Total**
Banaras Hindu University	10799	3869	**14668**	154	54	**208**
Aligarh Muslim University	-	-	-	156	46	**202**
Kurukshetra University	-	-	-	55	17	**72**
Osmania University	74237	61690	**135927**	49	11	**60**
University of Hyderabad	-	-	-	46	10	**56**
Jawaharlal Nehru University, New Delhi	-	-	-	48	6	**54**
South Gujarat University	-	-	-	34	16	**50**
Karnataka State Open University	-	-	-	36	13	**49**
Anna University	-	-	-	41	7	**48**
Acharya NG Ranga Agricultural University	2414	1448	**3862**	18	24	**42**

DISABILITY STUDENTS IN S.V.UNIVERSITY

Sri Venkateswara University

Established on September 2nd, 1954 as the brain-child of visionary luminaries Sri Prakasam Pantulu, Sri Neelam Sanjeeva Reddy and others, Sri Venkateswara University has been catering to the higher educational needs and aspirations of the people of Rayalaseema. Christened after the Lord of the Seven Hills, the University was launched with generous help from the Tirumala Tirupati Devastanams which donated 1200 acres of sprawling campus along with the then existing college buildings, besides a munificent annual grant of 10 lakhs which has been increased to one crore from the financial year 2008-09.

Efficiently nurtured by committed Vice-chancellors starting from Prof. S. Govindarajulu to the present Vice-Chancellor Prof. N. Prabhakar Rao, the University has grown from strength to strength, emerging as a premiere institution of learning, teaching, research, extension and consultancy.

The university has four constituent campus colleges, S.V.U. College of Arts, S.V.U. College of Sciences, S.V.U. College of Management Studies and S.V.U. College of Engineering, with 60 Departments offering 73 Post-Graduate Courses, 7 Engineering Under-Graduate Colleges spread over Chittoor, Kadapa and Nellore districts.

Affiliated to the University are 37 PG Colleges, 2 Engineering colleges, 23 MBA/MCA Colleges, 6 Law Colleges, 76 College of Education, 2 Physical Education Colleges, 3 Oriental Colleges, 1 College of Music and Dance, 166 Under-Graduate Colleges spread over Chittoor, Kadapa and Nellore districts.

The selection to all PG and Research programs is through entrance tests conducted by the Directorate of Admissions, EAMCET, ICET, Ed.CET, LAWCET etc.

The constituent colleges in the University campus and the Post-Graduate at Kavali together have 5000 students and 600 well qualified faculty members in various disciplines. The faculties have achieved national and international repute for their research output, quality teaching, and have been awarded several national and international fellowships in their respective fields.

Disability Students in SVU

TABLE-1 NO.OF CANDIDATES ADMITTED INTO PG COURSES IN SVU

YEAR	MALE	FEMALE	TOTAL	PH MALE	PH FEMALE	PHTOTAL (%)
2007-08	2377	1707	4084	73	28	101 (2.47)
2008-09	2021	1616	3637	48	16	64 (1.75)
2009-10	2902	2325	5227	67	29	96 (4.12)
2010-11	2047	1358	3405	43	16	59 (1.73)

From the above table we conclude that, the rate of admission of disability students in Sri Venkateswara University is decreasing from 2007-08 to 2010-11 except in the year 2009-10. In the year 2007-08, 2.47 per cent of disability students have taken admission into the different courses at P.G. level. In the year 2009-10, 4.12 per cent of disability students have taken admission. It is higher than the reservation quota of disability students, which is 3 per cent. Again, the rate of admission was decreased from 4.12 per cent in the year 2009-10 to 1.73 per cent in the year 2010-11.

Facilities for Disability Students in SVU

There is a separate Hostel for disability students (boys). Separate foot path (track) was constructed for free access of disability students at Central Library, Main Building and other departments. The university is taking care to provide three wheeler cycles and vehicles for poor disability students. There is a special priority for disability students in Earn and Lean Programme. The Department of Sociology, Social Work, Population Studies, Women Studies, Extension Studies and Adult & Continuing Education are taking special care towards welfare of disability students. There is a special fund for poor disability students in the university. Some NGOs like RASS, PASS, Abhayashketra and Akshayashketra etc. are visiting university to help disability students. The university reserved 3 per cent of total sheets to disability students as per the norms of government.

CASE STUDY

Introduction

The Researcher has conducted a case study on Mr. Venkataramana, a student of Department of Economics, Sri Venkateswara University, Tirupati.

Name of the Student : Venkataramana
Sex : Male
Date of Birth : 1986
Birth Order : 2nd
Native Place : Y.S.R. Kadapa, A.P.
Age : 24
Father Occupation : Agriculture
Mother Occupation : House Wife
Annual Income : Rs. 50, 000/-
Education : i) SSC - 63.33%
ii) Intermediate -70%
iii) Degree (HEP)-71%
iv) M.A., Economics-72% (I, II & III Sems), University 2nd S.V.University, Tirupati-517502.
Ambition : To become Group-I officer
Disability per cent : 90.5%

Ramana expressed that he is so happy with the support of friends, parents and teachers. He never faced any type of problems in the university. He never hurt by the peer group. He frankly says that, disability students want love and affection not mercy. In his words.... "We are equal with all the students in the class room. We don't want special interest towards disability. We also have courage and strength to do all types of jobs in the society. Will power is important for success. I have more will power". It shows that positive attitude is more important for success not only in career, but also in the life of all human beings.

CONCLUSION

Education in general and Higher Education in particular is more important not only for ability students, but also for disability students. Education is power. Education gives strength and confidence to the individual. The impact of globalization is very much on the individuals of the society. Boys and girls are moving with high-speed to reach their goals. Special attention and care is important towards students with disability. It is more important to follow rules and regulations for the welfare of disability students. Some universities are not taking care about students with disability. Effective monitoring is necessary to provide higher education for all disability students in the country. We hope India will be provided higher education for all students with disability by 2020.

REFERENCES

1. "*Status of Mainstream Education of Disabled Students in India*", a Research Study of 'National Centre for Promotion of Employment of Disabled people'.
2. Ministry of HRD, Government of India.
3. "*National Family Health Survey-III*" (2005-06): Ministry of Health and Family Welfare, Government of India.
4. University Grants Commission, Government of India.
5. Sri Venakteswara University, Tirupati.

29

Empowerment of Youth Through Education

INTRODUCTION

We are shining, we will be the 2nd largest economy by 2020, we are the largest pool of skilled man power on the earth, we are the emerging global IT superpower, we are the outsourcing hub of the world, we offer one of the largest consumer market across the world for MNC's, we boast of rich and varied heritage, we are growing at the GDP rate of impressive 8-9% per annum and aiming for a glittering double digit growth rate soon, we are India! It seems that the above facts are in our favor; we are shining, but are we really? Or our mindset of estimating standard of living of the population just by the glittering GDP growth rates is a sign of our biased mentality? The other side of the story – 25 per cent population still living below poverty line, most of the cities and villages without even suitable condition for a healthy living, proper health care centers, electricity, UNESCO is concerned about the child mortality rate in India, we are in the top countries from below in the Human Development Index and still we ignoring the reality or over shadowing the face of our country's ugly face.

Education has a prominent role in the development of any nation in the world. India has a large number of youth across the world. Many researchers say that there is a positive correlation between education and economic development. Development of youth leads to development of the nation. Education in general and quality education in particular is important for all the youth in the country. In the present high-tech world, we are facing so many problems viz., poverty, illiteracy, teenage pregnancy, corruption and environmental pollution. Through education it is possible to solve all these problems in the society. Education is the best way for youth empowerment.

YOUTH IN INDIA

Young people (aged 10–24) constituted almost 315 million and represented 31% of the Indian population in 2001. Not only does this cohort represent India's future in the socio-economic and political realms, but its experiences will largely determine India's achievement of its goal of population stabilization and the extent to which the nation will be able to harness its demographic dividend. While today's youth are healthier, more urbanized and better educated than earlier generations, social and economic vulnerabilities persist. In the course of the transition to adulthood, moreover, young people face significant risks related to sexual and reproductive health, and many lack the knowledge and power to make informed sexual and reproductive choices.

According to UN definition; persons between the ages of 15 years and 24 years are youth. The youth population in total population of India was 41.05 per cent in 2001. Between the years 2010-2030, India will add 241 Million people in working-age population. According to UNESCO-2002 the youth literacy rate of India was 73.3 per cent; where as China's youth literacy was 98.9 per cent. United Nations Statistic Division (2005) says that the youth unemployment of India was 10.5per cent. Through youth empowerment only the development of India is possible.

Many Youth are Illiterate or Have Very Low Educational Attainment

- Thirty-one per cent of young women and 14 per cent of young men are illiterate. However, literacy is much higher among the youngest youth age 15 years (77% among women and 92% per cent among men) than among youth only a decade older (63% among women and 84% among men).
- Despite improvements over time, educational attainment remains very low even among youth: only 29 per cent of young women and 38 per cent of young men have completed 10 or more years of education.
- Urban-rural differentials are much wider for women than men in literacy and educational attainment and the gender gap is also much greater in rural than in urban areas.
- Only 41 per cent of adolescents age 15-17 were attending school in the school year 2005-06, suggesting a very high school dropout

rate. School attendance rates for youth age 15-17 years increase sharply with household wealth. The gender gap is also much narrower in wealthier households than in poorer households.

Many Youth are Economically Active

- Thirty-four per cent of women and 67 per cent of men age 15-24 were employed at any time in the 12 months preceding the survey, with the vast majority being currently employed.
- Among men, the proportion employed increases sharply with age from 33 per cent among those age 15 to 92 per cent among those age 24; among women, by contrast, employment varies little with age.
- Employment is higher among rural than among urban youth and is much lower among youth with 10 or more years of education than among those with no education. Almost all men with no education are employed.
- The majority of employed women are agricultural workers; however, there is greater diversity in male employment.
- Less than two-thirds of employed women (64%) earn cash for their work, compared with 88 per cent of employed men.

EMPOWERMENT

Empowerment is a construct shared by many disciplines and arenas: community development, psychology, education, economics, and studies of social movements and organizations, among others. How empowerment is understood varies among these perspectives? In recent empowerment literature, the meaning of the term empowerment is often assumed rather than explained or defined. Rappoport (1984) has noted that it is easy to define empowerment by its absence but difficult to define in action as it takes on different forms in different people and contexts. Even defining the concept is subject to debate. Zimmerman (1984) has stated that asserting a single definition of empowerment may make attempts to achieve it formulaic or prescription-like, contradicting the very concept of empowerment.

A common understanding of empowerment is necessary, however, to allow us to know empowerment when we see it in people with whom we are working, and for program evaluation. According to Bailey (1992), how we precisely define empowerment within our projects and programs will depend upon the specific people and context involved.

As a general definition, however, we suggest that empowerment is a multi-dimensional social process that helps people gain control over their own lives. It is a process that fosters power (that is, the capacity to implement) in people, for use in their own lives, their communities, and in their society, by acting on issues that they define as important.

Researchers suggest that three basic components are important to define the concept of empowerment. Empowerment is multi-dimensional, social, and a process. It is multi-dimensional in that it occurs within sociological, psychological, economic, and other dimensions. Empowerment also occurs at various levels, such as individual, group, and community. Empowerment, by definition, is a social process, since it occurs in relationship to others. Empowerment is a process that is similar to a path or journey, one that develops as we work through it. Other aspects of empowerment may vary according to the specific context and people involved, but these remain constant. In addition, one important implication of this definition of empowerment is that the individual and community are fundamentally connected.

SWAMI VIVEKANANDA TO YOUTH

Supreme value of youth period is incalculable and indescribable. Youth life is the most precious life. Youth is the best time. The way in which you utilize this period will decide the nature of coming years that lie ahead of you. Your happiness, your success, your honor and your good name all depend upon the way in which you live now, in this present period. Remember this. This wonderful period of the first state of your life is related to you as the soft wet clay in the hands of the potter. Skillfully the potter gives it the right and correct shapes and forms, which he intends to give. Even so, you can wisely mould your life, your character, your physical health and strength, in short your entire nature in any way in which you make up your mind to do. And you must do this now.

O fortunate youth, recognize this great duty. Feel this wonderful privilege. Take up this adventure. God watches you graciously, ever ready to help and guide. I wish you to be great. The world has put its faith in you. Your elders keep their hopes in you. Now youth means to place your firm confidence in yourself and exercise your hopeful determination and resolution and willing good intentions in this beautiful task of self-culture. This will truly bring supreme satisfaction and fulfillment not only to you, but also to all concerned. The shaping of your life is indeed in your own hands.

Practice virtue, persevere in virtue. Become established in virtue. Shine as an embodiment of noblest virtue and heroic adherence to goodness. Youth is meant for this grand process. Youth life is the active development and fulfillment of these processes. This period of your time provides the suitable and favourable fields for the working out of this extremely important and most indispensable process in life. This is the special significance, the great importance and supreme value of youth life. It signifies the creation of noble personality. It is Atma-Viakasa. It is Atma –Nirmana. Please try to understand the correct implication of the term successful life. When you talk of success with reference to life, it does not merely mean succeeding in everything that you undertake or do; it does not merely mean succeeding in fulfilling all wants or getting whatever you desire; it does not just mean acquiring a name or attaining a position or imitating fashionable ways appearing modern or up-to-date. The essence of true success is what you make of yourself. It is the conduct of life that you develop, it is the character that you cultivate and it is the type of person you become. This is the central meaning of successful living. Therefore, you will see this important matter is not so much a question of success in life. (Jivan – Me- Safalta) but rather it is success of life. Such successful life is one that succeeds in producing an ideal individual, a noble man. Your success is not measured in terms of what all you obtained but in term of what you become, how you live and what actions you do. Upon this point reflect well and attain great happiness.

In our grand culture they conceived of life in four stage-preliminary stage, development stage, flowering or blossoming stage and the culminating fruitful stage. These can be described as he preparatory period, the practicing period for the satisfactory growth of the latter stage. Yours is the stage of preliminary preparations for right and successful living. Herein is its supreme value and great importance. This is like the ploughing and sowing of seeds in the field by a farmer. Now, you can easily understand, what is the significance and importance of this in connection with the harvest, which any one would wish to reap later on. And also, it is like the laying of the foundation for an important building you wish to construct. If this building is something very important to you, then you just think how much more important its proper foundation becomes in your view. The strong and continued existence of the building depends certainly upon the foundation. This is the stage you are now in. Let your preparations be wise, correct and of such kind that will lead to your true welfare, supreme good and lasting satisfaction and happiness. This must engage your active, enthusiastic attention throughout the period of your youth life. Our culture refers to this stage as the Brahmacharya Ashram or Vidyarthi Jivan. Here, you acquire knowledge of not only subjects like History, Geography, Mathematics, etc., but also about human nature, correct Vyavahara, science of Self- control, art of developing pure mind, Dharma, the duties of man and the proper relationship between you, your family, your society and the world.

YOUTH EMPOWERMENT THRODGH EDUCATION

The large and increasing relative share and absolute numbers of the youth population in India makes it even more necessary that the nation ensure that the youth of India become a vibrant, constructive force that can address social and economic issues and contribute to sustained and just governance and nation building. In recognition of the important role for youth in nation building, the preamble of India's 2003 National Youth Policy ¯reiterates the commitment of the entire nation to the composite and all-round development of the young sons and daughters of India and seeks to establish an All-India perspective to fulfill their legitimate aspirations so that they are all strong of heart and strong of body and mind in successfully accomplishing the challenging tasks of national reconstruction and social changes that lie ahead. The thrust of the policy is youth empowerment in different spheres of national life (National Youth Policy, 2003). Education, employment, and health, including sexual and reproductive health, are all key elements of youth empowerment.

Educational attainment not only affects the economic potential of youth, but also their effectiveness as informed citizens, parents, and family members. Article 26 of the 1948 Declaration of Human Rights gives everyone the right to education, and further states that, ¯Technical and professional education shall be made generally available and higher education shall be equally accessible to all on the basis of merit (United Nations, 1948). It points to continuing and unacceptable differentials in education by residence and gender. In particular, it recognizes the need to address the great disparity in primary and higher education between rural compared with urban areas, and for females compared with males. Contributing to low educational access and attainment, particularly of girls, is the low age at first marriage. Although, the age at first marriage has been increasing over time, a sizeable proportion of girls in India continue to be married at an age when they should still be in school or completing their education. Another important element contributing to low educational attainment is the mismatch between the numbers who need admission to quality higher level educational institutions and the ability of available institutions to them in large numbers.

Vivekananda realizes that mankind is passing through a crisis. The tremendous emphasis on the scientific and mechanical ways of life is fast reducing man to the status of a machine. Moral and religious values are being undermined. The fundamental principles of civilization are being ignored. Conflicts of ideals, manners and habits are pervading the atmosphere. Disregard for everything old is the fashion of the day. Vivekananda seeks the solutions of all these social and global evils through education. With this end in view, he feels the dire need of awakening man to his spiritual self wherein, he thinks, lies the very purpose of education.

Vivekananda points out that the defect of the present-day education is that it has no definite goal to pursue. A sculptor has a clear idea about what he wants to shape out of the marble block; similarly, a painter knows what he is going to paint. But a teacher, he says, has no clear idea about the goal of his teaching. Swamiji attempts to establish, through his words and deeds, that the end of all education is man making. He prepares the scheme of this man-making education in the light of his over-all philosophy of Vedanta. According to Vedanta, the essence of man lies in his soul, which he possesses in addition to his body and mind. In true with this philosophy, Swamiji defines education as 'the manifestation of the perfection already in man.' The aim of education is to manifest in our lives the perfection, which is the very nature of our inner self. This perfection is the realization of the infinite power which resides in everything and everywhere-existence, consciousness and bliss (satchidananda). After understanding the essential nature of this perfection, we should identify it with our inner self. For achieving this, one will have to eliminate one's ego, ignorance and all other false identification, which stand in the way. Meditation, fortified by moral purity and passion for truth, helps man to leave behind the body, the senses, the ego and all other non-self elements, which are perishable. He thus realizes his immortal divine self, which is of the nature of infinite existence, infinite knowledge and infinite bliss.

At this stage, man becomes aware of his self as identical with all other selves of the universe, i.e. different selves as manifestations of the same self. Hence education, in Vivekananda's sense, enables one to comprehend one's self within as the self everywhere. The essential unity of the entire universe is realized through education. Accordingly, man making for Swamiji stands for rousing mans to the awareness of his true self. However, education thus signified does not point towards the development of the soul in isolation from body and mind. We have to remember that basis of Swamiji's philosophy is Advaita which preaches unity in diversity. Therefore, man making for him means a harmonious development of the body, mind and soul.

In his scheme of education, Swamiji lays great stress on physical health because a sound mind resides in a sound body. He often quotes the Upanishadic dictum '*nayamatma balahinena labhyah*'; i.e. the self cannot be realized by the physically weak. However, along with physical culture, he harps on the need of paying special attention to the culture of the mind. According to Swamiji, the mind of the students has to be controlled and trained through meditation, concentration and practice of ethical purity.

All success in any line of work, he emphasizes, is the result of the power of concentration. By way of illustration, he mentions that the chemist in the laboratory concentrates all the powers of his mind and brings them into one focus-the elements to be analyzed-and finds out their secrets. Concentration, which necessarily implies detachment from other things, constitutes a part of Brahmacharya, which is one of the guiding mottos of his scheme of education. Brahmacharya, in a nutshell, stands for the practice of self-control for securing harmony of the impulses. By his philosophy of education, Swamiji thus brings it home that education is not a mere accumulation of information but a comprehensive training for life.

In 1984, the Government of India declared and decided to observe the Birthday of Swami Vivekananda (12th January, according to English calendar) as National Youth Day every year from 1985 onwards.

The given below teachings of Vivekananda help for good character building of youth in our country. It is more important to change the attitude of youth towards their strength and success.

- Education is the manifestation of the perfection already in man.
- If you have faith in all the three hundred and thirty millions of your mythological gods ... and still have no faith in yourselves, there is no salvation for you. Have faith in yourselves, and stand up on that faith and be strong; that is what we need.
- It is love and love alone that I preach, and I base my teaching on the great Vedantic truth of the sameness and omnipresence of the Soul of the Universe.
- My ideal, indeed, can be put into a few words, and that is: to preach unto mankind their divinity and how to make it manifest in every movement of life.
- Purity, patience, and perseverance are the three essentials to success, and above all, love.
- Religion is realization; not talk, not doctrine, nor theories, however beautiful they may be. It is being and becoming, not hearing or acknowledging; it is the whole soul becoming changed into what it believes.
- Religion is the manifestation of the Divinity already in man.
- So long as the millions live in hunger and ignorance, I hold every man a traitor who, having been educated at their expense, pays not the least heed to them.
- Strength, strength it is that we want so much in this life, for what we call sin and sorrow have all one cause, and that is our weakness. With weakness comes ignorance, and with ignorance comes misery.

- Teach yourselves, teach everyone his real nature, call upon the sleeping soul and see how it awakes. Power will come, glory will come, goodness will come, purity will come, and everything that is excellent will come when this sleeping soul is roused to self-conscious activity.
- The older I grow, the more everything seems to me to lie in manliness. This is my new Gospel.
- They alone live who live for others, the rest are more dead than alive.
- This is the gist of all worship – to be pure and to do good to others.
- We want that education by which character is formed, strength of mind is increased, the intellect is expanded, and by which one can stand on one's own feet.
- Whatever you think, that you will be. If you think yourselves weak, weak you will be; if you think yourselves strong, strong you will be.

CONCLUSION

Education plays a vital role in achieving human development, hence, universalisation of school education and complete eradication of illiteracy among the people in the age group of 15 to 35 years is one of the basic objectives of the Tenth Plan. We are at the end of 11th Five Year Plan. Still we are unable to provide education for all. Youth population of India is increasing year by year. It is fortunate for India. It is our duty to utilize energetic youth in the development process. Youth participation in development programme is necessary. Education in general and quality & value education in particular is important for all youth in our society. Through value education only it is possible to become good citizen. Education is power. Through education it is possible to solve all types of problems in the society. Education and employment have positive correlation. Through education only empowerment of youth is possible.

REFERENCES

1. "*A Profile of Youth in India*", National Family Health Survey (NFHS-3) 2005-06, Ministry of Health and Family Welfare, Government of India, New Delhi.
2. Anil Bordia (2009): "*Education of Youth and Adolescents in India*", NCERT, New Delhi.
3. "*Education and Youth Welfare*", Working paper, Government of India, New Delhi.
4. "*Empowering Youth through National Policies*", UNESCO.
5. "*India's New Opportunity-2020*", Confederation of Indian Industry, All India Management Association, India.
6. Pravin Visaria (1998): "*Unemployment among Youth in India: Level, Nature*

and Policy Implications", Employment and Training Department, International Labour Office, Geneva.

7. Rajput, J.S. "*Need for Moral Values to Indian Youth*", the Ramakrishna Mission Institute of Culture.
8. "*Youth in India: Situation and Needs 2006-07*", Ministry of Health and Family Welfare, Government of India, New Delhi.

30

Women in Higher Education in India

INTRODUCTION

India's distinctiveness rests on its great foundations, which were built by her ancient sages who relentlessly sought after the highest integral knowledge and perfection; as a result, her culture has been sustained, even through periods of decline, with surprising continuity since remote antiquity.

India's renaissance, which began in the last decades of the 19th century, has been marked by multisided awakening, creativity, renewal and reconstruction enabling the country to make valuable contributions in the services of her people and the peoples of the world. Our culture has always stood for universality and common fraternity of the entire human race, and our aspirations are reflected in the educational field in creating, strengthening and developing a national system that should be geared to the highest ideals of universal peace, unity and harmony.

We maintain that education is a liberating force as also an evolutionary force, which enables the individual to rise from mere materiality to superior planes of intellectual and spiritual consciousness. Education is a dialogue between the past, present and the future, so that the coming generations receive the accumulated lessons of the heritage and carry it forward. In the words of Sri Aurobindo, the foremost philosopher and sage of our times, "The past is our foundation, the present our material, the future our aim and summit. Each must have its due and natural place in a national system of education."

The Vedas, Puranas, Ayurveda, Yoga, Kautilya's Arthasahtra are only some of the milestones that the traditional Indian knowledge system boasts of. There are evidences of imparting formal education in ancient India under the Gurukul system. The education system in India has savored a special bond between the teacher and the pupil since time unknown.

HIGHER EDUCATION IN INDIA

Higher Education in India is one of the most developed in the entire world. There has in fact been considerable improvement in the higher education scenario of India in both quantitative and qualitative terms. In technical education, the IITs, and the IIMs have already marked their names among the top higher educational institutes of the world. Moreover the Jawaharlal University and Delhi University are also regarded as good higher educational institutes for doing postgraduates courses and research in science, humanities and social sciences. As a result, students from various parts of the world are coming today for higher education in India.

IMPORTANCE OF HIGHER EDUCATION

The enrollment of students in higher education in India is only 10 per cent where as in developed countries it is above 60 per cent. Prime Minister of India, Dr. Manmohan Singh has recognized the importance of higher education in India. He is planning to establish world class universities in India. The minister for HRD Mr. Kapil Sibal was welcomed the foreign universities to establish their campuses in India.

President of America, Obama has emphasized the importance of higher education, urging more Americans to get college degrees. Higher education can lead to prestigious careers and high salaries. It can also broaden one's experience, exposing the student to differing points of view, critical thinking and analytical skills, as well as appreciation of the arts or diverse cultures. These may rival career advancement in importance.

The importance of higher education lies in several areas, including the financial, social, emotional and intellectual realms. University professors Boyce Watkins and Richard Vedder, speaking in a discussion on National Public Radio's Tell Me More (Sept. 1, 2009), emphasized that students should carefully analyze the benefits they wish to gain from higher education.

DEMAND FOR HIGHER EDUCATION

The demand for higher education globally has increased and will continue to grow. There are more than 100 million college students worldwide, new campuses are being built, and existing campuses are expanding. Universities are competing internationally for resources, faculty, the best students, and education funding.

Overseas expansion creates opportunities for students and faculty in terms of exchange programs and expanded campus environments. China, India, and the Middle East have quickly become key areas for widespread campus growth. The learning model varies by country and institution, ranging from replicating the home campus, to building local capacity, to participating in faculty exchanges.

These global learning environments give students an opportunity to expand their portfolios to include experience that is valued in today's workforce. Universities in turn use their foreign campuses to attract top research talent and build international relationships, establishing a global presence and helping develop local capacity.

WOMEN IN HIGHER EDUCATION IN INDIA

Women constitute almost half of the population in the world. But the hegemonic masculine ideology made them suffer a lot as they were denied equal opportunities in different parts of the world. The rise of feminist ideas has, however, led to the tremendous improvement of women's condition throughout the world in recent times. Access to education has been one of the most pressing demands of theses women's rights movements. Women's education in India has also been a major preoccupation of both the government and civil society as educated women can play a very important role in the development of the country.

History of Women's Education: Although in the Vedic period women had access to education in India, they had gradually lost this right. However, in the British period there was revival of interest in women's education in India. During this period, various socio religious movements led by eminent persons like Raja Ram Mohan Roy, Iswar Chandra Vidyasagar emphasized on women's education in India. Mahatma Jyotiba Phule, Periyar and Baba Saheb Ambedkar were leaders of the lower castes in India who took various initiatives to make education available to the women of India. However women's education got a fillip after the country got independence in 1947 and the government has taken various measures to provide education to all Indian women. As a result women's literacy rate has grown over the three decades and the growth of female literacy has in fact been higher than that of male literacy rate. While in 1971 only 22% of Indian women were literate, by the end of 2001 54.16% female were literate. The growth of female literacy rate is 14.87% as compared to 11.72 % of that of male literacy rate.

Importance of Women's Education: Women's education in India plays a very important role in the overall development of the country. It not only helps in the development of half of the human resources, but in improving the quality of life at home and outside. Educated women not only tend to promote education of their girl children, but also can provide better guidance to all their children. Moreover educated women can also help in the reduction of infant mortality rate and growth of the population. **Obstacles:** Gender discrimination still persists in India and lot more needs to be done in the field of women's education in India. The gap in the male-female literacy rate is just a simple indicator. While the male literary rate is more than 75% according to the 2001 census, the female literacy rate is just 54.16%.

Prevailing prejudices, low enrollment of girl child in the schools, engagements of girl children in domestic works and high dropout rate are major obstacles in the path of making all Indian women educated.

TABLE-II PERCENTAGE OF FEMALE POPULATION BY EDUCATIONAL LEVEL

Percentage distribution of population by educational level

Educational level	1971		1981		1991*		2001**	
	Female	**Male**	**Female**	**Male**	**Female**	**Male**	**Female**	**Male**
1	2	3	4	5	6	7	8	9
Illiterate	81.30	60.60	75.20	53.10	67.83	47.25	54.85	36.76
Literate without educational level	6.80	12.20	8.60	14.40	8.94	12.53	14.58	17.40
Primary	7.10	13.70	8.10	13.60	10.09	14.38	12.73	15.70
Middle	3.00	7.50	4.20	8.40	6.55	11.19	6.91	10.50
Matriculate/Secondary	1.50	4.90	2.30	5.90	3.59	7.57	5.65	9.62
Higher secondary/Intermediate/ Pre-University	-	-	0.80	2.20	1.39	3.18	2.66	4.62
Non-technical diploma or certificate not equal to degree	-	0.10	-	-	0.06	0.10	0.03	0.05
Technical diploma or certificate not equal to degree	-	0.10	0.10	0.30	0.11	0.40	0.15	0.55
Graduate and above	0.30	0.91	0.70	2.10	1.44	3.40	2.44	4.80
All Levels	100.00	100.00	100.00	100.00	100.00	100.00	100.00	100.00

Note : The figures for 1981 exclude Assam where the census could not be conducted and the figures for 1991 excludes Jammu & Kashmir where census could not be conducted

* The figures for 1991 excludes Jammu & Kashmir where census could not be conducted

** India figures exclude those of the three sub-divisions viz. Mao Maram, Paomata and Purul of Senapati district of Manipur as census results divisions were cancelled of 2001 in these three sub-due to technical and administrative reasons

Source: Office of the Registrar General of India

Table-II shows that the percentage distribution of female population by educational level of graduate and above was increased from 0.30 in 1971 to 2.44 in 2001. It concludes that the number of women students in higher education is increasing year by year.

TABLE-III NUMBER OF FEMALES PER 100 MALES IN UNIVERSITY EDUCATION IN MAJOR DISCIPLINES

Number of females per 100 males in university education in major disciplines					
Year	Arts	Science	Commerce	Engineering & Technical	Medicine
1	2	3	4	5	6
1950-51	15.4	NA	0.5	0.3	18.5
1955-56	14.9	NA	0.7	0.2	18.9
1960-61	22.3	NA	1.1	0.4	25.6
1965-66	36.9	NA	4.9	2.2	29.4
1970-71	50.2	21.0	6.2	3.8	25.3
1975-76	44.7	27.1	9.9	5.2	22.0
1979-80	61.0	38.3	15.8	8.0	40.4
1980-81	59.7	38.9	18.5	6.8	40.4
1981-82	64.1	41.4	21.2	6.8	43.1
1982-83	63.0	41.6	22.9	6.8	46.1
1983-84	62.3	42.1	24.1	7.6	47.7
1984-85	66.8	45.8	25.9	8.6	51.4
1985-86	66.7	47.9	28.1	9.2	53.5
1986-87	65.6	47.5	29.2	8.4	43.4
1987-88[P]	64.5	44.3	27.9	8.60	48.40
1988-89[P]	63.9	47.1	28.5	8.60	48.60
1989-90[P]	63.3	56.8	30.0	11.90	52.60
1990-91[P]	65.5	58.3	31.6	12.20	52.10
1991-92[P]	65.3	45.7	33.8	9.50	53.30
1992-93[P]	64.7	48.0	35.9	11.9	52.4
1993-94[P]	64.7	49.1	36.5	12.5	57.5
1994-95[P]	65.5	50.1	38.9	15.1	51.2
1995-96[P]	70.3	56.8	40.8	16.6	52.7
1996-97[P]	70.7	54.2	41.4	17.4	54.8
1997-98[P]	70.6	55.4	44.0	20.3	56.5
1998-99[P]	80.1	55.3	46.1	24.3	62.1
1999-2000[P]	81.3	60.0	50.7	28.3	61.0
2000-2001[P]	81.4	61.4	55.3	28.7	68.2
2001-2002[P]	77.8	64.2	63.1	33.1	68.4
2002-2003[P]	82.2	60.6	58.0	29.2	71.2
2003-04[P]	85.7	75.9	51.2	17.5	72.5
2004-05[P]	87.3	84.3	51.6	31.1	53.1
2005-06	77.7	71.2	65.2	36.1	90.1*
2006-07 (P)	76.9	71.2	60.9	35.8	89.5*

Source : Department of Secondary & Higher Education, Ministry of Human Resource Development

Note : Arts and Science figures are combined for the years 1955-56 , 1960-61 and 1965-66.

NA : Not available

Figures in respect of Engineering, Technical and Medicine relate to only for degree level, not post graduate for the years 1987-88 to 1991-92

P. Provisional,

*: includes dentistry, nursing, pharmacy, Ayurvedic and Unani

Table-III gives full information about the number of females per 100 males in university education in major disciplines from 1950-51 to 2006-07.

CONCLUSION

In the 21st century, technology will play an increasing role in higher education. Institutions will adopt innovative solutions that will change the way students learn, communicate, produce, collaborate, and study both on and off campus—solutions that will also improve interactions among faculty, staff, and students. Creating innovative services from current and future technologies requires a powerful, reliable, expandable, and secure IT infrastructure that has adequate bandwidth, quality of service, and storage. Many colleges and universities have already developed short- and long-term plans to ensure success in meeting their current and future needs. ICT based higher education is necessary for all female students in India for their better future. It is the duty of our government to provide quality higher education for all students of India in general and female students in particular.

References:

1. All India Council for Technical Education, Government of India, New Delhi.
2. Department of Secondary & Higher Education, Ministry of Human Resource Development, Government of India, New Delhi.
3. Ministry of Human Resource Development, Government of India, New Delhi.
4. Registrar General of India.
5. UNESCO World Conference on Higher Education in the Twenty-First Century, Paris, 5-9 October 1998.
6. University Grants Commission, Government of India, New Delhi.

31

On-line Material for Teacher Educators at Elementary Level

INTRODUCTION

Since Independence, successive Indian governments have had to address a number of key challenges with regard to education policy, which has always formed a crucial part of its development agenda. Currently, while Indian institutes of management and technology are world-class, primary and secondary schools, particularly in rural areas, face severe challenges.

Education has been around for as long as man has been, though its structure and perception has varied over centuries and civilizations. Now we are living in the highly scientific and technological world. Enormous changes are occurring in the day to day life of human beings because of globalization, privatization and liberalization. Education is seen as central to economic competitiveness, the reduction of poverty and inequality and environmental sustainability. So, it is necessary to provide education for all; then only India will become developed country by 2020.

The development of any nation depends mainly on the standards of its educational institutions. Education is the most powerful and effective instrument for inducing radical changes in the behaviour of students. Education is a powerful instrument of national development-social, economic and cultural. The teacher occupies pivotal position in the system of education. Teaching has been one of the oldest and most respected professions in the world. Technology increases the strength of the teacher.

OBJECTIVES OF THE STUDY

The study is designed with the following specific objectives:

1. To study the influence of on-line material on professional development of teacher educators at elementary level.
2. To study the availability of on-line material for teacher educators at elementary level.
3. To study the importance of on-line material for teacher educators at elementary level.

NEED AND IMPORTANCE OF THE STUDY

"Of all the different factors which influence the quality of education and its contribution to national development; the quality, competence and character of teachers are undoubtedly the most significant......."

...**Kothari Education Commission (1964-66)**

Education is important for every individual in a nation. It plays a vital role to change the stare of a country. No country could bring a revolution in it unless it's everybody are educated enough to meet the challenges. Education makes a man realize about himself and his goals and how to achieve that goals. We are living in the modern age of science where we found Technologies in every aspect of life. What makes life so brain friendly for us simply; these are the Technologies which we use for our ease and comforts. Not only in our daily life but also in the research centre, in defensive measured of a country, biological aspects etc. No nation could generate the progress unless it promotes technical aspects in its fields.

To improve teacher education system in the country, National Council for Teacher Education (NCTE), which sets norms and standards for quality teacher education and ensure planned and coordinated of teacher education, is conducting a nationwide study on the demand and supply of teachers and teacher educators at the school level, for the year 2007-08 to 2016-17. Without strengthening teacher education it is not possible to give quality education for school students. To reach the above goal usage of technology is important. With the help of internet we can read and watch any type of information relating to teacher education in the forms of e-library, e-newsletter, databases, on-line forum, portal, audio, video and features. The sharing of on-line material is not only time saving and cheap but also effective.

REVIEW OF THE STUDY

The world of separate nation-states is said to be ending enabling the process of globalization to run its logical course. The new technology, based on the computer and satellite communication have indeed revolutionized our traditional conception of the media, both print and electronic. Books, newspapers, radio, television and video programme are now being transposed into the multimedia world of the cyber space and available to all people of the world wherever they may live. Ajayi (2001) remarks that globalization is about competition and struggle for dominance which encourages more than anything else, the continuation and expansion of western imperialism in the new millennium.

The public is keeping abreast with the technology changes. More than ever, individuals value the importance of technology changes in education. Take a look at the following releases of public and student opinion on technology and education:

Public Opinion

In a January, 1995 survey by Microsoft, public opinion recognizes the importance of:

- 89 per cent of parents (84 per cent of general population) believe computer skills are important to educational success.
- 86 per cent of computer-using children believe computers skills are important to getting good grades in school.
- 92 per cent of children think computer skills will help them earn higher salaries in future jobs.
- 77 per cent of teachers (67 per cent of general public) think computers help each child learn at his/her own pace.
- 61 per cent of American (56 per cent of teachers) believe that computers help develop kids' creativity.

Student Opinion

In a once-per-decade poll of teens about school, the National Association of Secondary School Principals found the following (Education Daily, August 19, 1996):

- In 1974 and 1983, math and English ranked as the most important courses offered in school. Computer use barely made the list.
- In 1996, student ranked computer use and programming a close third in importance to math and English. 96 per cent of the student ranked math as very or fairly important, 93 per cent ranked English as very or fairly important and 92 per cent ranked computer use and programming as very or fairly important.

With over 400 educators, parents, interested community members, and business leaders present in a Department of Education forum in 1995, a vision for education was cultivated to guide districts and school systems. This section will show you their conclusions.

Learning in the 21st Century

The following requirements were identified for learning in the 21st Century:

- A greater dependence on new communication and computing technologies that support new levels of student creativity and research.
- A change in the role of teachers from "sages on the stage" to mentors, researchers, publishers, technology users, knowledge producers, risk takers and lifelong learners.
- Involvement of parents to play a major role in the education of their children and to work actively with teachers to connect formal and informal education.
- Partnering of local businesses and other community organizations so they become actively involved in the schools.
- Collaborations that bring students, teachers, and researchers together to create new curriculum for K-12 learners and adult Learners.

Building Schools of the Future

- The following conditions were recognized as critical elements of future schools:
- Schools of the future must be open and flexible.
- New communication should promote new collaborations and a higher level of cooperation and creative problem-solving.
- Teachers must be supported in their use of new technologies for learning and also in their use of technology for professional development and collaboration.
- Learners must be able to use technology to achieve new levels of learning and to acquire new information age skills and abilities.
- Educational managers need to use technology as a tool for managing schools and learner communities.
- Free from one geographic location.
- Supportive of all learning styles.
- Teachers must be researchers and mentors.
- New skills required in info-society: abilities to quickly adapt to new situations and new technologies and to be able to process vast amounts of information

- "'The only way a school or district will get sustained support for quality professional development in technology is when the line administrators and top administrators are active technology users'" Van Wilinson
- Administrators and managers need professional development as much as their staff.
- Principals, superintendents and school boards must provide teachers with adequate training and support to effectively use the technology in their classrooms. They need to understand how the current structure of a teacher's and learner's day impact on their effective use of the technology. In effect, managers must provide the vision of change that includes empowering teachers and learners in new ways and then must learn how to effectively manage these empowered teachers and learners".
- New on-line communities
- "'Education needs to SELL its beliefs to industry and start a cooperative partnership'". Perry Brown, Anderson County Schools office of Technology in Clinton, Tennessee. "If we can make students life-long learners, then industries would not have to pay 20% of their manpower budget on retaining! The point is, if we can do the job right, then industry would be SMART to help fund us – we would be saving them money in several ways".
- Give to the community as well as asking from it. Create a vision and a reality in which the school is creating value for the community and the technology is enabling the technology to be created.

METHODOLOGY

a. Locale and Size of the Sample

The sample of the study consisted of 60 Teacher Educators belonging to twelve D.Ed. Colleges (private) of three regions of Andhra Pradesh State (Andhra, Rayalaseema and Telangana). The stratified random sampling was applied. All the 12 colleges were situated in urban areas of different districts of A.P.

a. Tools for the collection of the data

The investigator searched for the tools for on-line material for professional development of teacher educators at primary level. The investigator has not found suitable tool for on-line material for professional development of teacher educators at primary level. Hence, the investigator planned to develop a tool for on-line material for professional development of teacher educators.

On the basis of review of literature, a list of 27 items was prepared on on-line material for professional development of teacher educators at primary level. These items were given to some experts. The experts had checked the suitability and vocabulary used in the items. 7 items were deleted on the advice of the experts and 20 items rctained were suitable to measure on-line material for professional development of teacher educators at elementary level. Each item of the inventory was arranged on a 2 point scale with responses: good, not good or useful, not useful etc.

c. Date collection and analysis

The investigator visited personally and collected data from 38 Male and 22 Female Teacher Educators from 12 D.Ed. colleges. The analysis was carried by using simple statistical techniques.

On-line material for Professional Development of Teacher Educators at Elementary Level:

The given bellow table gives full information about the feelings of teacher educators towards on-line material for professional development.

S.No.	Statement	Answer	%
1	Availability of on-line material in your college.	Good	43.33
		Not good	56.67
2	Quality of on-line material in your college.	Good	50.00
		Not good	50.00
3	Computer lab in your college.	Good	50.00
		Not good	50.00
4	Internet facility in your college.	Good	18.33
		Not good	81.67
5	Student co-operation for the use of on-line material.	Good	90.00
		Not good	10.00
6	Responses of students after using on-line material.	Good	91.66
		Not good	08.34
7	The content in the on-line material.	Good	53.33
		Not good	46.67
8	Co-operation among teacher educators for the exchange of on-line material.	Good	50.00
		Not good	50.00
9	The usage of on-line material in your college.	Good	50.00
		Not good	50.00
10	Infrastructure of computer lab in your college.	Good	66.66
		Not good	33.37
11	Advanced computer education for teacher educators.	Necessary	90.00
		Not necessary	10.00

12	Need of on-line material for professional development.	Necessary	51.66
		Not necessary	48.34
13	Advanced training for internet usage.	Necessary	90.00
		Not necessary	10.00
14	Training for usage of technology other than internet.	Necessary	41.66
		Not necessary	58.37
15	Books for on-line material collection.	Necessary	90.00
		Not necessary	10.00
16	Seminars and workshops on on-line material.	Necessary	96.66
		Not necessary	03.37
17	Re-fresher course on on-line material usage.	Necessary	91.66
		Not necessary	08.37
18	Feedback on on-line material usage.	Necessary	98.33
		Not necessary	01.67
19	On-line material for professional development.	Useful	91.66
		Not useful	08.34
20	Encouragement of the management for the usage of on-line material.	Encouragement	60.00
		No encouragement	40.00

RESULTS AND DISCUSSION

After analysis of the collected data the following results were found.

1. Availability of the on-line material.

Gender	Good (%)	Not good (%)
Male Teacher Educator	30	33.33
Female Teacher Educator	13.33	23.33

Only 43.33% of teacher educators were expressed that the availability of on-line material was good and remaining 56.67 per cent were said that the availability of on-line material was not good.

2. Need of the on-line material.

Gender	Necessary (%)	Not necessary (%)
Male Teacher Educator	33.33	30
Female Teacher Educator	18.33	18.33

51.66 per cent of teacher educators were expressed their views that, need of on-line material was necessary and remaining 48.34 per cent of teacher educators were felt that the on-line material was not necessary for professional development.

3. On-line material for professional development.

Gender	Useful (%)	Not useful (%)
Male Teacher Educator	58.33	5
Female Teacher Educator	33.33	3.33

91.66 per cent of total teacher educators were said that on-line material is useful for professional development and remaining 8.34 per cent of teacher educators were felt that they have no useful.

4. On-line material- Encouragement of the management.

Gender	Encouragement (%)	No encouragement (%)
Male Teacher Educator	30	33.33
Female Teacher Educator	30	6.66

60 per cent of teacher educators are getting encouragement from the management to use on-line material and 40 per cent of teacher educators are not getting any type of encouragement for theirs' professional development.

5. Advanced Training for Internet usage.

Gender	Necessary (%)	Not necessary (%)
Male Teacher Educator	56.67	6.67
Female Teacher Educator	33.33	3.33

90 per cent of teacher educators were felt that, advanced training for internet usage is necessary for professional development and only 10 per of teacher educators were felt that, advanced training for internet usage is not necessary for professional development.

SUGGESTIONS AND CONCLUSION

Only 50 per cent of the teacher educators were computer operators and internet users and the remaining 50 per cent teacher educators have no interest to know computer/internet. Majority of the teacher educators are working part-time job along with regular job. They are not spending much time for professional development. Low salary is also one of the causes for un-satisfaction of the job of teacher educators. 75 per cent of teacher educators have no personal computer. After seeing the data and real position of colleges and teacher educators, the following suggestions were recommended;

1. Increase the salary of teacher educators.
2. Provide on-line services with low cast for teacher educators.
3. Proper training is necessary for internet use of teacher educators at primary level.
4. Government should take necessary steps towards use of on-line material in private teacher educators.
5. The availability of on-line material will be in the local language.
6. Separate portal for teacher educators at elementary level.
7. Seminars/workshops/conferences relating to on-line material are necessary

BIBLIOGRAPHY

1. HRD, Govt. of India, New Delhi.
2. NCTE, New Curriculum Framework for Teacher Education, New Delhi.
3. Scholte, Jan Aart (2000), "*Globalization: A Critical Introduction*" (New York: St. Martin's).
4. SSA, Govt. of India, New Delhi.

32

Human Health in India – An Appraisal

INTRODUCTION

Now, what is health, indeed? Since it is often overcast with too many intellectual and idealistic notions that are not testable under objective norms, it is essential to define health under a norm of minimum objective criteria. World Health Organization defines health as a state of complete physical, mental and social well-being and not merely the absence of disease or infirmity.

HEALTH CARE IN INDIA

'Health is Wealth'. 'A sound mind in a sound body'. The above sentences are showing the importance of health. Healthcare in India is the responsibility of constituent states and territories of India. The Constitution charges every state with "raising of the level of nutrition and the standard of living of its people and the improvement of public health as among its primary duties". The National Health Policy was endorsed by the Parliament of India in 1983 and updated in 2002.

The art of Health Care in India can be traced back nearly 3500 years. From the early days of Indian history the Aryurvedic tradition of medicine has been practiced. During the rule of Emperor Ashoka Maurya (third century B.C.E.), schools of learning in the healing arts were created. Many valuable herbs and medicinal combinations were created. Even today many of these continue to be used. During his reign there is evidence that Emperor Ashoka was the first leader in world history to attempt to give health care to all of his citizens, thus it was the India of antiquity which was the first state to give it's citizens national health care.

In recent times India has eradicated mass famines, half of children in India are underweight, one of the highest rates in the world and nearly the same rate of Sub-Saharan Africa. Water supply and sanitation in India continue to be a challenged, only one of three Indians has access to improved sanitation facilities such as toilet. India's HIV/AIDS epidemic is a growing threat. The maternal mortality in India is the second highest in the world.

Providing healthcare and disease prevention to India's growing population of more than a billion people becomes challenging in the face of increased competition for resources. 2.47 million People in India are estimated to be HIV positive. India is one of the four countries worldwide where polio has not as yet been successfully eradicated and one third of the world's tuberculosis cases are in India. Three out of four children who died from measles in 2008 were in India.

According to the World Health Organization 900,000 Indians die each year from drinking contaminated water and breathing in polluted air. As India grapples with these basic issues, new challenges are emerging for example there is a rise in chronic adult diseases such as cardiovascular illnesses and diabetes as a consequence of changing lifestyles.

There are vast disparities in people's health even among the different states across the country largely attributed to the resource allocation by the state governments where some states have been more successful than others. Better efforts are needed by the local governments to ensure that the health services provided are actually reaching the poor in worst-affected areas.

However, at the same time, India's health care system also includes entities which are world class. India is a magnet for medical tourists, who are able to get medical treatments and surgeries at a fraction of the cost of these procedures in western countries. The Apollo set of hospitals, for example, thrives on this business. Each hospital, however, must also set aside a number of beds for the poor. Majority people of South-East Asian countries are visiting India to get low-cost and good treatment.

HEALTH STATUS IN INDIA

The health status is usually measured in terms of life expectancy at birth, infant mortality rate, fertility rate, crude birth rate and crude death rate. These indicators of health are determined by numerous factors such as per capita income, nutrition, housing, sanitation, safe drinking water, social infrastructure, health and medical care services provided by government, geographical climate, employment status, incidence of poverty and the like (Reddy and Selvaraju 1994; Dadibhavi and Bagalkoti 1994). It is, de facto, the quality of human health upon which the realization of life goals and objectives of a persona, the community or nation as whole depends.

Health status is multidimensional in nature and difficult to measure precisely. It is captured through a range of indicators such as mortality, morbidity, anthropometric measures, nutritional status or calorie intake, and life expectancy at birth. Among these, mortality and life expectancy at birth are widely used to measure the health status of a population, as they are easily observed, objective and less prone to measurement errors. However, morbidity may be a more useful indicator than mortality, since it is related to the pain and sufferings of the people, while mortality is a terminal event. But the problem with morbidity is that it is difficult to measure without bias. Despite these well- recognized problems and difficulties of measurement, there can be little doubt that good information on morbidity is extremely useful (Sen, 1998).

Enhancing the quality of growth is an important objective of the development paradigm in many developing countries. Better health, education, equal and wider job opportunities to all, trustworthy and transparent people's intuitions, sustainable and cleaner environment, dignity, self-esteem and life security, among others, are key manifestations of the quality of growth (WB 2000). If the quality of human capital is not good, physical capital and natural resources can't be properly utilized and growth neither be sustained nor be qualitative. Health is major segment of human capital.

Experts generally believe that the level of health status of persons in a nation is a robust reflection of the state of development of the nation. Based on experience and logical thought process, it can be concluded with a fair amount of certainty that a nation with good health tends to be productive and that productivity tends to uplift economic and societal developments. Economic and societal developments, in turn, tend to improve the indicators of health status and quality of life.

Health is an important entitlement that enhances "capabilities" of the poor people leading to increase in "commodities" and further improvement in health status (Dadibhavi and Bagalkoti 1994; Bloom et al 2004). As investment on health increases, the productive capacity of the working population, and hence the level of income tends to rise and to that extent it contributes to a decline in the incidence of poverty (Reddy and Selvaraju 1994). With rapid improvement in health particularly of the poor "vicious circle" of poverty can be converted into "virtuous circle" of prosperity (Mayer 1999; Mayer 2000; Bloom et al 2004). Although there has been a two-way relationship, a strong causal link from adult health to economic growth is observed by many studies (Mayer 1999; Knowles and Owen 1997; Jamison and Wang 1998). Further, Knowles and Owen (1997) and Jamison and Wang (1998) find that life expectancy contributes to economic growth more than education. In addition to its direct impact on productivity, health has other effects on economic development and demographic transition. Good infant health and nutrition directly increase the benefits of education (WB 1993; WHO 1999). Further, Barro (1996) points out that by increasing longevity, health reduces the depreciation rate of human capital, making investment in education more attractive.

It is a well-known fact that India is, next only to China, the second largest country in terms of population in the world. But the health status of a great majority of the people is far from satisfactory as compared to China and other developed countries. However, over the last five decades or so, India has built up health infrastructure and manpower at primary, secondary and tertiary care in government, voluntary and private sectors and made considerable progress in improving the health of its population (Ray 2003; Bhat and Babu 2004).

Health risk due to high prevalence of alcohol and tobacco consumption is also increasing. India's dream of "World Class" health care delivery system is difficult to achieve. On the other hand, the economic reforms that have been introduced in the country since 1991 have brought changes in all the sectors of the Indian economy. It is the social sector, particularly health and education, which is financially getting affected, among others. The share of public expenditure as a percentage to GDP on health and education at higher level has been gradually declining (Panchamukhi 2000; Dev and Mooij 2002). The health sector, therefore, faces "dual" challenges: while control of communicable and non-communicable diseases is of paramount importance, the budget allocation by the government is low when compared to developed countries in the world. Hence, India faces the daunting challenge of meeting health care needs of its vast population and ensuring accessibility, efficiency, equity and quality of healthcare and thereby achieving the objective of growth with equality and social justice.

Family Health Survey of India (2005-06)

The results of the latest National Family Health Survey (NFHS-3) conducted in 2005-06 provide disturbing information. The proportion of underweight children under the age of three was 47 per cent in 1996-97; according to the 2005-06 survey it has fallen to 46 per cent.

In some of the more economically backward States it was even higher, such as Madhya Pradesh with 60 per cent, Bihar with 58 per cent, Jharkhand with 59 per cent and Chhattisgarh with 52 per cent. In several of these States, the proportion of underweight children actually increased between 1996-97 and 2005-06. In Bihar, it went up from 54 to 58 per cent; in Jharkhand from 54 to 59 per cent.

The more surprising fact is that such degeneration was not confined to the poorer and more backward States, but happened even in some of the more prosperous States. Thus, in Gujarat, which is one of the richest States and has shown one of the highest rates of economic growth over this period, the proportion of underweight children increased from 45 to 47 per cent.

Data on anaemia provide some evidence of the quality of nutrition and therefore address the point that some analysts try to make about calorie consumption or even weight for age/height not being correct indicators. According to the NFHS-3, the prevalence of anemia is not only alarmingly high but has actually got significantly worse since the mid-1990s.

In the latest survey, nearly four out of five children in the age group of 6 to 35 months had anaemia, while nearly three out of every five ever-married women and pregnant women also were anaemic. The prevalence of severe anaemia also remains high.

Poor nutrition obviously increases vulnerability to disease and, therefore, preventive health services would have to be even more active in order to prevent the adverse tendencies arising from worsening nutrition. But here too the evidence is not really of improvement but suggests some deterioration. While the pattern obviously varies across States, a number of State governments have actually shown declines - sometimes significant - in per capita health expenditures, especially in public health areas such as immunization.

This is now showing in the most worrying changes in basic indicators such as immunization rates of small children. The percentage of children in the age group of 12 to 23 months who have been immunized fully (by receiving vaccines for BCG, measles, and three doses each of polio/DPT) has gone up very slightly between 1996-97 and 2005-06, but it is still only 43.5 per cent. That means more than half of the children in India still do not receive full immunization and are, therefore, prey to completely eradicable diseases.

In three of the richest States - Maharashtra, Punjab and Gujarat - per capita public spending on health has declined in constant price terms after 2000. And the NFHS-3 results indicate that in these three States, immunization rates of children in the age group of 12 to 36 months have actually fallen in 2005-06 compared with 1998-99.

In some cases, the decline is dramatic – from 78 per cent to only 59 per cent in Maharashtra, for instance.

This is not just a severe indictment of public health policies, but poses grave risks for the future. Lack of full immunization can turn into a future public health disaster, with the possible re-emergence and spread of diseases polio, tetanus and diphtheria – all of which are easy to prevent with proper public health management.

HEALTH EXPENDITURE IN INDIA

India spends a high proportion of its gross domestic product (GDP) on health care but still it is poor in terms of health outcomes as compared to countries at similar level of development. It is therefore, extremely important to understand the financial dimensions of the health sector in order to allow policy makers to make wise decisions in this sector. National Health Accounts (NHA) provide an important tool to describe and measure the flow of health expenditures outlining total spending, contributions to spending by different sources and claims on spending by different uses of funds. NHA thereby gives a consistent framework for modeling reforms and for monitoring the effects of financing health care. It helps in the optimal management of the allocation and mobilization of health resources.

Table-1Health Expenditure in India (2004-05)

Type of Expenditure	Expenditure	Distribution of total Health Expenditure %)	Share of GDP (%)
Public Expenditure	263, 132, 133	19.67	0.84
Private Expenditure	1, 044, 135, 932	78.05	3.32
External Flow	30, 495, 141	2.28	0.10
Total Health Expenditure	1, 337, 763, 206	100	4.25
Gross Domestic Product	31, 494, 120, 000		

Sources: *Demand for Grants of Ministry of Health & Family Welfare & Other Central Ministries, (2006-07), Government of India.*

It is well known that health expenditure in India is dominated by private spending. To a large extent this is a reflection of the inadequate public spending that has been a constant if unfortunate feature of Indian development in the past half century.

The given data from the above table-1 shows that; the public expenditure on health is very low (0.84 per cent of total GDP) when compared to private expenditure (3.32 per cent of total GDP). It is important to increase public expenditure on health in India to improve health status of people's.

Indian Budget Expenditure on Health 2009-10

The Government of India giving high priority for health sector. The allocation for health sector increases last few years. Allocation under National Rural Health Mission (NRHM) increased by Rs.2, 057 crore over Interim B.E. 2009-10 of Rs.12, 070 crore.

All BPL families to be covered under Rashtriya Swasthya Bima Yojana (RSBY).Allocation under RSBY increased by 40 per cent over previous allocation to Rs.350 crore in B.E. 2009-10.

Table-2 2009-10 Budget Expenditure on Medical & Public Health (Rs. in crore)

Medical & Public Health	Head of Development	2008-09 Budget	2008-09 Revised	2009-10 Budget
	22, 210	5, 200.54	4, 988.41	6, 175.95

Source: *Parliament Library, New Delhi, 2009.*

The given data from the above table-2 shows that; the budget expenditure on medical and public health increased Rs.1187.54 crore from the year 2008-09 to 2009-10.

Table-3 Per Capita Expenditure on Health in India

Per Capita Expenditure on Health in India (1993-1994 to 2003-04)			
S.No.	Year	Real	
		Health Expenditure (Rs. in crore)	Per Capita Expenditure
1	1993-94	7938.36	89
2	1994-95	7921.58	87
3	1995-96	8521.14	91.82
4	1996-97	8876.16	93.83
5	1997-98	9772.64	101.38
6	1998-99	10884.42	110.73
7	1999-2000	12068.52	120.56
8	2000-01	12078.79	118.54
9	2001-02	11795.52	113.75
10	2002-03	12790.28	121.23
11	2003-04	13091.70	122.01

Source: *Planning Commission, Govt. of India.*

From the above table-3 we conclude that the per capita expenditure on health increases year by year except in 2001-02.

Table-4 State-wise Per Capita Health Expenditure and Number of Government Hospital Beds Available per 100,000 Populations

S.No	States / UTs	Per Capita Health Expen. 2008-09 (Rs.) (#)	No. of Govt. hospital beds available per 100,000 Population (@)	Reference Period*
States which are above National Average of Per Capita Health Exp. 2008-09				
1	Mizoram	1611	128	1/1/2008
2	Sikkim	1446	173	1/1/2009
3	Andaman & Nicobar (UT)	1347	233	1/1/2009
4	Puducherry (UT)	1333	284	1/1/2009
5	Lakshadweep (UT)	1315	274	1/1/2008
6	Goa	1149	178	1/1/2009
7	Himachal Pradesh	884	123	1/1/2009
8	Jammu & Kashmir	845	36	1/1/2008
9	Delhi (UT)	840	141	1/1/2009
10	Chandigarh (UT)	798	225	1/1/2008
11	Nagaland	794	85	1/1/2009
12	Arunachal Pradesh	771	188	1/1/2008
13	Tripura	740	66	1/1/2008
14	Manipur	695	94	1/1/2008
15	Meghalaya	690	106	1/1/2007
16	Uttarakhand	630	84	1/1/2009
States which are below National Average of Per Capita Health Exp. 2008-09				
17	Assam	471	11	1/1/2004
18	Kerala	454	82	1/1/2008
19	Dadra & Nagar Haveli (UT)	430	87	1/1/2009
20	Karnataka	419	86	1/1/2009
21	Andhra Pradesh	410	43	1/1/2007
22	Tamil Nadu	410	72	1/1/2008
23	Daman & Diu (UT)	405	105	1/1/2004
24	Chhattisgarh	378	41	1/1/2008
25	Punjab	360	40	1/1/2008
26	Jharkhand	328	18	1/1/2008
27	Uttar Pradesh	293	18	1/1/2007
28	Rajasthan	287	51	1/1/2008
29	Harayana	280	32	1/1/2009

30	Maharashtra	278	28	1/1/2009
31	Gujarat	270	53	1/1/2009
32	Orissa	263	37	1/1/2009
33	West Bengal	262	58	1/1/2008
34	Madhya Pradesh	235	29	1/1/2008
35	Bihar	173	24	1/1/2008
All India		**503****	**43**	

Source: # *Calculations are based on the Health Expenditure by Central & State Governements in 2008-09 publised in National Health Accounts India-2004-05 (with provisional estimates from 2005-06 to 2008-09) and Population figures published in Census of India 2001-Population Projections for India and States 2001-2026 (Report of the Technical Group on Population Projections-May 2006)*

(@) Calculations are based on data (Population served per Government Hospital Bed) published in the National Health Profile 2008 - Central Bureau of Health Intelligence

* Reference period relates to Population per Government Hospital Bed based on which figures in Col. No. 4 have been arrived at.

** All India Average is based on expenditure on health by States/UTs and Central Government.

The date was given in the above table-4 shows that the per capita expenditure on health is different from state to state. It was high in Mijoram (Rs. 1611) and low in Bihar (Rs. 173). The number of Government Hospital beds available per 1, 00,000 population was high in Pondichery (284) and low in Assam (11).

HEALTH IN INDIA- INTERNATIONAL COMPARISION

Quantity and Quality are the two important dimensions of human population in any country. In general, all the countries are committed to improving quality of population, a better welfare standard measure. Health is a prerequisite for human development and is an essential component for the well being of the mankind. Health is at the heart of the Millennium Development Goals (MDGs). Goals 4, 5 and 6 specifically focus on health, but all the MDGs have health-related aspects; achieving them will not be possible without progress on food security, gender equality, the empowerment of women, wider access to education and better stewardship of the environment.

Health Expenditure of India-International Comparison

Table-5 International Comparison of Health Expenditure

Health spending across selected countries based on available data shows a mixed picture as given below.

S.No.	Country	Total Health of Exp. as % GDP		Government Exp. on Health as % of Total Exp. on Health	
		2004	2005	2004	2005
1	USA	15.4	15.2	44.7	45.1
2	Germany	10.6	10.7	76.9	76.9
3	France	10.5	11.2	78.4	79.9
4	Canada	9.8	9.7	69.8	70.3
5	UK	8.1	8.2	86.8	87.1
6	Brazil	8.8	7.9	54.1	44.1
7	Mexico	6.5	6.4	46.4	45.5
8	China	4.7	4.7	38.0	38.8
9	Malaysia	3.8	4.2	58.8	44.8
10	Indonesia	2.8	2.1	34.2	46.6
11	Thailand	3.5	3.5	64.7	63.9
12	Pakistan	2.2	2.1	19.6	17.5
13	Sri Lanka	4.3	4.1	45.6	46.2
14	Bangladesh	3.1	2.8	28.1	29.1
15	Nepal	5.6	5.8	26.3	28.1
16	India	5.0	5.0	17.3	19.0

Source: *World Health Statistics, (2007&2008), World Health organization.*

The data from the above table-5 reveals that; the total health expenditure (% on GDP) of India is better than other Asian countries except Nepal and lower than other countries mentioned above. But, in case of Government expenditure on health is lower than all the above countries.

DISEASES

Although India accounts for 16.5 per cent of the world's population, it contributes to more than 20 per cent of the world's share of diseases. And far from getting better, this burden of disease is projected to increase considerably in the near future. Even as diseases and deaths on account of malaria, tuberculosis (TB), diarrhoea and other infectious diseases may reduce, human immunodeficiency virus/acquired immune deficiency syndrome (HIV/AIDS) and TB and drug-resistant malaria are projected to increase.

Table-6 Selected Infectious Diseases

S.No.	Disease (2007) *2008	Country			
		China	India	UK	USA
1	Cholera	168	2635	32	7
2	Diptheria	0	3354	3	0
3	H_5N_1 Influenza*	3	—	—	—
4	Japanese encephalitis	4330	4017	0	—
5	Leprosy	1528	137685	—	—
6	Malaria	—	1476562	—	—
7	Measles	109023	36900	1022	30
8	Meningitis	—	—	—	—
9	Mumps	252701	—	2569	715
10	Pertussis	—	70729	1163	8739
11	Plague	—	—	—	7
12	Polio-myelitis	0	873	0	0
13	Congenital rubella syndrome	—	—	1	0
14	Rubella	74746	—	31	11
15	Neonatal tetanus	2112	937	0	0
16	Total tetanus	2112	7005	4	20
17	Tuberculosis	465877	592587	1639	4864
18	Yellow fever	—	—	0	—

The date given in the above table-6 tells that; the total number of diseased population was high in India than China, United Kingdom and United States of America.

Table-7 Health, Workforce, Infrastructure, essential medicines

S.No.	Category		Country			
			China	India	UK	USA
1	**Physicians** (2000-07)	Number	1862630	645825	126126	730801
		Density (per 10000 population)	14	6	23	26
2	**Nursing & Midwifery Personnel**(2000-07)	Number	1259240	1372059	740731	2669603
		Density (per 10000 population)	10	13	128	94
3	**Dentistry Personnel**(2000-07)	Number	136520	61424	25914	463663
		Density (per 10000 population)	1	1	10	16

4	**Community health workers**(2000-07)	Number	—-	50393	—-	—-
		Density (per 10000 population)	—-	1	—-	—-
5	**Other health service providers**(2000-07)	Number	1724620	1752027	1205694	5039244
		Density (per 10000 population)	13	16	208	177
6	**Hospital bed per 10000 population**(2000-2008)	Number	22	7	39	31

Source for Table-6 & 7: *World Health Organization Statistics 2009.*

From the table-7 we conclude that; the availability of Physicians, Nursing & Midwifery personnel, Dentistry personnel, Community health workers and other health service providers were lesser in India than China, United Kingdom and United State of America. The number of hospital bed per 10000 populations is also lower in India (7) than China (22), United Kingdom (39) and United States of America (31).

CONCLUSION

'Health is Wealth'. Health means happiness. Health is one of the most precious possessions we have and we should learn to preserve it. The golden ingredients to preserve and maintain good health are food, exercise, work and recreation. Above all, the contribution of mental peace should not be ignored. Prevention is better than cure. It is important to educate people in both rural and urban areas of India towards good health. It is necessary to minimize corruption in the health sector. The budget allocation on health sector is very low when compared to developed countries. The State Government of Andhra Pradesh in India was launched a new programme 'AROGYASREE' for all the people of below poverty level by Dr. Y.S. Rajashekara Reddy, former Chief Minister of Andhra Pradesh. This type of programme is necessary for all over India for better health of all people without regarding caste, colour, region, religion and economic status. Without heath it is impossible for anyone to do good work. So, 'Health is Wealth'.

REFERENCES

1. Barro, R. (1996), "Health and Economic Growth", Annex I of the Convocatoria para propuestas de investigacion sobre Inversion en Salud y Crecimiento Economico de la Organizacion Panamericana de la Salud.
2. Bhat, Ramesh and Sumesh K. Babu (2004), "Health Insurance and Third Party Administrators: Issues and Challenges", Economic and Political Weekly, Vol. 39, No 28, July 10-16.

3. Bhat, Ramesh and Sumesh K. Babu (2004), "Health Insurance and Third Party Administrators: Issues and Challenges", Economic and Political Weekly, Vol. 39, No 28,
4. Bloom, David E., David Canning and Dean T. Jamison (2004), "Health, Wealth and Welfare", Finance and Development, Vol. 41, No. 1, March.
5. Census of India 2001.
6. Dadibhavi, R. V and S. T. Bagalkoti (1994), "Inter-State Disparities in Health Status in India", Yojana, December 31.
7. Dev, S. Mahendra and Jos Mooij (2002), "Social Sector Expenditure in the 1990s: An Analysis of Central and State Budget", Economic and Political Weekly, Vol. 37 No. 9, March 2.
8. Diczfalusy E. Reproductive physiology, reproductive health and the last decade of the millennium. In Ghosh D, Sengupta J (Eds.), Frontiers in Reproductive Physiology. Wiley Eastern, New Delhi, 1992; pp 1–19.
9. Furedi F. Population and Development. Polity Press, Cambridge, 1997.
10. Jamison, Lau and Wang (1998), "Health's Contribution to Economic Growth, 1965- 1990", in Health, Health Policy and Health Outcomes: Final Report, Health and Development Satellite WHO Director-General Transition Team.
11. Mayer, D. (1999), "The Long-Term Impact of Health on Economic Growth in Latin America", in Health, Growth and Income Distribution in Latin America and the Caribbean: A Study of Determinants and Regional and Local Behavior, Project Report for the Pan American Health Organization.
12. Mayer, David (2000), "On the Role of Health in the Economic and Demographic Dynamics of Brazil, 1980-1995", paper presented at the conference on Population Dynamics and the Macro Economy organized by Harvard Centre for Population and Development Studies and IFS, September.
13. National Family Health Survey 2005-06, The Ministry of Health and Family Welfare, Government of India, New Delhi.
14. National Health Accounts 2004-05, Ministry of Health and Family Welfare, Government of India.
15. Panchamukhi, P. R. (2000), "Social Impact of Economic Reforms in India: A Critical Appraisal, Economic and Political Weekly, March 4.
16. Parliament Library, New Delhi, 2009.
17. Planning Commission, Government of India, New Delhi.
18. Reddy, K. N. and V. Selvaraju (1994), "Determinants of Health Status in India: An Empirical Investigation, The 76th Annual Conference Volume of the Indian Economic Association, Indira Gandhi Institute of Development Research, Bombay.
19. Union Budget of India 2009-10, Government of India.
20. W B (1993), "World Development Report 1993: Investing in Health", Oxford University Press, New York.
21. World Health Organization, World Statistics2007, 2008 and 2009.

33

Life Skills and Health Education

INTRODUCTION

Education in general and quality education in particular is more important for wealthy and healthy life. Education is power. Education gives strength to the individual. The development of any nation depends mainly on the standards of its educational institutions. Teacher has a prominent role in the development of nation. Human resource is valuable. Psychological, sociological and economical awareness is important for all human beings. Health is important for all human beings. The impact of media is very much not only on youth, but also on other human beings. Life skills and health education is most important in the present scenario.

LIFE SKILLS

Definition of Life Skills

Life skills are abilities for adaptive and positive behaviour, which enable individuals to deal effectively with the demands and challenges of everyday life. Described in this way, skills that can be said to be life skills are innumerable, and the nature and definition of life skills are likely to differ across cultures and settings. However, analysis of the life skills field suggests that there is a core set of skills that are at the heart of skills-based initiatives for the promotion of the health and well-being of children and adolescents.

UNICEF defines life skills as "a behaviour change or behaviour development approach designed to address a balance of three areas: knowledge, attitude and skills".

Life skills are essentially those abilities that help promote mental well-being and competence in young people as they face the realities of life. Most development professionals agree that life skills are generally applied in the context of health and social events. They can be utilized in many content areas: prevention of drug use, sexual violence, teenage pregnancy, HIV/AIDS prevention and suicide prevention. The definition extends into consumer education, environmental education, peace education or education for development, livelihood and income generation, among others. In short, life skills empower young people to take positive action to protect them and promote health and positive social relationships.

Types of Life Skills

There are different types of life skills in general. The most important top 10 life skills are given below:

1. **Decision making:** Decision making helps us to deal constructively with decisions about our lives. This can have consequences for health if young people actively make decisions about their actions in relation to health by assessing the different options, and what effects different decisions may have.
2. **Problem solving:** Problem solving enables us to deal constructively with problems in our lives. Significant problems that are left unresolved can cause mental stress and give rise to accompanying physical strain.
3. **Creative thinking:** Creative thinking contributes to both decision making and problem solving by enabling us to explore the available alternatives and various consequences of our actions or non-action. It helps us to look beyond our direct experience, and even if no problem is identified, or no decision is to be made, creative thinking can help us to respond adaptively and with flexibility to the situations of our daily lives.
4. **Critical thinking:** Critical thinking is an ability to analyze information and experiences in an objective manner. Critical thinking can contribute to health by helping us to recognize and assess the factors that influence attitudes and behaviour, such as values, peer pressure, and the media.
5. **Effective communication:** Effective communication means that we are able to express ourselves, both verbally and non-verbally, in ways that are appropriate to our cultures and situations. This means being able to express opinions and desires, but also needs and fears. And it may mean being able to ask for advice and help in a time of need.

6. **Interpersonal relationship skills:** Interpersonal relationship skills help us to relate in positive ways with the people we interact with. This may mean being able to make and keep friendly relationships, which can be of great importance to our mental and social well-being. It may mean keeping good relations with family members, which are an important source of social support. It may also mean being able to end relationships constructively.
7. **Self-awareness:** Self-awareness includes our recognition of ourselves, of our character, of our strengths and weaknesses, desires and dislikes. Developing self-awareness can help us to recognize when we are stressed or feel under pressure. It is also often a prerequisite for effective communication and interpersonal relations, as well as for developing empathy for others.
8. **Empathy:** Empathy is the ability to imagine what life is like for another person, even in a situation that we may not be familiar with. Empathy can help us to understand and accept others who may be very different from ourselves, which can improve social interactions, for example, in situations of ethnic or cultural diversity. Empathy can also help to encourage nurturing behaviour towards people in need of care and assistance, or tolerance, as is the case with AIDS sufferers, or people with mental disorders, who may be stigmatized and ostracized by the very people they depend upon for support.
9. **Coping with emotions:** Coping with emotions involves recognizing emotions in us and others, being aware of how emotions influence behaviour, and being able to respond to emotions appropriately. Intense emotions, like anger or sorrow can have negative effects on our health if we do not react appropriately.
10. **Coping with stress:** Coping with stress is about recognizing the sources of stress in our lives, recognizing how this affects us, and acting in ways that help to control our levels of stress. This may mean that we take action to reduce the sources of stress, for example, by making changes to our physical environment or lifestyle. Or it may mean learning how to relax, so that tensions created by unavoidable stress do not give rise to health problems.

Main Components of Life Skills

World Health Organization (WHO) categorizes life skills into the following three components:

1. Critical thinking skills/Decision-making skills
2. Interpersonal communication skills
3. Coping and self-management skills

Importance of Life Skills

Life skills are more important for all human beings. With life skills, one is able to explore alternatives, weigh pros and cons and make rational decisions in solving each problem or issue as it arises. It also entails being able to establish productive interpersonal relationships with others. Life skills enable effective communication, for example, being able to differentiate between hearing and listening and ensuring that messages are transmitted accurately to avoid miscommunication and misinterpretations.

Life skills & Lifelong Pledge

The following life skills are important for all human being for healthy and wealthy life. It is our duty to follow these skills for happy life.

S.No.	Type of Skill	General Meaning
1	Integrity	To be honest and sincere and do the right thing
2	Initiative	To do something because it needs to be done
3	Flexibility	The ability to alter plans when necessary
4	Perseverance	To stay with something until it is complete
5	Organized	To plan, arrange, keep things together
6	Caring	To feel concern for others
7	Friendship	To make and keep a friend
8	Common Sense	To use good judgment
9	Problem Solving	To seek solutions in difficult situations
10	Responsibility	To be accountable for your actions
11	Patience	To wait calmly for someone or something
12	Effort	To try your hardest
13	Curiosity	A desire to learn or know about things
14	Cooperation	To work together toward a common goal
15	Sense of Humor	To laugh and be playful without hurting others
16	Courage	To act according to one's beliefs
17	Pride	To be proud of oneself and what you can do

LIFE SKILLS & HEALTH EDUCATION

Health

Health is the general condition of a person in all aspects. It is also a level of functional and/or metabolic efficiency of an organism, often implicitly human. Health is a state of complete physical, mental and social well-being, and not merely the absence of disease or infirmity (**World Health Organization**).

Skills-based Health Education

In skills-based health education, content refers to the specific health knowledge and attitudes toward self and others, as well as the skills necessary to influence behaviour and conditions related to a particular health issue. Skills-based health education should enable a young person to apply knowledge and develop attitudes and skills to make positive decisions and take actions to promote and protect one's health and the health of others.

OTHER INFLUENCES

Understanding skills-based health education & life skills

Life skills education is designed to facilitate the practice and reinforcement of psychosocial skills in a culturally and developmentally appropriate way; it contributes to the promotion of personal and social development, the prevention of health and social problems, and the protection of human rights.

Knowledge refers to a range of information and the understanding thereof. To impart this knowledge, teachers may combine instruction on facts with an explanation of how these facts relate to one another (Greene & Simons-Morton, 1984). For example, a teacher might describe how HIV infection is transmitted and then explain that engaging in sexual relations with an intravenous drug user elevates the risk of HIV infection.

Attitudes are personal biases, preferences, and subjective assessments that predispose one to act or respond in a predictable manner. Attitudes lead people to like or dislike something, or to consider things good or bad, important or unimportant, worth caring about or not worth caring about. For example, gender sensitivity, respect for others, or respecting one's body and believing that it is important to care for attitudes that are important to preserving health and functioning well (adapted from Greene & Simons-Morton, 1984). The domain of attitudes comprises a broad range of concepts, including values, beliefs, social norms, rights, intentions, and motivations.

Skills are grouped into life skills and other skills. In general, skills are abilities that enable people to carry out specific behaviours. The phrase other skills refers to practical health skills or techniques such as competencies in first aid (e.g., bandaging, resuscitation, sterilising utensils), in hygiene (e.g., hand washing, brushing teeth, preparing oral rehydration therapy), or sexual health (e.g., using condoms correctly).

Life skills are abilities for adaptive and positive behaviour that enable individuals to deal effectively with the demands and challenges of everyday life (WHO definition). In particular, life skills are psychosocial competencies and interpersonal skills that help people make informed decisions, solve problems, think critically and creatively, communicate effectively, build healthy relationships, empathise with others, and cope with managing their lives in a healthy and productive manner. Life skills may be directed toward personal actions or actions toward others, or may be applied to actions that alter the surrounding environment to make it conducive to health.

Life Skills for Health Education

COMMUNICATION ANDINTER-PERSONAL SKILLS	DECISION-MAKING AND CRITICAL THINKING SKILLS	COPING AND SELF-MANAGEMENT SKILLS
• **Interpersonal Communication Skills** Ø verbal/nonverbal communication Ø active listening Ø expressing feelings; giving feedback (without blaming) and receiving feedback • **Negotiation/Refusal Skills** Ø negotiation and conflict managementü Ø assertiveness skillsü Ø refusal skills • **Empathy Building**o ability to listen, understand another's needs and circumstances, and express that understanding • **Cooperation and Teamwork**· expressing respect for others' contributions and different styles· assessing one's own abilities and contributing to the group • **Advocacy Skills**ü influencing skills and persuasionü networking and motivation skills	• **Decision-making/Problem solving Skills** Ø information-gathering skills Ø evaluating future consequences of present actions for self and others-determining alternative solutions to problems Ø analysis skills regarding the influence of values and of attitudes about self and others on motivation • **Critical Thinking Skills** Ø analysing peer and media influences Ø analysing attitudes, values, social norms, beliefs, and factors affecting them Ø identifying relevant information and sources of information	• **Skills for Increasing Personal Confidence** and Abilities to Assume Control, Take Responsibility, Make a Difference, or Bring About Change Ø building self-esteem/ confidenceü Ø creating self-awareness skills, including awareness of rights, influences, values, attitudes, rights, strengths, and weaknessesü Ø setting goals Ø self-evaluation / self-assessment/ self-monitoring skills • **Skills for Managing Feelings** Ø managing anger Ø dealing with grief and anxiety Ø coping with loss, abuse, and trauma • **Skills for Managing Stress**o time managemento positive thinkingo relaxation techniques

Life Skills made specific to major Health Topics

HEALTHTOPICS	**COMMUNICATION ANDINTERPERSONAL SKILLS**	DECISION-MAKING ANDCRITICAL THINKING SKILLS	COPING AND SELFMANAGEMENT SKILLS
ALCOHOL, TOBACCO, ANDOTHER DRUGS	• **Communication Skills:** Students can observe and practice ways to: Ø inform others of the negative health and social consequences and personal reasons for refraining from alcohol, tobacco, and drug use Ø ask parents not to smoke in the car when they ride with them • **Empathy Skills:** Students can observe and practice ways to: Ø listen to and show understanding of the reasons a friend may choose to use drugs Ø suggest alternatives in an appealing and convincing manner • **Advocacy Skills:** Students can observe and practice ways to: Ø persuade the headmaster to adopt and enforce a policy for tobacco-free schools Ø generate local support for tobacco-free schools and public buildings • **Negotiation/Refusal Skills:** Students can observe and practice ways to: Ø resist a friend's repeated request to chew or smoke tobacco, without losing face or friends • **Interpersonal Skills:** Students can observe and practice ways to: Ø support persons who are trying to stop using tobacco and other drugs Ø express constructive positive intolerance for a friend's use of substances. *"It is not okay for you to do that..."*	• **Decision-making Skills:** Students can observe and practice ways to: Ø gather information about consequences of alcohol and tobacco use Ø weigh the consequences against common reasons young people give for using alcohol or tobacco Ø identify their own reasons for not using alcohol or other drugs and explain those reasons to others Ø suggest a decision to drink non-alcoholic beverages at a party where alcohol is served - make and sustain a decision to stop using tobacco or other drugs and seek help to do so • **Critical Thinking Skills:** Students can observe and practice ways to: Ø analyze advertisements directed toward young people to use tobacco and see how they are playing upon the need to seem "cool," appeal to girls, or be attractive to boys - develop counter-messages that include the cost of buying cigarettes and how else that money could be used Ø assess how tobacco use takes advantage of poor people Ø analyze what may be driving them to use substances and aim to find a healthy alternative	• **Skills for Managing Stress:** Students can observe and practice ways to: Ø analyze what contributes to stress Ø reduce stress through activities such as exercise, meditation, and time management Ø make friends with people who provide support and relaxation

HEALTHY NUTRITION	• **Communication Skills:** Students can observe and practice ways to: Ø persuade parents and friends to make healthy food and menu choices • **Refusal Skills:** Students can observe and practice ways to: Ø counter social pres-sures to adopt unheal-thy eating practices • **Advocacy Skills:** Students can observe and practice ways to: Ø present messages of healthy nutrition to others through posters, ads, performan-ces, and pre-sentations Ø gain support of influential adults such as headmas-ters, teachers, and local physicians to provide healthy foods in the school environment	• **Decision-making Skills:** Students can observe and practice ways to: Ø choose nutritious foods and snacks over those less nutritious Ø convincingly demon-strate an understanding of the consequences of unbalanced nutrition (deficiency diseases) • **Critical Thinking Skills:** Students can observe and practice ways to: Ø evaluate nutrition claims from advertise-ments and nutrition-related news stories	• **Self-awareness and Self - manage-ment Skills:** Students can observe and practice ways to: Ø recognize links between eating disorders and psychological and emotional factors Ø identify personal preferences among nutritious foods and snacks Ø develop a healthy body image
SEXUAL ANDREPRODU-CTIVEHEALTH ANDHIV/ AIDSPREVENTION	• **Communication Skills:** Students can observe and practice ways to: Ø effectively express a desire to not have sex Ø influence others to abstain from sex or practice safe sex using condoms if they cannot be influenced to abstain Ø demonstrate support for the prevention of discrimi-nation related to HIV/AIDS • **Advocacy Skills:** Students can observe and practice ways to: Ø present arguments for access to sexual and repro-ductive health information, services, and counselling for young people • **Negotiation/Refusal Skills:** Students can observe and practice ways to: Ø refuse sexual inter-course or negotiate the use of con-doms • **Interpersonal Skills:** Students can observe and practice ways to: Ø show interest and listen actively to others Ø be caring and compassion-ate, including when inter-acting with someone who is infected with HIV	• **Decision-making Skills:** Students can observe and practice ways to: Ø seek and find reliable sources of information about human anato-my; puberty; concep-tion and pregnancy; STIs, HIV/AIDS, and local prevalence rates; and available methods of contraception Ø analyze a variety of potential situations for sexual interaction and determine a variety of actions they may take and the consequences of such actions • **Critical Thinking Skills:** Students can observe and practice ways to: Ø analyze myths and misconceptions about HIV/AIDS, contracep-tives, gender roles, and body image that are perpetuated by the media Ø analyze social-cultural influences regarding sexual behaviours	• **Skills for Managing Stress:** Students can observe and practice ways to: Ø seek services for help with reproduc-tive and sexual health issues, e.g., contraception, condoms to prevent HIV or unplanned pregnancy, sexual abuse, exploita-tion, discrimina-tion, (gender-based) violence, or other emotional trauma • **Skills for Increasing Personal Confi-dence and Abili-ties to Assume Control, Take Re-sponsibility, Make a Difference, or Bring About Change:** Students can observe and practice ways to: Ø assert personal val-ues when encoun-tering peer and other pressures

REDUCING HELMINTH (WORM) INFECTIONS	• **Communication Skills:** Students can observe and practice ways to: Ø communicate messages about worm infection to families, peers, and members of the community Ø encourage peers, siblings, and family members to take part in deworming activities and to avoid re-infection • **Advocacy Skills:** Students can observe and practice ways to: Ø advocate for an environment and behaviour that are not conducive to helminth infections Ø share positive results of deworming activities	• **Decision-making/problem solvingSkills:** Students can observe and practice ways to: Ø identify and avoid behaviours and environmental conditions that are likely to cause infection, such as ingestion of or contact with contaminated soil, and adopt behaviours that are likely to prevent infection, such as keeping human faces from polluting the ground or surface water - use safe water and uncontaminated food	• **Self-Monitoring Skills:** Students can observe and practice ways to: Ø engage in behaviours that are not conducive to contracting helminth and worm infections, such as avoiding contaminated water
VIOLENCE PREVENTION OR PEACE EDUCATION	• **Communication Skills:** Students can observe and practice ways to: Ø state their position clearly and calmly, without blaming Ø listen to each other's point of view Ø communicate positive messages Ø use "I" statements and not accuse others • **Negotiation Skills:** Students can observe and practice ways to: Ø intervene and discourage others from conflict before it escalates • **Advocacy Skills:** Students can observe and practice ways to: Ø get involved in community activities that promote non-violent behaviour Ø join, support, and inform others about non-violent activities and organisations Ø advocate for programmes to buy back weapons or create weapon free zones Ø discourage viewing violent television movies and video games	• **Decision-making Skills:** Students can observe and practice ways to: Ø understand the roles of aggressor, victim, and bystander • **Critical Thinking Skills:** Students can observe and practice ways to: Ø identify and avoid situations of conflict Ø evaluate both violent and non-violent solutions that appear to be successful as depicted in the media Ø analyze their own stereo types, beliefs, and attributions that support violence Ø help reduce prejudice and increase tolerance for diversity	• **Skills for Managing Stress:** Students can observe and practice ways to: Ø identify and implement peaceful ways of resolving conflict Ø resist pressure from peers and adults to engage in violent behaviour

In efforts to achieve specific behavioural outcomes, programmes aimed at developing young people's life skills without a particular context such as a health behaviour or condition are less effective than programmes that overtly focus on applying life skills to specific health choices and behaviours (Kirby et al, 1994). To influence behaviour effectively, skills must be applied to a particular topic, such as a prevalent health issue. Not to be overlooked, however, is the importance of building life skills to equip young people in other aspects of their development as well, such as maintaining positive interpersonal relations with teachers, students, and family members.

CONCLUSION

All of you know about the importance of health. *'Health is wealth'. 'A sound mind in a sound body'*. All these quotations show the importance of health. According to Gandhi, the Father of Indian Nation ...'When wealth is lost, nothing is lost; when health is lost, something is lost; when character is lost, everything is lost'. It is our duty to give more importance for health and character. Skills-based health education is important. Skills in general and life skills in particular are important for happy and healthy life. Today's children are tomorrow's citizens. It is our duty to take care about present generation. We are living in the highly technological and scientific society. The impact of peer group and media is very much on the students of the knowledge society. Without good health it is not possible for anyone to do something. Health education is not only important for youth, but also for other human beings. Skills-based health education curriculum is necessary in the present day situation. Teacher has a prominent role to promote good health skills in the students.

REFERENCES

1. Life Skills Guide for Grade 6, 7, & 8.
2. Padmini Nagesh Pai (2006). 'life Skills Education for School Effectiveness and Improvement', Round Table Presentation at International Congress for School Effectiveness and Improvement(3rd to 6th January 2006), Fort Lauderdale- Florida – U.S.A
3. Peace Corps (2001.'Life Skills Manual', Information Collection and Exchange Publication No. M0063.
4. UNICEF - Life skills - Focusing resources on effective school health.
5. UNICEF-Report of Workshop on 'Life Skills-based Hygiene Education', 12th -15th September, 2000, New York.
6. WHO/GPA. (1994). School health education to prevent AIDS and STD: *A resource package for curriculum planners.* World Health Organisation/Global Programme on AIDS, Geneva. As cited in WHO, 1994.
7. WHO/UNFPA/UNICEF. (1995). Programing fore adolescent health. Discussion paper prepared for the Study Group on Programing for

Adolescent Health. Saillon, Switzerland, 29th November – 4th December, 1995.

8. World Health Organisation [WHO]. (1999). WHO Information Series on School Health. Preventing HIV/AIDS/STI and related discrimination: *An important responsibility of Health Promoting Schools*. WHO/HPR/HEP/98.6. Geneva: WHO.
9. World Health Organization (WHO), (1998). 'WHO's Global School Health Initiative: Health-Promoting Schools'. WHO/HPR/HEP/98.4. Geneva: WHO.
10. Young, M., Kelley, R., & Denny, G. (1997). Evaluation of selected life-skills modules from the contemporary health series with students in grade 6. Perceptual and Motor Skills. 84, 811-818.

34

Spiritual Development through Education-swami Vivekananda

INTRODUCTION

Swami Vivekananda (1863 - 1902), a great thinker and reformer of India, embraces education, which for him signifies 'man-making', as the very mission of his life. Vivekananda realizes that mankind is passing through a crisis. The tremendous emphasis on the scientific and mechanical ways of life is fast reducing man to the status of a machine. Moral and religious values are being undermined. The fundamental principles of civilization are being ignored. Conflicts of ideals, manners and habits are pervading the atmosphere. Disregard for everything old is the fashion of the day. Vivekananda seeks the solutions of all these social and global evils through education. With this end in view, he feels the dire need of awakening man to his spiritual self wherein, he thinks, lies the very purpose of education.

2. GOAL OF EDUCATION

Vivekananda points out that the defect of the present-day education is that it has no definite goal to pursue. A sculptor has a clear idea about what he wants to shape out of the marble block; similarly, a painter knows what he is going to paint. But a teacher, he says, has no clear idea about the goal of his teaching. Swamiji attempts to establish, through his words and deeds, that the end of all education is man making. He prepares the scheme of this man-making education in the light of his over-all philosophy of Vedanta. According to Vedanta, the essence of man lies in his soul, which he possesses in addition to his body and mind. In true with this philosophy, Swamiji defines education as 'the manifestation of the perfection already in man.' The aim of education is to manifest in our lives the perfection, which is the very nature of our inner self. This perfection is the realization of the infinite power which resides in everything and everywhere-existence, consciousness and bliss (satchidananda). After understanding the essential nature of this perfection, we should identify it with our inner self. For achieving this, one will have to eliminate one's ego, ignorance and all other false identification, which stand in the way. Meditation, fortified by moral purity and passion for truth, helps man to leave behind the body, the senses, the ego and all other non-self elements, which are perishable. He thus realizes his immortal divine self, which is of the nature of infinite existence, infinite knowledge and infinite bliss.

At this stage, man becomes aware of his self as identical with all other selves of the universe, i.e. different selves as manifestations of the same self. Hence education, in Vivekananda's sense, enables one to comprehend one's self within as the self everywhere. The essential unity of the entire universe is realized through education. Accordingly, man making for Swamiji stands for rousing mans to the awareness of his true self. However, education thus signified does not point towards the development of the soul in isolation from body and mind. We have to remember that basis of Swamiji's philosophy is Advaita which preaches unity in diversity. Therefore, man making for him means a harmonious development of the body, mind and soul. Education for him means that process by which character is formed, strength of mind is increased, and intellect is sharpened, as a result of which one can stand on one's own feet.

3. EDUCATION OF THE MASSES

According to Swami Vivekananda a nation's progress is depending on the spread of education among the masses. The bane of India's progress is that the whole education and intelligence of the land became the monopoly of a handful of men. Unless and until we care for the spread of education among the masses^ no progress will be achieved in this country. Priest power and foreign rule have exploited the poor people to such an extent that they don't even think they are human beings. In a sad situation like this we have to open their eyes and make them see what is happening in the world around. "Our duty is to put the ideas into their heads, they will do the rest." He contended.

Swami blamed 'the cruel society which is interested to shower blows upon the poor man instead of coming to his help in this terrible situation.

Next he takes to task the educated of our country. "So long as the millions live in hunger and ignorance I hold every man a traitor who, having been educated at their expense, pays not the least heed to them', said Vivekananda. He regarded the neglect of the masses as a great national sin.

Vivekananda was fully convinced that only through education the lot of the poor can be improved here. Through education we should develop in them their lost individuality, once they become conscious of their human dignity, they would naturally try to rise up from their miserable state. But he was very much disappointed to see that nothing substantial has been done for educating the people. The germs of spirituality stored in our sacred books have to be brought to the common man. This can be done by spreading education among the masses through the medium of mother tongue. Ideas can easily be understood and assimilated even by the common-eat man if they are taught through their own mother-tongue. Our duty is to give those ideas and culture. "Without giving them culture, there can be no permanence in the raised condition of the masses", Vivekananda warned. Besides, they must be instructed in simple words about the necessities of -life and in trade, commerce, agriculture etc.

Once the poor man is made conscious of his strength, that he is the 'Omnipotent' and the 'Omniscient', the rest of the work becomes easy. The moment a fisherman thinks that he is spirit; he will be a better fisherman. Likewise a student becomes a better student, too. But so long as the novelty of the people is not banished, the hope of mass education remains a pious wish. For, even if free schools are opened in villages, the children would rather so to help their parents in their work or try to make a living than going to the school, if the poor bony cannot come to school for education, education must go to him.

4. SPIRITUAL DEVELOPMENT THROUGH EDUCATION

There are different types of education for spiritual development viz., Religious Education, Yoga Education, Moral Education...etc.

4.1. Religious Education – Spiritual Development

Hinduism is the world's oldest religious tradition; it goes back to the very dawn of history. The hymns composed some 5,000 years ago are still recited today.

Hinduism is the third largest of the world's religions, after Christianity and Islam. Nearly one-seventh of humanity calls Hinduism their spiritual home. Millions more in South and Southeast Asia and in the Far East trace their spiritual roots to Hinduism.

Hinduism is also the world's largest pluralistic tradition. A multiplicity of spiritual paths and ways are recognized as valid in Hinduism. Hinduism is not based on the teachings of a single Prophet or a single Book. The teachings of many different sages and saints find home within Hinduism. God may be worshiped both in male and female forms. Hinduism has much in common with the earth based religious traditions of the world.

Hinduism is not a creedal religion, based on dogma. Its emphasis is not on correct belief but on search for the Truth. The scripture describes several paths to spiritual development. The mountain peak may be reached by taking any of the several paths.

Sri Aurobindo (1872-1950), the great Indian seer of the first half of the twentieth century declared that Hinduism (also known as *Sanatan Dharma* or the eternal tradition) was rising not for India alone but for the world. Arnold Toynbee in his *A Study of History* was of the view that Hinduism will gain the status of a world religion in the new century.

Hindus believe that Reality is One – Ekam Sat. This Reality is everywhere, in everything, in every being. It is one and many at the same time and it also transcends them both. At the popular level, the One Reality is worshipped as the Trinity: Brahma the creator, Vishnu the preserver and Shiva the dissolver. Brahma, Vishnu and Shiva are not different gods, but they represent different faces of the One Supreme. Brahma, Vishnu and Shiva have their respective female consorts: Saraswati, Lakshmi and Durga. Even though God is One, Hindus worship God in a number of both male and female forms. Ram Swarup puts the matter this way:

Spiritual life is one but it is vast and rich in expression. The human mind conceives it differently. If the human mind was uniform without different depths, heights and levels of subtlety; or if all men had the same mind, the same psyche, the same imagination, the same needs, in short, if all men were the same, then perhaps One God would do. But a man's mind is not a fixed quantity and men and their powers and needs are different. So only some form of polytheism alone can do justice to this variety and richness.

—The Word As Revelation: Names of Gods, 1980.

FOUR PATHS: Hinduism prescribes four ways of spiritual salvation, depending on the personality of the seeker.

1. For the active person, there is Karma yoga, the path of selfless works.
2. For the contemplative and intellectual person, there is Jnana Yoga, the path of Knowledge.
3. For the emotional person, there is Bhakti yoga, the path of love and surrender. Bhakti yoga is said to be similar to the Christian path of love.

4. Finally, Raja yoga is the path of meditative exercises including concentration and one-pointedness. This path focusing on meditation has become popular in the West

Yoga Education – Spiritual Development

The Eight Limbs (Ashtanga) of Raja Yoga

The eight "limbs" or steps prescribed in the second *pada* of the Yoga Sutras are: *Yama, Niyama, Asana, Pranayama, Pratyahara, Dharana, Dhyana* and *Samadhi.*

Ashtanga yoga consists of the following steps: The first five are called external aids to Yoga (bahiranga sadhana)

- o **Yama** refers to the five abstentions. These are the same as the five vows of Jainism.
  - **Ahimsa**: non-violence, inflicting no injury or harm to others or even to one's own self, it goes as far as nonviolence in thought, word and deed.
  - **Satya**: truth in word & thought.
  - **Asteya**: non-covetousness, to the extent that one should not even desire something that is not his own.
  - **Brahmacharya**: abstain from sexual intercourse; celibacy in case of unmarried people and monogamy in case of married people. Even this to the extent that one should not possess any sexual thoughts towards any other man or woman except one's own spouse. It's common to associate Brahmacharya with celibacy.
  - **Aparigraha**: non-possessiveness
- o **Niyama** refers to the five observances
  - **Shaucha**: cleanliness of body & mind.
  - **Santosha**: satisfaction; satisfied with what one has.
  - **Tapas**: austerity and associated observances for body discipline & thereby mental control.
  - **Svadhyaya**: study of the Vedic scriptures to know about God and the soul, which leads to introspection on a greater awakening to the soul and God within,
  - **Ishvarapranidhana**: surrender to (or worship of) God.
- o **Asana**: Discipline of the body: rules and postures to keep it disease-free and for preserving vital energy. Correct postures are a physical aid to meditation, for they control the limbs and nervous system and prevent them from producing disturbances.
- o **Pranayama**: control of breath. Beneficial to health, steadies the body and is highly conducive to the concentration of the mind.

- o **Pratyahara**: withdrawal of senses from their external objects.

The last three levels are called internal aids to Yoga (antaranga sadhana)

- o **Dharana**: concentration of the citta upon a physical object, such as a flame of a lamp, the midpoint of the eyebrows, or the image of a deity.
- o **Dhyana**: steadfast meditation. Undisturbed flow of thought around the object of meditation (pratyayaikatanata). The act of meditation and the object of meditation remain distinct and separate.
- o **Samadhi**: oneness with the object of meditation. There is no distinction between act of meditation and the object of meditation. Samadhi is of two kinds:

Samprajnata Samadhi conscious samadhi. The mind remains concentrated (ekagra) on the object of meditation; therefore the consciousness of the object of meditation persists. Mental modifications arise only in respect of this object of meditation.

This state is of four kinds:

- § Savitarka: the Citta is concentrated upon a gross object of meditation such as a flame of a lamp, the tip of the nose, or the image of a deity.
- § Savichara: the Citta is concentrated upon a subtle object of meditation , such as the tanmatras
- § Sananda: the Citta is concentrated upon a still subtler object of meditation, like the senses.
- § Sasmita: the Citta is concentrated upon the ego-substance with which the self is generally identified.

Asamprajnata Samadhi supraconscious. The citta and the object of meditation are fused together. The consciousness of the object of meditation is transcended. All mental modifications are checked (niruddha), although latent impressions may continue.

Combined simultaneous practice of Dhâranâ, Dhyâna & Samâdhi is referred to as Samyama and is considered a tool of achieving various perfections, or Siddhis.

Yoga and Religion

Yoga is not a religion. It has no creed or fixed set of beliefs, nor is there a prescribed godlike figure to be worshipped in a particular manner. Religions for the most part seem to be based upon the belief in and worship of things (God or godlike figures) that exist outside one-self. The core of Yoga's philosophy is that everything is supplied from within the individual.

Thus, there is no dependence on an external figure, either in the sense of a person or god figure, or a religious organization.

The common belief that Yoga derives from Hinduism is a misconception. Yoga actually predates Hinduism by many centuries. Ancient seals unearthed in the Indus Valley provide clear evidence of widespread Yoga practice earlier than 3,000 B.C.E. The techniques of Yoga have been adopted by Hinduism as well as by other world religions. Yoga is a system of techniques that can be used for a number of goals, from simply managing stress better, learning to relax, and increasing limberness all the way to becoming more self-aware and acquiring the deepest knowledge of one's own self.

The practice of Yoga will not interfere with any religion. Many American Yoga Association students who have practiced Yoga intensively for many years continue to follow the religious traditions they have grown up in or adopted without conflict.

5. SWAMI VIVEKANANDA SPIRITUAL QUOTES

1. *Anything that brings spiritual, mental or physical weakness, touch it not with the toes of your feet.*
2. *Be brave! Be strong! Be fearless! Once you have taken up the spiritual life, fight as long as there is any life in you. Even though you know you are going to be killed, fight till you "are killed." Don't die of fright. Die fighting. Don't go down till you are knocked down.*
3. *BY the study of different RELIGIONS we find that in essence they are one.*
4. *By the Vedas no books are meant. They mean the accumulated treasury of spiritual laws discovered by different persons in different times. Just as the law of gravitation existed before its discovery, and would exist if all humanity forgot it, so is it with the laws that govern the spiritual world*
5. *External nature is only internal nature writ large.*
6. *Give up all desire for enjoyment in earth or heaven. Control the organs of the senses and control the mind. Bear every misery without even knowing that you are miserable. Think of nothing but spiritual freedom.*
7. *GOD is to be worshipped as the one beloved, dearer than everything in this and next life.*
8. *God is very merciful to those whom He sees struggling heart and soul for spiritual realization. But remain idle, without any struggle, and you will see that His grace will never come.*
9. *GOD of truth, be Thou alone my guide...*

10. *Let us put forth all our energies to acquire that which never fails—our spiritual perfection. If we have true yearning for realization, we must struggle, and through struggle growth will come. We shall make mistakes, but they may be angels unawares.*
11. *Never think there is anything impossible for the soul. It is the greatest heresy to think so. If there is sin, this is the only sin? To say that you are weak, or others are weak.*
12. *Our supreme duty is to advance toward freedom—physical, mental, and spiritual—and help others to do so.*
13. *Records of great spiritual men of the past do us no good whatever except that they urge us onward to do the same, to experience religion ourselves.*
14. *Renunciation is the background of all religious thought wherever it be, and you will always find that as this idea of renunciation lessens, the more will the senses creep into the field of religion, and spirituality will decrease in the same ratio.*
15. *Salvation is not achieved by inactivity but by spiritual activities.*
16. *Save the spiritual store in your body by observing continence.*
17. *"Seek ye first the kingdom of God, and everything shall be added unto you".This is the one great duty, this is renunciation. Live for an ideal, and leave no place in the mind for anything else. Let us put forth all our energies to acquire that which never fails—our spiritual perfection. If we have true yearning for realization, we must struggle, and through struggle growth will come. We shall make mistakes, but they may be angels unawares.*
18. *Take up one idea. Make that one idea your life - think of it, dream of it, live on that idea. Let the brain, muscles, nerves, every part of your body, be full of that idea, and just leave every other idea alone. This is the way to success that is way great spiritual giants are produced.*
19. *The animal has its happiness in the senses, the human beings in their intellect, and the gods in spiritual contemplation. It is only to the soul that has attained to this contemplative state that the world really becomes beautiful.*
20. *The first sign of your becoming religious is that you are becoming cheerful*
21. *The greatest help to spiritual life is meditation. In meditation we divest ourselves of all material conditions and feel our divine nature. We do not depend upon any external help in meditation. The touch of the soul can paint the brightest color even in the dingiest places; it can cast a fragrance over the vilest thing; it can make the wicked divine—and all enmity, all selfishness is effaced.*

22. *The more we come out and do good to others, the more our hearts will be purified, and God will be in them.*
23. *This is the great lesson that we are here to learn through myriads of births and heavens and hells—that there is nothing to be asked for, desired for, beyond one's spiritual Self (atman).*
24. *Tremendous purity, tremendous renunciation, is the one secret of spirituality. "Neither through wealth, nor through progeny, but through renunciation alone is immortality to be reached," say the Vedas. "Sell all that thou hast and give to poor, and follow me," says the Christ. So all great saints and prophets have expressed it, and have carried it out in their lives. How can great spirituality come without renunciation?*
25. *We are what our thoughts have made us; so take care about what you think. Words are secondary. Thoughts live; they travel far.*
26. *What is material and what is not material? When the world is the end and God the means to attain that end, then that is material. When God is the end and the world is only the means to attain that end, spirituality has begun.*
27. *Where can we go to find God if we cannot see Him in our own hearts and in every living being.*
28. *You cannot believe in God until you believe in yourself.*
29. *You have to grow from the inside out. None can teach you, none can make you spiritual. There is no other teacher but your own soul.*

6. CONCLUSIONS

Inculcation of Spiritual values in each and every student is important. Today we are facing so many problems like terrorism, poverty, corruption, illiteracy, alcoholism and teenage pregnancy. Terrorism is the most dangerous problem in the modern world. The only cause for all these problems is lack of spiritual knowledge. We are giving priority or importance for external world. "*Brahma Satyam, Jagat Mithya, and Jivo Brahmaiva naparah*"... according this the ultimate reality is Brahman. There is no difference between self and Brahman. If anyone loves God, definitely he loves fellow human beings. Love and affection towards fellow human beings, animals and plants is more important. Spiritual knowledge gives discriminative power- what is right? What is wrong? Which is good? Which is bad? What is right way? Etc. It is the duty of parents and teacher to develop spiritual values in the students. Education is power. Through Education it is easy to inculcate spiritual knowledge in the students. According to swami Vivekananda education means that character is formed, strength of mind is increased, and intellect is sharpened, as a result of which one can stand on one's own feet. It is the fore most duty of government to provide such type of education for all.

7. REFERENCES

1. Amareswaran, N. (2010). "*Moral Values of Intermediate Students*", Discovery Publication, New Delhi.
2. Amareswaran, N. (2011): "*Importance of Yoga for Human Wellbeing*", edited by Anjana Kaul, Discovery Publication, New Delhi.
3. Madan Lal Goel. "*Religious Tolerance and Hinduism*", unpublished article.
4. Sudipa dutta Roy (2001). "*Education in the Vision of Swami Vivekananda*", published in 'e-Samskriti: The Essence of Indian Culture', online article.

Index

A

B

C

Q

R

S

T

V

W

X

Y

Z